Psyche's Prophet

In this collection spanning 65 years as a clinical psychologist, Nicholas A. Cummings selects articles that heralded, often far in advance, each phase of clinical psychology's evolution to the present. A pioneer in effecting change, Cummings established the first freestanding professional school of clinical psychology, demonstrated that medical utilization was reduced with psychotherapy, was an early proponent of universal healthcare, fought for the inclusion of psychotherapy in national health insurance, established American Biodyne, the first privately managed care firm for mental health coverage, and battled to maintain psychological services for children against the trend toward medication. This resource will teach not just the history of psychology, but what lies ahead.

Nicholas A. Cummings, PhD, ScD, is a former president of the American Psychological Association (APA) who for the past half century has been predicting the course of psychology and forming organizations designed to meet challenges as each occurred. He holds an extensive psychotherapy practice, is the author of 54 books and more than 450 journal articles, and has had a profound effect on the course of the profession.

For a full list of titles in this series, please visit www.routledge.com

The World Library of Mental Health celebrates the important contributions to mental healthcare made by leading experts in their individual fields. Each author has compiled a career-long collection of what they consider their finest pieces: extracts from books, journals, articles, major theoretical and practical contributions, and salient research findings.

For the first time ever the work of each contributor is presented in a single volume so readers can follow the themes and progress of their work and identify the contributions made to, and the development of, the fields themselves.

Each book in the series features a specially written introduction by the contributor giving an overview of their career, contextualizing their selection within the development of the field, and showing how their own thinking developed over time.

Titles in this series:

Soul: Treatment and Recovery – The selected works of Murray Stein
Murray Stein

A Developmentalist's Approach to Research, Theory, and Therapy – The Selected Works of Joseph D. Lichtenberg
Joseph D. Lichtenberg

Existential Psychotherapy and Counselling after Postmodernism: The selected works of Del Loewenthal
Del Loewenthal

Love the Wild Swan: The selected works of Judith Edwards
Judith Edwards

Conscience and Critic: The selected works of Keith Tudor
Keith Tudor

Psyche's Prophet
The Selected Writings of Nicholas A. Cummings

Edited by Nicholas A. Cummings

 Routledge
Taylor & Francis Group

NEW YORK AND LONDON

First published 2017
by Routledge
711 Third Avenue, New York, NY 10017

and by Routledge
2 Park Square, Milton Park, Abingdon, Oxon, OX14 4RN

*Routledge is an imprint of the Taylor & Francis Group, an informa
business*

Library of Congress Cataloging-in-Publication Data
A catalog record for this book has been requested

ISBN: 978-1-138-79502-0 (hbk)
ISBN: 978-1-315-75872-5 (ebk)

Typeset in Times New Roman
by Apex CoVantage, LLC

Contents

Bibliography of Featured Articles

Article 1. Cummings, Nicholas A. The California School of Professional Psychology: One Alternative to the Extinction of Professional Psychology. *Journal of Clinical Issues in Psychology*, Vol. 1, No. 1, October 1969, pp. 8–10.

Article 2. Follette, William T. & Cummings, Nicholas A. Psychiatric Services and Medical Utilization in a Prepaid Health Plan Setting I. *Medical Care*, Vol. 5, No. 1, January–February 1967, pp. 25–35.

Article 3. Cummings, Nicholas A. & Follette, William T. Psychiatric Services and Medical Utilization in a Prepaid Health Plan Setting II. *Medical Care*, Vol. 6, No. 1, January–February 1968, pp. 31–41.

Article 4. Cummings, Nicholas A. The Anatomy of Psychotherapy under National Health Insurance. *American Psychologist*, Vol. 32, No. 9, September 1977, pp. 711–718.

Article 5. Cummings, Nicholas A. Turning Bread into Stones: Our Modern Antimiracle. *American Psychologist*, Vol. 34, No. 12, December 1979, pp. 1119–1129.

Article 6. Cummings, Nicholas A. Arguments for the Financial Efficacy of Psychological Services in Healthcare Settings. In *Handbook of Clinical Psychology in Medical Settings* (Chapter 8), edited by Jerry J. Sweet, Ronald G. Rozensky, & Steven M. Tovian. Plenum Publishing Corporation, 1991, pp. 113–126.

Article 7. Cummings, Nicholas A. & Wiggins, Jack G. A Collaborative Primary Care/ Behavioral Health Model for the Use of Psychotropic Medication with Children and Adolescents: The Report of a National Retrospective Study. *Issues in Interdisciplinary Care*, Vol. 3, No. 2, 2001, pp. 121–128.

Article 8. Cummings, Nicholas A. The Next Phase in the Evolution of Behavioral Care and Its Re-empowerment of the Practitioner. *The Independent Practitioner*, Summer 2000, Vol. 20, No. 3; Bulletin of the Psychologists in Independent Practice, a Division of the American Psychological Association.

Article 9. Cummings, Nicholas A. A New Vision of Healthcare for America. In *Integrated Behavioral Healthcare: Prospects, Issues, and Opportunities*, edited by N. A. Cummings, H. Dörken, M. S. Pallak, & C. J. Henke. Academic Press, 2001, chapter 2.

Article 10. Cummings, Nicholas A. Behavioral Health in Primary Care: Dollars and Sense. In *Behavioral Health in Primary Care: A Guide for Clinical Integration*, edited by N. A. Cummings, J. L. Cummings, & J. N. Johnson. Psychosocial Press, 1977, pp. 3–21.

Article 11. Cummings, Nicholas A. Medical Costs, Medicaid, and Managed Mental Health Treatment: The Hawaii Study (Michael S. Pallak, PhD, Nicholas A. Cummings, PhD, Herbert Dörken, PhD, & Curtis J. Henke, PhD). *Managed Care Quarterly*, Vol. 2, No. 2, 1994, pp. 64–70.

Tables and Figures

Figures

Introduction

Nicholas A. Cummings, PhD, ScD

When Dr. George Zimmar of Routledge asked me to be one of several colleagues to select and submit for publication 14 of my articles, I thought this to be a most interesting assignment. Then it struck me: How was I to select just 14 out of more than 450 articles published over my 65-year career? After some thought, the answer became obvious.

Beginning with the post–World War II era when psychologists numbered a mere 5,000 to the present constituency of more than 150,000, at each step of its evolution I was able to predict the course of our profession, even though at each juncture my predictions were not only rejected, but most often were met with resistance and even ridicule. My accuracy was so astounding that the professional publication *Psychotherapy Networker* affectionately dubbed me "psychology's soothsayer" (Simon, 2009). I would submit for each of psychology's evolutionary eras one article that was representative of my ignored predictions, all the way to 2015 when all of my predictions belatedly were acknowledged by a large sector of my colleagues.

Psychology is slow to change and is often seemingly dragged into acknowledging societal and healthcare changes long after the fact. This unfolding of 65 years of history may now not seem real, but it occurred just as described, and the acceptance of the predictions came painfully slowly. For example, my insistence in 1964 that the practice of psychology is a business was fiercely resisted until 2009 when then APA president James Bray made this acknowledgment a focal point of his administration (Bray, 2011).

As I look back, none of these so-called predictions seems prescient to me now, as they also did not seem so then. As one by one they unfolded, they seemed so obvious that each time I was startled and troubled by my colleagues' blindness, and even more so by their hostility. Even after and in the midst of each prediction having taken place, psychology's leadership quieted its constituency by the ostensibly soothing message that the occurrence was merely a passing fancy. Rogers Wright as board chair of the Practice Directorate and Brian Welch as its executive director reassured its psychology community by unabashedly ridiculing me in speeches and in print. But as events in the healthcare sector began to unfold, the discourse settled down to a more professional debate, with my predicting the growth of managed care while Rogers continued to insist this would be avoided by the rationing of healthcare, thus eliminating unnecessary services (Cummings & Wright, 1991).

During World War II mental healthcare came of age. William "Will" Menninger, MD, was appointed brigadier general in command of psychiatry for the U.S. Army, a position that had not existed before his appointment in 1943. Heretofore healthcare in the military consisted of only medicine and surgery, and the creation of the service of psychiatry was a giant step forward. Will Menninger was the brother of prescient writer Karl Menninger, and together they had founded the famous state-of-the-art Menninger Clinic in Topeka, Kansas. General Will, as he was affectionately known, founded the School of Military Neuropsychiatry on Long Island, New York, where he sent young physicians just out of medical school, even before their internships. There they received a 90-day crash course in psychiatry and then went to field hospitals just behind the front lines to treat the so-called battle neuroses. It was Menninger's contention that if these men were treated immediately, this would prevent the formation of the permanent mental disabilities that resulted in the lifelong residents of veterans' mental hospitals after World War I.

The task was an insightful but overwhelming one, and to aid these fledgling psychiatrists he inducted master's-level clinical psychologists and, to a lesser degree, social workers and put them through a similar crash course, after which they were deployed to the front lines themselves rather than behind the lines as were the newly minted psychiatrists. The strategy was masterful. It worked so well that in the immediate postwar-era society, the latest heroes were psychiatrists and psychologists. So much so that an astounding number of returning veterans used the G.I. Bill to enter the new doctoral clinical psychology programs in the many universities taking advantage of the funds provided by the Veterans Administration and the freshly created National Institute of Mental Health (NIMH). I was one of these veterans, and for a full account, see Austad (2014).

The Professional School Movement

Since its inception, the profession of psychology has been fractionated by the numerous competing theoretical positions of general psychology. Unlike theories in physics that can be tested by such accomplishments as putting a man on the moon, thus resulting in principles becoming laws, experimental psychology has no such endpoint. Rather, there continue to be "schools" of psychology that can and do design experiments that "prove" each school's theoretical position. In the post–World War II years, the parlaying of experiments, each proving their authors' positions (Hull, Tolman, Spence, Skinner, Guthrie) filled the pages of psychology journals. Learning theories, all based on rat-maze experiments, dominated psychology, and students in doctoral programs of clinical psychology were indoctrinated in whatever rat-running theory was extant in the university in which they were trying to learn clinical psychology.

So-called clinical psychology doctorates were predominately experimental programs, with varying degrees of scarcity of real clinical courses. Universities were not really interested in the emerging profession of clinical psychology, but they wanted the money given to psychology departments for having clinical programs. Those of us in training in the latter part of the 1940s bootlegged our real clinical training. Secretly we met evenings in the homes of friendly psychiatrists who taught us psychotherapy practice. In the beginning we each paid a fee, but later we received the training in exchange for psychological testing of these psychiatrists' prospective patients. In that era, psychotherapy was never undertaken before the patient was administered the standard battery of psychological tests: Wechsler Bellevue Intelligence Scale, Rorschach, Thematic Apperception Test (TAT), Bender-Gestalt, and Machover Draw-a-Person. Had our faculty known of the way we were bootlegging our training, we surely would have been dismissed from the program.

By the 1960s, the APA had developed certain requirements for approval to grant doctorates in clinical psychology. But a little-discussed reality is that these approved programs varied significantly in accordance with the theoretical position dominating that particular university program. This continues to this day, with differing theoretical positions from program to program, each designing experiments "proving" each theoretical position. The profession also seems to go through phases of popularity. One position may achieve dominance only to be replaced with an emerging, more convincing theory. As cognitive therapy became the gold standard, suddenly meditation became the fashion, to be followed by acceptance-commitment therapy (ACT), and so on and on. In the immediate postwar era, psychoanalysis was in vogue and it was fashionable to have a picture of Sigmund Freud hanging in one's office.

Well into the third decade following World War II, when psychotherapy had evolved from a strictly psychoanalytic bias, it was still prolonged, with no firm landmarks denoting when enough was enough. The burgeoning prepaid health insurance industry regarded it as unmanageable and thus could not be included in prepaid insurance, often describing the potential duration of psychotherapy as "how long is a piece of string?" But in the early 1960s, as previously noted, I had established that brief, targeted psychotherapy could be included in health insurance because of the cost savings in subsequent medical/surgical care. It became apparent to me that we needed professional schools that taught efficient-effective practice in a curriculum that was strictly clinical and not hampered by competing theoretical psychology. After all, medicine, nursing, optometry, podiatry, and even social work had professional schools, and it was time psychology did also.

Repeated attempts to convince the university-dominated APA of the importance of professional schools that would teach true clinical psychology practice proved futile. After much frustration, it occurred to me that I should establish the first such school, freestanding if need be. As president of the California Psychological Association (CPA) in 1968, I was able to convince the state association that the time was right to found a freestanding professional school of psychology, and with a carefully appointed board of directors I did so in 1969 with the first doctoral classes commencing in 1970 in Los Angeles and San Francisco, to be followed 2 and 3 years later by campuses in San Diego and Fresno. Named the California

School of Professional Psychology (CSPP), it captured the imagination of clinically trained practitioners dissatisfied with the mediocre clinical training they had received in their own doctoral programs. The second published paper included in this series (Cummings, 1969) is one of several early publications announcing the formation of CSPP, and it was followed by several others as I stomped the professional psychology national circuit. Rapidly CSPP was followed by freestanding schools in several states, and soon my own doctoral mentor, Dr. Gordon Derner, upgraded Adelphi's professional program into the first professional school on a university campus. The creation of a professional school at Rutgers University quickly followed.

By 1979, more than 20 professional schools of psychology existed, and I formed the National Council of Schools of Professional Psychology (NCSPP) that same year. I had obtained permission from the U.S. Department of Education for the NCSPP, rather than the APA, to serve as the accrediting body of the new professional schools of psychology. At the APA convention in 1977, I convened representatives from all the professional schools, and we adopted articles of incorporation and bylaws. I conducted an election where Gordon Derner was elected NCSPP's first president. I then left the room, for I was no longer president of CSPP and it would be inappropriate for me to stay on. An unforeseen series of events followed. Gordon had run four times for the presidency of the APA and planned to run again, so he had an interest in bringing NCSPP into the APA education and training list of approved schools. He convinced the assembly to approve this plan, and in doing so, he destroyed the intent and autonomy of the professional school movement.

The professional schools were designed to have a very small core faculty, perhaps only two and possibly three, and a large core faculty of psychologists in the community who would teach one course—that aspect of psychology in which he or she made a living. Thus, child therapy would be taught by a practicing child therapist, industrial psychology would be taught by a practicing industrial psychologist, and so on. Since several part-time faculty members cost less than one full-time faculty member, the school could be financed by tuition, which would be its sole source of income. CSPP not only so financed itself, but had enough income left over to allow one fourth of its students tuition-free scholarships. In obtaining APA approval, the professional schools were required to have full-time faculty, which destroyed the financial concept I had created. Now professional schools support themselves by admitting large numbers of master's-level students who on graduating flood the market, resulting in too many practitioners, which in turn results in depressed fees and incomes. The ultimate paradox is that Gordon Derner ran a fifth time and was defeated, while I was elected APA president that same year, which was my first and only run.

Medical Cost Offset

In 1959, I was hired as the chief psychologist of the fast-growing Kaiser Permanente Health Plan in San Francisco, the nation's first extensive prepaid capitated health system that fostered innovation, and the first to make psycho-therapy a prepaid/covered benefit. Because all health services were conducted in-house, it was there that Kaiser Permanente founder Sidney Garfield, MD, discovered that 60% of patients visiting their primary physician on any given day had significant mental health issues that were manifesting themselves in physical complaints, or psychological issues that were complicating existing medical conditions or making them worse. My years of research there revealed unequivocally that brief, targeted psychotherapy (average 7.5 visits) reduced outpatient visits, hospital days, and laboratory tests significantly the first year following psychotherapy, and this reduction increased and remained on a 5-year follow-up. Eventually, what was termed the "medical cost offset effect" was shown to persist in follow-up research that spanned 17 post-treatment years (Follette & Cummings, 1967; Cummings & Follette, 1968; Cummings & Van-denBos, 1981).

When scholars first published this research, the APA and psychology practition-ers generally heralded the findings as proving that psychotherapy was a needed part of healthcare. They ignored the fact that the medical cost offset effect derived from targeted interventions in which the psychotherapist was far more active than was extant in the psychotherapy practice of the era. Although the long-term, psychoanalytically oriented therapy of the day might eventually reduce medical utilization, cost savings in healthcare were more than outweighed by the costs of long-term psychotherapy. My pleas that my findings not be so misquoted were totally dismissed, and in time the misrepresentations backfired. The end result was that healthcare companies, all except for Kaiser Permanente and later Geisinger in Pennsylvania, ignored my research. Instead of promoting training in targeted, brief psychotherapy, they imposed arbitrary session limits determined by a case manager who, in most cases, was not a practitioner. Practitioners untrained in targeted interventions merely did what they always did: begin long-term psycho-therapy that was arbitrarily terminated within the imposed number of sessions, resulting in no demonstrable improvement in the patients. Besieged by patient complaints that the limited number of sessions did not ameliorate their conditions, the managed care companies welcomed and fostered the eventual replacement of much of psychotherapy by psychotropic medications. Once again, psychologists did much to foster their own demise, but instead of acknowledging this, they projected the blame. I was accused of having caused third-party payers to largely abandon psychotherapy in favor of medication.

Although this history goes back several decades, I have chosen a more recent article to describe this time inasmuch as subsequent years have cast more insight into the era (Cummings, 1991). Even more significant is that it reveals a continued need to heed the warnings decades after the initial findings. It is the first article in this collection. Finally, in Follette and Cummings (1967), as well as in Cummings and Follette (1968), even the titles indicate that it is a *pre-paid health plan setting*, a fact psychologists misquoting the studies continue to ignore when they mistakenly advocate that all psychotherapy reduces medical and surgical utilization.

Medical Cost Offset

It is only fitting to conclude this selection of my articles by including the prescient 1960s research that launched me on the lifelong journey of exploration into developing, succeeding phases of psychotherapy *practice*. The first of these reported the finding that brief, targeted psychotherapy could reduce medical costs significantly and impressively beyond the costs of providing the psychotherapy (Follette & Cummings, 1967). The mental health professions seized on this discovery and used it extensively to "prove" that the long-term therapy that was the mode at the time would reduce medical costs. Eventually it was shown that medical cost savings did not equal the costs of long-term psychotherapy, and, unfortunately, the significance and importance of the fact that short-term psychotherapy is not only psychologically effective, but it is also more than economically viable.

Medical Cost Offset Continued

In Part 2 of this early research (Cummings & Follette, 1968), it was shown that attempts at early detection of emotional problems did not generate more psychiatric clinic patients than those generated through routine medical practice in a setting where physicians were already sensitive to mental and emotional symptoms, and trained to address them. This preceded by 45 years current medical practice in which primary care physicians address the majority of emotional problems within their ongoing practices, often with the involvement of a social worker, psychologist, or psychiatric nurse.

Arrival of the Drug Culture

By my APA presidential year in 1979, the drug culture was well entrenched and overdoses and other untoward events had become common. The 1960s ushered in the "hippie culture" with its quaint dress, long hair for men, and straight hair for women that looked as if it had been done on the ironing board. Dr. Timothy Leary, a former Harvard psychologist, became the era's guru with his admonition, "Tune in, turn on, and drop out." In parks and other such gathering places, seeing young people smoking pot while "lying on the hip" became commonplace, as indeed many did drop out, living on the dole or otherwise scrounging an existence. It must be remembered that military conscription took place during the Vietnam War, causing many to flee to Canada, where the government refused to extradite so-called draft dodgers back to the United States. Attempts to seal the border to Canada to prevent fleeing young people faced with conscription failed as well-meaning citizens opposed to the war created illegal exit corridors, called "underground railroads," in the states of Washington on the West Coast and Vermont on the East Coast.

On a lecture visit to Vancouver, British Columbia, I witnessed hundreds of American youths sitting on the courthouse steps and lying in parks, doing nothing but smoking marijuana and living on money regularly sent by sympathetic parents. I personally knew Dr. Timothy Leary, whom I succeeded as chief psychologist at Kaiser Permanente after he was fired. This was before he became the pot-smoking guru. He was fired because he and his staff were busy doing research, to the neglect of patients waiting to be seen in psychotherapy. He had not yet discovered marijuana, but he was a heavy drinker, which so often precedes marijuana addiction. He then accepted a position at Harvard, where subsequently he became the nation's first guru. I renewed my acquaintance after he had left Harvard and was arrested and sentenced to prison after paradoxically trying to smuggle marijuana *into* Mexico. I visited him at the federal prison in Lompoc, California, where it was apparent that he had completely destroyed his mind. He told me he was a visitor from the 25th century, where people like himself had superior intellects, and that when he finished his mission in our present he would fly back to the 25th century.

Incredible as it may seem now, many influential colleagues of the era became hippies, growing full beards and long hair, while dressing in a manner that today would be laughable. Esalen Institute on the Monterey, California, peninsula became *the* mecca, attracting numerous hippie psychologists from across the nation. Those attending regularly sat in redwood hot tubs for hours, each in turn reciting his or her "enlightenment." The outlandish Dr. Frederick "Fritz" Perls, the guru known for his gestalt therapy in which he was very active, was a regular attendee. So was the seemingly opposite guru, Prof. Carl Rogers, who promulgated client-centered therapy, and was known as one who never got angry. I was present at a session during which the two debated each other, which quickly degenerated into Fritz taunting Carl, challenging him to get angry. I was sitting behind Carl and could only see the back of his totally bald head, but I had a full view of the smirking Fritz, who kept jeering, "Come on, Carl, get mad at me." It worked, for soon I saw the back of Carl's neck turn red as the color slowly rose to engulf his entire bald pate, after which he began blurting, "Wow, is this what anger feels like?"

In looking back, that all this nonsense was then regarded as appropriate and important psychological insight is now difficult to comprehend. It would explain why psychology fell from its lofty height in the early postwar years to its present level. Yes, I well remember that for the 10 postwar years a national poll conducted in a popular women's magazine named psychologists as the men women most wanted to marry (remembering that in those years psychology was almost exclusively a male profession rather than the largely female profession it has become).

It was in this era that I chose to address the drug culture, especially that within psychology, as the subject of my APA presidential address in 1979 (Cummings, 1979). I chose the title "Turning Bread into Stones," using the parlance of the day in which bread was money and stones were drug users. It also played on the biblical miracle in which Jesus turned stones into bread. My intent was surprising beyond all expectation. Heretofore, when treating drug addiction was relegated mostly to those colleagues who could not otherwise make a living, seemingly overnight hundreds of psychologists began treating addiction. In times past when there were fewer than a dozen requests for a reprint of a presidential address, my speech was eventually reprinted four times in response to more than 7,000 requests. This was truly the exception to the usual response of my colleagues, who do not want to espouse my usual prescience, and the article is included here in its entirety as Number 3.

Psychology and National Health Insurance

The fourth article chosen (Cummings, 1977) addressed the then burgeoning issue of national health insurance. At the time, the words "health insurance," rather than "healthcare," were in extensive use inasmuch as prepaid health insurance burst on the national scene with a vengeance. Interesting, it was a Republican president, Richard Nixon, rather than a Democrat, who first became enamored of the concept, but quickly it became the primary health objective of Senator Edward (Ted) Kennedy. Being first a member of the Senate from California, Nixon was well acquainted with the tremendous success of Kaiser Permanente in providing first-class, prepaid, in-house, affordable healthcare to millions of Californians, and he saw it as a solution to rapidly escalating costs. With the cooperation of Congress, he provided 3-year start-up funds to healthcare groups eager to found replicas of the Kaiser Permanente system. Rapidly more than two dozen companies sprang up across the United States, sparking optimism that prepaid healthcare would provide affordable services for all Americans.

An early proponent was Senator Kennedy, who held hearings on the subject of prepaid healthcare. Early on, I was called to testify before the Senate Health Committee, which he chaired. I described how the Kaiser Permanente Health Plan had saved substantial healthcare costs by providing free psychotherapy services to all high utilizers of healthcare services because such patients were unconsciously translating emotional distress into physical symptoms. As I wrote it in 1959 and as it was adopted as a prepaid benefit the following year, it was the first instance in which the universally excluded benefit of psychotherapy became a covered benefit. The subsequent positive experience at Kaiser Permanente captured Senator Kennedy's attention, and he asked me to serve as an unpaid advisor to his committee.

Senator Ted, as he allowed me to address him, was convinced that the time for prepaid universal healthcare had arrived, and he worked enthusiastically toward that end. His office frequently called me at my Kaiser Permanente office in San Francisco, and I was regularly asked to go to Washington for strategy meetings and Senate hearings. Those 3 years were an exciting time for me that suddenly and unexpectedly came to an abrupt end when the political climate in Washington drastically changed. President Nixon was in trouble and was soon to resign. The chair of the Senate Subcommittee on Health was suddenly yanked out from under him and given to conservative Southern senator Herman Talmadge, who promptly wiped away all the progress we had made toward universal health insurance. The political climate had greatly shifted, and being a novice politico I was confused and devastated. I wondered out loud why all this happened, when Senator Kennedy replied in words I shall never forget, "Nick, universal healthcare will arrive in America when General Motors wants it." I thought to myself at the time that such would never happen. But now that the senator has passed away, we have seen General Motors come out in favor of the Affordable Care Act, commonly known as Obamacare, which was enacted in 2012 and is in the process of being implemented in successive steps.

The article I have chosen as representative of this era does not describe this history, but *The Anatomy of Psychotherapy under National Health Insurance* (Cummings, 1977) renders a good picture of how universal prepaid psychotherapy would have been conducted had Senator Edward Kennedy's dream been enacted. It also underscores that I was predicting the inevitable arrival of integrated healthcare in 1964, more than 4 decades before APA president James Bray made it official policy in 2009.

The Triumph of Psychotropic Medications over Psychotherapy

As previously addressed, in the lucrative era of the 1990s, psychotherapists did not want to hear that this all was about to end. As a result, they resisted adopting briefer, more cost-effective treatments while psychiatry promised rapid, far less expensive relief through psychotropic meds. The outcome was inevitable: by 2014, more than 90% of patients with mental and emotional problems were prescribed one of the many psychotropic medications, and when psychotherapy was prescribed, it was in conjunction with meds and secondary to them. Alarmed, my coauthors and I published several books warning psychotherapists and suggesting effective alternatives (see, for example, Wright & Cummings, 2005; Cummings & O'Donohue, 2008; Cummings & O'Donohue, 2011).

Attempts to sound the alarm through journal articles met fierce rejection by the editors. This is why my article with Jack Wiggins (2001) appeared in an obscure journal. Included in the reference section, it published the results of the American Biodyne study that treated more than 300,000 children and adolescents who were diagnosed with ADHD with targeted psychotherapy, without medication and with remarkable results. Not only was psychology not addressing the psychotropic revolution, it resisted effective psychotherapeutic alternatives. This was the epitome of keeping one's head in the sand!

Behavioral Health in Primary Care: Dollars and Sense

By the mid-1990s, I was in my 70s, and, tiring of fighting both mainstream psychology and the burgeoning hostility of psychiatry, I decided to retire. After first getting assurance from my successors that they would continue delivering services in the prepaid manner of the small salaried group practices that had not only succeeded financially, but had not a single malpractice suit in my 10 years as CEO, I vacated my position. My successor and cofounder, Albert Waxman, could not admit not knowing how to administer the staff model, and after 6 months of floundering and refusing to acknowledge this, he transformed the company into a network model. Almost overnight the company had its first lawsuit. A patient in Detroit who was refused psychiatric hospitalization ran his car into a freeway abutment, killing his wife and two children. Miraculously, he survived, recovered, and sued the company. Seeing that the company had betrayed my trust, I sold my stock and did not participate in the successive morphing that has concluded in the current Magellan Health.

It became very apparent that not only my successors, but the several innovators who tried to emulate American Biodyne, had not the ability to deliver the innovative services that made the approach possible and profitable. In response, I published a how-to paper, "Behavioral Health in Primary Care: Dollars and Sense" (Cummings, 1997). As part of a comprehensive guide to behavioral health in primary care, it was widely read by physicians, but not psychologists. It introduced the reader to the concept of somatization, its effect on the medical system, and its treatment.

A New Vision of Healthcare in America

The dawning of the new millennium came after a 50-year history of often drastic changes in healthcare. From the founding in the 1930s of BlueCross/BlueShield as the first prepaid health insurance company, followed by the rise and failed attempt in the Nixon era to adopt capitated-prepaid healthcare such as was so successful at Kaiser Permanente, to the rejection of thrusts toward national healthcare by Senator Edward Kennedy, as slow as these changes in physical healthcare were, they seemed rapid as compared to the torturously slow pace of changes in mental healthcare (Cummings, 2001a).

At the turn of the millennium, however, psychologists were enjoying an unexpected financial bonanza. Psychiatrists had abandoned psychotherapy, replacing it with a burgeoning psychotropic medication practice. This left psychologists as the premier psychotherapists in the lucrative era that preceded the nation's current abandonment of behavioral interventions. To me, the two possible courses were obvious: (1) If psychologists adopted brief, but effective psychotherapy, as the sole dispensers of behavioral interventions they would capture a very lucrative field and thus prosper. On the other hand, (2) if they persisted in doing long-term psychotherapy it would not be long before the needy public would essentially move from psychology with its atavistic practices to psychiatry, which promised overnight improvement through medication. Because of the giant leaps in medicine, the public was lulled into the belief that such advances were possible also in medically controlled psychiatry. Seeing this coming, I tried in vain to point out how this demise could be avoided in a new era of prosperity with effective, brief psychotherapy (Cummings, 2001b, included herein as Number 5).

My thrust in enabling psychology to capture the burgeoning mental health treatment market was always to emphasize the value and efficacy of brief psychotherapy. If we did not espouse and promote the new advances in the brief psychotherapies research was demonstrating as remarkably effective, the public would understandably turn to medication psychiatry that promised overnight relief. The value added to the healthcare industry would be impressive savings in medical cost offset, that is, impressive dollar savings in medical and surgical costs.

In discussing medical/surgical cost savings, I introduced into the psychological literature the principles of the supply side versus the demand side of economics. Although well established in economics generally, the idea that reductions in demand can trump increases in supply was foreign to psychology in general, and contrary to the beliefs of long-term therapists. It went over like a lead balloon.

Knowing how foreign economic concepts were in my profession, I described with painstaking clarity successful published examples such as in bereavement and Alzheimer's counseling, and further described remarkable successful demonstrations in placing therapists in primary care settings. It only invoked a deaf ear from the overwhelming number of my colleagues. They even scoffed at the prediction that brief psychotherapy was *the* future.

The Next Phase in the Evolution of Behavioral Care and the Re-empowerment of the Practitioner

Undaunted, I continued my predictions, and began by not only describing what these would be, but flatly stating they were unavoidable no matter how long it would take. As not to be mired in vague generalities, a characteristic of most futurists, I made very specific, precise predictions from which I could not wiggle out of had any of these not materialized. My plethora of detractors was delighted. At once they thought I was foolish, and were pleased I had chosen to make myself vulnerable to inevitable disgrace. Far-reaching changes take time to evolve, and during these years the chorus of derision grew louder. My audiences at the APA and other psychology meetings grew smaller and smaller. But I kept speaking and writing, even though my audiences diminished and journals increasingly rejected my writings. This later was countered by my writing books asserting the predictions while continuing to expand on them, and reemphasizing organized psychology's myopia.

I am a gregarious sort and I do not take these kinds of attacks personally. For this I am grateful, as throughout I maintained my closeness to all my friends and we continued to enjoy each other even though most had been severe critics. Typical was the warm remark by Dr. Donald Friedman, after I had delivered a rousing but failed speech on managed care in the APA Council of Representatives, "Nick, that was terrific. I would rather hear a great speech by someone I completely disagree with than a boring speech by someone I totally agree with."

In delineating what I saw as the inevitable, I have chosen as typical "The Next Phase in the Evolution of Behavioral Care and Its Re-empowerment of the Practitioner" (Cummings, 2000). The profession had gone far afield from the era of prepaid, capitated staff-model behavioral healthcare with only three such large-scale delivery systems remaining: Kaiser Permanente on the West Coast, by far the largest in the world; Geisinger Health Care in Pennsylvania; and the smaller but impressive Cherokee Health System in Tennessee. Even the company I had founded, in spite of promises not to abandon the staff model, morphed through a series of iterations and acquisitions to what is now Magellan Health, a national company with seven different health divisions, of which mental health is only one. All of its divisions utilize national networks of respective providers. Interesting, my son Andrew Cummings, American Biodyne's first in-house lawyer, remained with the company from its earliest days and is now senior executive vice president in charge of operations for all seven of its divisions.

Since networks are far more difficult to control than close-knit staff systems, my writings in this era emphasized cost and therapeutic effective models that could survive the period in which practitioners had lost control of healthcare delivery. It addressed the new healthcare delivery system that was subject to a plethora of government and industrial regulations, most of which hampered effective healthcare delivery in spite of its intent to facilitate it. In attempts to prevent abuses by corporate healthcare giants, government regulation too often interfered with the exercise of practice.

A New Vision of Healthcare for America

Seeing that the still lucrative but isolated long-term psychotherapy profession simply ignored the concept of behavioral health's inevitable integration into primary care, I published my "New Vision of Healthcare for America" (Cummings, 2001b). It projected a positive tone for the future as psychotherapy became an integral part of healthcare.

Years earlier, my former psychology comrade, Dr. Rogers Wright, had discerned that American Biodyne was the wave of the future, and offered to join me. I was delighted and eager to have him on board. Rog had for years been providing brief therapy to his patients, but he knew nothing about integrated care. I offered him a starting position in one of our centers, and indicated I was certain that within 6 months he would not only have learned the system, but his long-proven administrative abilities would see him promoted to that of a center director. He was incensed, shouting that he was a senior practitioner and he either started at the top or not at all. Not getting his way made him a vociferous enemy of managed care. To this day I am convinced that had Rog come on board in the late 1980s, his national standing as a spokesperson for clinical psychology would have precluded the years of professional hostility toward what was inevitable. Rather than in 2009 when APA president James Bray, on behalf of the APA, officially espoused integrated behavioral/primary care, the inevitable would have occurred 15 years earlier (see Bray, 2011).

My 2001 article took notice of the rapidly changing health system and delineated just how behavioral health would function within primary care. It provided several examples of proven programs such as bereavement and Alzheimer's counseling right in the primary care setting, all of which Bray supported and included in his pronouncement.

Medical Costs and Managed Mental Health Treatment

As we entered the second decade of the 21st century with its newfound interest in integrated behavioral and primary care, the thirst for "how-to" knowledge heightened. In response, the methods of the highly successful Hawaii Medicaid Project were revisited (see, for example, Pallak et al., 1994). "Understanding the Behavioral Healthcare Crisis" (edited by Cummings & O'Donohue, 2011) was widely circulated. There was suddenly a remarkable abatement of hostility toward me.

On the other hand, seemingly overnight, a large number of advocates for integrated care seemed to come out of the woodwork, all claiming to be experts. Along with the Johnny-come-latelies, who exaggerated their past experience, were the former antagonists who now claimed to be long-term advocates. All of these ignored our years of advocacy and proffered themselves as newly proclaimed leaders of this new age. Even Bray, the first time around in the writing of his 2011 chapter, wrote as if he not only proclaimed integrated care, but invented it. This was rectified at the insistence of the coeditor. Regardless, integrated care will undoubtedly move forward with the Affordable Care Act, although as in all thrusts, there will be glitches and setbacks.

Resolving the Dilemmas in Mental Healthcare Delivery

The often-quoted statement of George Bernard Shaw more than a century ago regarding economists could not be more accurate than it is in healthcare: "If all economists were laid end to end, they still wouldn't reach an agreement." The soon to be enacted Affordable Care Act, along with the 2009 espousal of integrated care by both APAs, would only open the door to heated debates about access, stigma, fragmentation, conflicting research, and politics, as well as an inevitable as yet unpredictable array of disagreements (Cummings, 2005). This prediction, made several years before these advances were enacted, could not have been more prescient.

Access and stigma turned out to be essentially self-created artifacts. Inasmuch as 80% of mental healthcare is delivered by primary care physicians, only 10% of patients had to cross the chasm of stigma by actually seeing a mental health professional. An APA study (Saunders, 2003) of focus groups revealed that cost and lack of insurance were the main barriers. Stigma was a surprisingly distant second. Needless to say, the APA did not disseminate its own findings.

Predictably, the mental health organizations ignored this information, as well as the entire array of problems of fragmentation, conflicting research, and, most of all, political infighting. This head-in-the-sand behavior prompted me to write several articles addressing the increasing instances of defeatism in the face of the rapidly changing healthcare system.

Psychology's Inadvertent Vow of Poverty

Interesting, at this time, more and more mental health professionals grew concerned that their livelihoods were slipping away. Resistance to my writings diminished as colleagues began to read such in-your-face pieces as my *Eleven Blunders that Cripple Psychotherapy in America* (Cummings & O'Donohue, 2008). Dismay increased over the mental health professional societies' lack of effective response, and feeling helpless, they voted with their feet. Our professional societies were subjected to a surprisingly enlarged number of practitioners who dropped their memberships, or who upon graduation did not join in the first place. The APA tried to counter this by giving new graduates free memberships, which they accepted only not to renew when the freebie expired.

This was now the era of increased online publications, and I made much use of this. Typical is our paradoxical online article, "We Are Not a Healthcare Business: Our Inadvertent Vow of Poverty" (Cummings, Cummings, & O'Donohue, 2008), which was widely disseminated and continued to be over several years.

Addendum

After I had founded an integrated behavioral/primary care curriculum in three successive universities, only to see each made ineffectual by their respective psychology departments, I was not encouraged by APA president James Bray's 2009 declaration fostering integrated care. Neither was Arizona State University's (ASU) president, Michael Crow, who had been named by *Time* magazine "America's University President" for his prescience. He and the chair of the board of trustees, Robert Bulla, were well acquainted with my work and invited me to found a training program at ASU. They overcame my thrice-burned resistance by offering to place the program in Health Solutions, ASU's newly formed medical array, which included the medical school consortium with Mayo Rochester, the School of Nursing, and other innovative healthcare programs. He brought in Provost Elizabeth "Betty" Phillips (nee Capaldi), who paved the way and created a firewall between the new program and the psychology department. It would not be a PhD, which would have been in the College of Letters and Sciences. Rather, it was a new degree in healthcare. Thus in 1979, the Nicholas A. Cummings Doctor of Behavioral Health Program (DBH degree) was founded with 25 students.

As of this writing, the program has been so successful it had to be capped at 300 students to prevent dilution of its one-to-one teaching. It is flooded with applications, so we can pick the best of the best. To apply, one must have a master's degree and be licensed in social work, counseling, psychiatric nursing, or some such related mental health field, plus no fewer than 7 years of experience. The average for our students is 11 years of experience. We look for students who are out-of-the-box thinkers, akin for psychotherapists to the iconoclasts of Silicon Valley who changed the Internet world.

And so, indeed, they are changing the business of mental healthcare. Where PhD and PsyD graduates in psychology suffer a high unemployment or underemployment rate, our DBH graduates are snapped up immediately upon graduation because of their relevance to today's primary mental healthcare needs. They are hired to create and administer integrated care in clinics, hospitals, and medical practices. Four of our graduates are CEOs of huge statewide or national healthcare systems. Still others have created brand new delivery systems, such as integrated pharmacy. Because they are already licensed to practice when they come into the program, they need no further licensure after graduation.

With the retirement of Provost Capaldi Phillips, the new provost began the process of returning the DBH program to the traditional College of Letters and Sciences. This necessitated pulling the Cummings program out of ASU and establishing an independent, freestanding university. Named the Cummings Graduate Institute, it was launched in 2015 with me as founding board chair, and my daughter Dr. Janet Cummings as the president heads an extensive, innovative, and prescient faculty and administration.

Interesting, the APA, the National Association of Social Work, and the American Counseling Association have not acknowledged that the DBH program even exists. That it is remarkably successful at a time when so much of mental healthcare delivery is taking a back seat to medication is being ignored or even hushed up. As for me, now in my 90s, I am having a ball.

References

Austad, C. S. (2014). *Psychology's provocateur: Nicholas A. Cummings*. Ithaca, NY: Ithaca Press.

Bray, J. H. (2011). Reforms in treating children and families. In N. A. Cummings & W. T. O'Donohue (Eds.), *Understanding the behavioral healthcare crisis: The promise of integrated care and diagnostic reform* (pp. 343–365). New York: Routledge.

Cummings, N. A. (1969, October). California school of professional psychology. *Journal of Clinical Issues in Psychology, 1*(1), 1–30.

Cummings, N. A. (1977). The anatomy of psychotherapy under national health insurance. *American Psychologist, 32*(9), 711–718.

Cummings, N. A. (1979). Turning Bread into Stones: Our Modern Anti-miracle. American Psychologist, 34(12), 1119–1129.

Cummings, N. A. (1991). Arguments for the financial efficacy of psychological services in healthcare settings. In J. J. Sweet, R. G. Rozensky, & S. M. Tovian (Eds.), *Handbook of clinical psychology in medical settings* (pp. 113–124). New York: Plenum.

Cummings, N. A. (1997). Behavioral health in primary care: Dollars and sense. In N. A. Cummings, J. L. Cummings, & J. N. Johnson (Eds.), *Behavioral health in primary care: A guide for clinical integration* (pp. 3–20). Madison, CT: Psychosocial Press.

Cummings, N. A. (2000, Summer). The next phase in the evolution of behavioral care and its re-empowerment of the practitioner. *The Independent Practitioner*, 171–175.

Cummings, N. A. (2001a). A history of behavioral healthcare: A perspective from a lifetime of involvement. In N. A. Cummings, W. O'Donohue, S. C. Hayes, & V. Follette (Eds.), *Integrated behavioral healthcare: Positioning mental health practice with medical/surgical practice* (pp. 1–18). San Diego, CA: Academic Press.

Cummings, N. A. (2001b). A new vision of healthcare for America. In N. A. Cummings, W. O'Donohue, S. C. Hayes, & V. Follette (Eds.), *Integrated behavioral healthcare: Positioning mental health practice with medical/surgical practice* (pp. 19–38). San Diego, CA: Academic Press.

Cummings, N. A. (2005). Resolving the dilemmas in mental healthcare delivery: Access, stigma, fragmentation, conflicting research, politics and more. In N. A. Cummings, W. T. O'Donohue, & M. A. Cucciare (Eds.), *Universal healthcare: Readings for mental health professionals* (pp. 47–74). Reno, NV: Context Press.

Cummings, N. A., Cummings, J. L., & O'Donohue, W. (2008). We are not a healthcare business: Our inadvertent vow of poverty. *Journal of Contemporary Psychotherapy*.

Cummings, N. A., & Follette, W. T. (1968). Psychiatric services and medical utilization in a prepaid health plan setting: Part 2. *Medical Care, 6*, 31–41.

Cummings, N. A., & O'Donohue, W. T. (2008). *Eleven blunders that cripple psychotherapy in America: A remedial unblundering.* New York: Routledge.

Cummings, N. A., & O'Donohue, W. T. (Eds.). (2011). *Understanding the behavioral healthcare crisis.* New York: Routledge.

Cummings, N. A., & VandenBos, G. R. (1981). The twenty year Kaiser Permanente experience with psychotherapy and medical utilization: Implications for national health policy and national health insurance. *Health Policy Quarterly, 1*(2), 159–175.

Cummings, N. A., & Wright, R. H. (1991, Spring). Managed mental healthcare: Two perspectives. *Advance Plan*, 1–2, 14–15.

Follette, W. T., & Cummings, N. A. (1967). Psychiatric services and medical utilization in a prepaid health plan setting. *Medical Care, 5*, 5–25.

Pallak, M. S., Cummings, N. A., Dörken, H., & Henke, C. J. (1994). Medical costs, Medicaid, and managed mental health treatment: The Hawaii Study. *Managed Care Quarterly, 2*(2), 64–70.

Saunders, T. R. (2003). Personal communication.

Simon, R. (2009, January 2). Psychology's soothsayer: Nick Cummings foretells your future. *The Psychotherapy Networker,* www.psychotherapynetworker.org/ . . . 499-psychotherapy-soothsayer.

Wright, R. H., & Cummings, N. A. (Eds.). (2005). *Destructive trends in mental health: The well-intentioned path to harm.* New York: Routledge.

1 The California School of Professional Psychology

One Alternative to the Extinction of Professional Psychology

Nicholas A. Cummings[*]

As society's need for journeyman mental health professionals grows, and as the public clamor for more professional psychologists increases, we have witnessed the curious and alarming trend for leading universities to abandon their clinical psychology programs. This "Harvard-Stanford Phenomenon," named after the universities that led the way, is expected to gather momentum. Meanwhile, the lesser colleges and universities expected to fill the deficit by initiating professional psychology programs have found it difficult, if not impossible, to surmount costs, APA scientific (rather than professional) requirements for approval, and, above all, faculty apathy and unresponsiveness to the needs in this area. Alarmed by what appears to be a serious situation, the California State Psychological Association (CSPA) launched a full-scale investigation and discovered that there was, indeed, a crisis. The most populous state, with the greatest complex of public universities and colleges the world has ever seen, and which culminates in a system of city colleges that places a junior college in virtually every community of 20,000 or more, graduated fewer than one dozen clinical psychologists in 1968! Looking to the future, CSPA was dismayed to learn that the University of California (UC) reduced its 1968–1969 class of clinical psychology students to three! The state colleges interested in granting doctorates in psychology have been virtually stymied. The other UC campuses have plans mostly along academic-physiological-experimental models, almost as if Berkeley has cast a long, ominous shadow of disapproval toward any budding daughter campus that might entertain thoughts of heretic, non-scientific training. And even more curious, while this atrophy continues, the interest of potential graduate students is remarkably high and seemingly unmindful of psychology's apparent determination for self-attrition. Year after year, doctoral programs receive upward of 20 to 30 applicants for each graduate student opening.

So, in spite of enthusiastic public and student acceptance, we are likely to be the first professional species to enter extinction because we could not master the

---

[*] Portions of this paper have been printed in the California State *Psychologist* and the Annual Report of the National Council on Graduate Education in Psychology.

simple facts of self-reproduction. This curious phenomenon is not limited to the state of California. The hundreds of letters we have received have led us to believe that if state associations were to examine the educational crisis facing professional psychology within their own borders, they would come to a similar conclusion.

The facts have always been before us, but because we cherish our profession, we have frantically denied that we have heard the death-rattle. And, for many of us, the prospect of challenging both our rejecting mother-university who reluctantly spawned us, and our impotent APA-father who has been dominated by her, was too painful a confrontation. So, a profession that was able to solve the problems of licensure, that was successful in building viable state associations, and that is about to win the struggle for insurance reimbursement, was content to feed these facts into an AGNOSTICON, a computer that does not know what it is supposed to do but that, nonetheless, prescribes large doses of AGNOSTAMINE, a palliative for when you don't know what ails you. In other words, we have pleaded, reasoned, cajoled, and courted the university system year after year, all the time hoping that the courteous non-response and the frequent hostility were only temporary.

Just as the professions of law, medicine, social work, and engineering achieved their destinies by owning their educational processes, CSPA believes professional psychology must decisively determine by its service-experience the quality of education required to prepare the graduate, rather than merely purport to prepare him, for his service to society. Let me tell you what CSPA has done in this regard.

Two years ago, a blue-ribbon committee chaired by Professor Sheldon Korchin, director of clinical training at UC, was asked to once again assemble the facts to make certain we had not deluded ourselves. This panel of distinguished psychologists performed an admirable job of documenting a bleak picture, rendered even more bleak by their inability to offer solutions within the academic system. This past year we have earnestly spoken with university and college chancellors, presidents, and psychology department heads, as well as to the governor's advisor on education, and we have ascertained that there are no plans that would significantly increase the approximately one dozen clinical psychologists who are graduated with PhDs annually in the entire state of California. We have spent countless hours talking with graduate students and have been appalled to learn that important, meaningful clinical training is, with but a few notable exceptions, as difficult to come by now as it was 20 years ago when many of us were frantically bootlegging our real training outside the gates of the university. We have met with administrators of public and private agencies and institutions and empathized with them as they recounted their mounting staff shortages. We appointed another blue-ribbon committee, which this time included the California Psychology Examining Committee, to think through the entire issue of a sub-doctoral cadre as one solution to the shortage of trained psychologists. Its scholarly report soundly reaffirmed the PhD as the journeyman level in psychology, and underscored the need for supervision and training of sub-professionals, which will necessitate the creation of even more professional psychologists if we are not to abrogate still another psychological function to our medical colleagues. And, finally, CSPA investigated the legalities and feasibility of founding its own school, chartered by the state to confer degrees, including the PhD itself.

Weighing all of these facts and developments, the CSPA Executive Board last December unanimously approved a two-faceted course of direct action. The first was to continue enthusiastic support of the NCCEP drive for university professional programs independent of psychology departments. The second was the establishment of a state association–sponsored, state-chartered, independent, PhD-granting professional school. Two months later, in February 1969, the California School of Professional Psychology (CSPP) was incorporated.

The response to what will be the first autonomous professional psychology school has been instantaneous and electric. But those of us charged with implementing our goal feel deeply the responsibility, the challenge, and the unprecedented opportunity. The avalanche of offers and suggestions must be patiently and cautiously investigated. In its first month of existence, CSPP has made the following progress and has affirmed the following principles.

Governing Structure

The school must always reflect the needs and evolution of the profession of psychology without being subject to its whims. It must also be responsive to its faculty, and it must accord a voice to its students. Although autonomous of CSPA, the school must recognize that in California, the profession of psychology is represented by the state association. Therefore, of the eventual 16-member board of directors, CSPA has elected 9, while the faculty will elect 5 and the student body will elect 2.

Degrees and Curriculum

The professional school will seek to meet the requirements of society for both professional and sub-professional personnel, with training at the 2-, 4-, 6-, and 8-year levels, leading to the AA, BA, MA, and PhD degrees, respectively. From the beginning the program would encourage upward mobility with the opportunity to qualify for the next educational level, either immediately or after a period of employment. An important feature would be the opportunity for minority or culturally disadvantaged students to enter a realistic program that provides an educational ladder, rather than to merely lock in such students on the lowest level of the mental health manpower scale. On the doctoral level, priority would be given to the thousands of master's-level working psychologists who would eagerly enter a realistic professional program if such were available.

Initially the school will concentrate on the first 2 and the last 2 years of the 8-year program, offering an associate in arts as the basis of a sub-doctoral cadre, and a 2-year doctoral program to qualified applicants who already possess a solid master's degree in psychology. These two extremes reflect the greatest need and the best opportunity for funding. Currently we are in serious discussion with the California Society of Psychiatric Technicians, which is interested in our assuming the 2-year training program, which in California culminates in a state license as a psychiatric technician.

Freed from the strangulation of the university psychology department, and unfettered by archaic APA requirements, we are determined to develop the best possible professional curriculum. Entering classes for the PhD will number 25 on each campus, and the students will move in unison along a regular schedule, rather than be demoralized by the possibility of taking prelims at some vague point of preparation at an even more obscure time interval. Dr. Hedda Bolgar, one of the school's directors, is chairing a subcommittee charged not only with devising the best possible curriculum, but to dovetail it with existing academic programs and to coordinate it with the Psychology Examining Committee so that our graduates will be eligible to be licensed under the laws of the State of California. This is a difficult and complex undertaking, and we are innovating with what paradoxically might be described as "cautious boldness."

Campuses

There will be two campuses serving the population centers of California: Los Angeles and San Francisco. Currently we are investigating several offers from existing, but relatively inoperative colleges that have offered affiliation and their existing state charters to grant higher degrees. Whether we shall accept one of these offers, or whether we shall start from scratch, will be determined by the direction that accords the best combination of viability and autonomy.

No one is more mindful than we of the enormity of the task that confronts us. Yet our timetable, which will have CSPP fully operative within 3 years, is a realistic and carefully determined goal. We have even received letters of support from chairmen of psychology departments that suggest that once the academe has surmounted his initial rage, he may be grateful to be relieved of training year after year clinical students who are hostile and disinterested in his ideas. CSPA does not regard the autonomous professional school as a solution only in California, for we offer it as a precedent and a model to the entire profession. We need the interest and support of professional psychologists everywhere, and within the next few months we shall be meeting with psychologists in a series of regional and state meetings to discuss our undertaking. There are excellent probabilities of grants and foundation gifts, but the profession will have to bear a share of the initial funding. The many enthusiastic letters we have received from all parts of the nation have demonstrated that CSPP is a realistic alternative to the extinction of professional psychology.

2 Psychiatric Services and Medical Utilization in a Prepaid Health Plan Setting I

William T. Follette and Nicholas A. Cummings[**]

In two previous studies,[1,2] the psychiatric practitioner's contention that emotionally disturbed patients do not seek organic treatment for their complaints following the intervention of psychotherapy have been investigated. Although it has long been recognized that a large number of the physical complaints seen by the physician are emotionally, rather than organically, determined, the more precise relationship between problems in living and their possible expression through apparent physical symptomatology has been difficult to test experimentally. As noted in the previous study, the GHI Project[3] demonstrated that users of psychiatric services were also significantly frequent users of medical services, but the Project was not able to answer the question of whether there is a reduction in the use of medical services following psychotherapy.

Because the facilities and structure of the Kaiser Foundation Health Plan accord an experimental milieu not available to Avnet, the original pilot project in San Francisco was able to demonstrate a significant reduction in medical utilization between the year prior to psychotherapy, and the 2 years following its intervention. Certain methodologic problems inherent to tie pilot study indicated caution and the need for refinement and replication to avoid arriving at premature conclusions. The lack of a control group of what might be termed psychologically disturbed high-utilizers who did not receive psychotherapy was a serious omission

[**] Presented at one of the Contributed Papers Sessions sponsored by the Medical Care Section at the 94th annual meeting of the American Public Health Association, San Francisco, California, October 31–November 4, 1966.

This study was primarily financed by Grant PH 108–64–100 (P), U.S. Public Health Service. The authors gratefully acknowledge the assistance and cooperation of Mr. Royal Crystal, Deputy Chief, Health Economics Branch. Secondary financial support for this study was through Grant No. 131–7241, Kaiser Foundation Research Institute.

This paper is a report of the first of two investigations seeking to develop and test methods of assessing the effect of psychiatric services on medical utilization in a comprehensive medical program. Part II deals with prospective, rather than retrospective, methodology, and will be reported later.

in the first experiment.[†] Furthermore, an error in the tabulation of inpatient utilization was discovered after the experiment had been concluded.[††] In addition, the question was raised whether the patients studied might, subsequent to the 2 years following psychotherapy, revert to previous patterns of somatization or, as a new pattern, merely substitute protracted and costly psychotherapy for previous medical treatment.

The Problem

This study investigated the question of whether there is a change in patients' utilization of outpatient and inpatient medical facilities after psychotherapy, comparing the patients studied to a matched group who did not receive psychotherapy.

Psychotherapy was defined as any contact with the Department of Psychiatry, even if the patient was seen for an initial interview only. The year prior to the initial contact was compared with the 5 subsequent years in both groups.

The problem can be stated simply: Is the provision of psychiatric services associated with a reduction of medical services utilization (defined as visits to other medical clinics, outpatient laboratory and x-ray procedures, and days of hospitalization)?

Methodology

The setting: the Kaiser Foundation Health Plan in the Northern California region is a group-practice prepayment plan offering comprehensive hospital and professional services on a direct service basis. Professional services are provided by the Permanente Medical Group—a partnership of physicians. The Medical Group has a contract to provide comprehensive medical care to the subscribers, of whom there were more than a half million at the time of this study. The composition of the Health Plan subscribers is diverse, encompassing most socioeconomic groups. The Permanente Medical Group comprises all major medical specialties; referral from one specialty clinic to another is facilitated by the organizational features of group practice, geographical proximity, and use of common medical records. During the years of this study (1959–1964), psychiatry was essentially not covered by the Northern California Health Plan on a prepaid basis, but in some areas of the Northern California region psychiatric services were available to Health Plan subscribers at reduced rates. During the 6 years of the study, the psychiatric clinic staff in San Francisco consisted of psychiatrists, clinical psychologists,

---

[†] The authors acknowledge their debt to Dr. M. F. Collen for this and other suggestions, and to Mr. Arthur Weissman, medical economist, Kaiser Foundation Medical Care Entities, for his expert consultation.

[††] At that time days of hospitalization per patient and by year were tabulated from each patient's outpatient medical records. Subsequent investigation has revealed that only about a third of the outpatient charts reviewed contained summaries of hospital admissions, and that tabulation of inpatient utilization must be made directly through the separately kept inpatient records.

psychiatric social workers, resident psychiatrists at the third- or fourth-year level, and psychology interns, all full-time. The clinic operates primarily as an outpatient service for adults (age 18 or older), for the evaluation and treatment of emotional disorders, but it also provides consultation for non-psychiatric physicians and consultation in the general hospital and the emergency room. There is no formal "intake" procedure, the first visit with any staff member being considered potentially therapeutic as well as evaluative and dispositional. Regardless of professional discipline, the person who sees the patient initially becomes that patient's therapist unless there is a reason for transfer to some other staff member, and he continues to see the patient for the duration of the therapy. An attempt is made to schedule the first interview as soon as possible after the patient calls for an appointment. There is also a "drop-in" or non-appointment service for emergencies so that patients in urgent need of psychiatric help usually can be seen immediately or at least within an hour or two of arrival at the clinic.

One of the unique aspects of this kind of associated health plan and medical group is that it tends to put a premium on health rather than on illness, i.e., it makes preventive medicine economically rewarding, thereby stimulating a constant search for the most effective and specific methods of treatment. The question of how psychiatry fits into comprehensive prepaid medical care is largely unexplored; there are not many settings in which it can be answered. Another feature of group practice in this setting is that all medical records for each patient are retained within the organization.

Subjects: The experimental subjects for this investigation were selected systematically by including every fifth psychiatric patient whose initial interview took place between January 1 and December 31, 1960. Of the 152 patients thus selected, 80 were seen for one interview only, 41 were seen for two to eight interviews (mean of 6.2) and were defined as "brief therapy," and 31 were seen for nine or more interviews (mean of 33.9) and were defined as "long-term therapy."

To provide a control group, the medical records of high medical utilizers who had never presented themselves to the Department of Psychiatry were reviewed until a group was selected that matched the psychotherapy sample in age, sex, socioeconomic status, medical utilization in the year 1959, Health Plan membership including at least the years 1959 through 1962, and criteria of psychological distress. Thus, each experimental patient was matched with a control patient in the criteria above, but without reference to any other variable. Both samples ranged in age from 24 to 62, with a mean of 38.1. Of these, 52% were women and 63% were blue-collar workers or their dependents. The satisfaction of so many criteria in choosing a matched control group proved a tedious and time-consuming procedure.

Review of the medical records of the psychiatric sample disclosed consistent and conceptually useful notations in the year prior to the patients' coming to psychotherapy, which could be considered as *criteria of psychological distress*. These consisted of recordings, made by the physicians on the dates of the patients' visits, which were indicative of those patients' emotional distress, whether or not the physicians recognized this when they made the notations. These (38) criteria were assigned weights from 1 to 3 in accordance with the frequency of their appearance in medical records and in accordance with clinical experience about the significance of the criteria when encountered in psychotherapeutic practice. The criteria, with weights assigned, are presented in Table 2.1. In comparing the charts of the psychiatric patients with those of Health Plan patients randomly drawn, it was determined that although some criteria were occasionally present in the medical records of the latter, a weighted score of 3 within 1 year clearly differentiated the psychiatric from the non-psychiatric groups. Accordingly, therefore, in matching the control (non-psychotherapy) group to the experimental (psychotherapy) group, the patients selected had records that indicated scores of 3 or more points for the year 1959. The mean weights of the three experimental groups and the control group in terms of the 38 criteria of psychological distress are presented in Table 2.2: note that there was no significant difference between this dimension of the two groups in 1959.

In order to facilitate comparison of the experimental (psychotherapy) and control (non-psychotherapy) groups, one last criterion for inclusion in the matched group was employed. Each subject in the control group had to be a Health Plan member for the first 3 consecutive years under investigation inasmuch as the experimental group, though demonstrating attrition in continued membership after that time, remained intact for those years.

Dependent variable: Each psychiatric patient's utilization of health facilities was investigated first for the full year preceding the day of his initial interview, then for each of the succeeding 5 years beginning with the day after his initial interview.

The corresponding years were investigated for the control group, which, of course, was not seen in the Department of Psychiatry. This investigation consisted of a straightforward tabulation of each contact with any outpatient facility, each laboratory report, and x-ray report.* In addition, a tabulation of number of days of hospitalization was made without regard to the type or quantity of service provided. Each patient's utilization scores consisted of the total number of separate outpatient and inpatient tabulations.

Results

The results of this study are summarized in Table 2.3, which shows the differences by group in utilization of outpatient medical facilities in the year before and the 5 years after the initial interview for the psychiatric sample, and the utilization of outpatient medical services for the corresponding 6 years for the non-psychotherapy sample.

The data of Table 2.3 are summarized as percentages in Table 2.4, which indicates a decline in outpatient medical (not including psychiatric) utilization for all

---

* These procedures were counted as one even if there was more than one laboratory or x-ray procedure per report in the chart.

Table 2.1 Criteria of Psychological Distress with Assigned Weights

One point	Two points	Three points
1 Tranquilizer or sedative requested. 2 Doctor's statement pt. is tense, chronically tired, was reassured, etc. 3 Patient's statement as in no. 2. 4 Lump in throat. * 5 Health Questionnaire: yes on one or two psych. questions. 6 Alopecia areata. 7 Vague, unsubstantiated pain. 8 Tranquilizer or sedative given. 9 Vitamin B_{12} shots (except for pernicious anemia). 10 Negative EEG. 11 Migraine or psychogenic headache. 12 More than four upper respiratory infections per year. 13 Menstrual or premenstrual tension; menopausal sex. 14 Consults doctor about difficulty in childrearing. 15 Chronic allergic state. 16 Compulsive eating (or overeating). 17 Chronic gastrointestinal upset; aereophagia. 18 Chronic skin disease. 19 Anal pruritus. 20 Excessive scratching. 21 Use of emergency room: two or more visits per year. 22 Brings written list of symptoms or complaints to doctor.	23 Fear of cancer, brain tumor, venereal disease, heart disease, leukemia, diabetes, etc. * 24 Health Questionnaire: yes on three or more psych, questions. 25 Two or more accidents (bone fractures, etc.) within 1 yr. Pt. may be alcoholic. 26 Alcoholism or its complications: delirium tremens, peripheral neuropathy, cirrhosis. 27 Spouse is angry at doctor and demands different treatment for patient. 28 Seen by hypnotist or seeks referral to hypnotist. 29 Requests surgery, which is refused. 30 Vasectomy: requested or performed. 31 Hyperventilation syndrome. 32 Repetitive movements noted by doctor: tics, grimaces, mannerisms, torticollis, hysterical seizures. 33 Weightlifting and/or health faddism.	34 Unsubstantiated complaint there is something wrong with genitals. 35 Psychiatric referral made or requested. 36 Suicidal attempt, threat, or preoccupation. 37 Fear of homosexuals or of homosexuality. 38 Nonorganic delusions and/or hallucinations; paranoid ideation; psychotic thinking or psychotic behavior.

* Refers to the last four questions (relating to emotional distress) on a modified Cornell Medical Index—a general medical questionnaire given to patients undergoing the Multiphasic Health Check in the years concerned (1959–1962).

Table 2.2 Scores for Criteria of Psychological Distress, for the Experimental Groups and the Control Group during the Year Prior to Psychotherapy (1959)

Group	Total score	No. of patients	Average score
One session only	264	80	3.30
Brief therapy	134	41	3.27
Long-term therapy	246	31	7.94
All experimental (psychotherapy) groups	644	152	4.24
Control (non-psychotherapy) group	629	152	4.13

Table 2.3 Utilization of Outpatient Medical Services (Excluding Psychiatry) by Psychotherapy Groups for the Year before (1-B) and the 5 Years after (1-A, 2-A, 3-A, 4-A, 5-A) the Initial Interview, and the Corresponding Years for the Nonpsychiatric Group

Group	1-B	1-A	2-A	3-A	4-A	5-A
One session only, unit score	911	815	612	372	321	217
No. of pts.	80	80	80	57	53	49
Average	11.4	10.2	7.7	6.5	6.1	4.4
Brief therapy, unit score	778	471	354	202	215	155
No. of pts.	41	41	41	32	30	27
Average	19.0	11.5	8.6	6.3	7.2	5.7
Long-term therapy, unit score	359	323	279	236	151	108
No. of pts.	31	31	31	27	24	19
Average	11.6	10.4	9.0	8.7	6.5	5.7
All experimental (psychotherapy) groups, unit score	2,048	1,609	1,245	810	687	480
No. of pts.	152	152	152	116	107	95
Average	13.5	10.6	8.2	6.4	6.4	5.1
Control (non-psychotherapy) group, unit score	1,726	1,743	1,718	1,577	1,611	1,264
No. of pts.	152	152	152	127	111	98
Average	11.4	11.5	11.3	12.4	14.5	12.9

three psychotherapy groups for the years following the initial interview, while there is a tendency for the non-psychotherapy patients to increase medical utilization during the corresponding years. Applying t-tests of the significance of the standard error of the difference between the means of the "year before" and the means of each of the 5 "years after" (as compared to the year before), the following results obtain. The declines in outpatient (non-psychiatric) utilization for the "one session only" and the "long-term therapy" groups are not significant for the first year following the initial interview, while the declines are significant at either the 0.05 or 0.01 levels for the remaining 4 years. In the "brief therapy" group,

Table 2.4 Comparison of the Year Prior to the Initial Interview with each Succeeding Year, Indicating Percent Decline or Percent Increase (Latter Shown in Parentheses) in Outpatient Medical (Non-psychiatric) Utilization by Psychotherapy Grouping, and Corresponding Comparisons for the Control Group, with Levels of Significance

Group	1-A		2-A		3-A		4-A		5-A	
	% change	Signif.	% change	Signif.	% change	Signif.	change	Signif.	% change.	Signif.
One session only	10.5	NS	32.8	0.05	44.75	0.05	46.5	0.05	61.4	0.01
Brief therapy	39.5	0.05	53.2	0.05	66.8	0.01	62.1	0.01	70.0	0.01
Long-term therapy	10.0	NS	22.3	0.05	25.0	0.05	43.0	0.05	50.9	0.05
All experimental (psychotherapy) groups	21.4	0.05	39.2	0.01	48.2	0.01	52.3	0.01	62.5	0.01
Control (non-psychiatric) group	None	—	None	—	(8.8)	NS	(27.2)	0.05	(13.2)	NS

there are statistically significant declines in all 5 years following the initial interview. As further indicated in Table 2.4, there is a tendency for the control group to *increase* its utilization of medical services, but this proved significant for the "fourth year after" only.

The question was raised as to whether the patients demonstrating declines in medical utilization have done so because they have merely substituted protracted psychotherapy visits for their previous medical visits.

As shown in Table 2.5, the number of patients in the one-session-only group who return in the third to fifth years for additional visits is negligible. Comparable results are seen in the brief-therapy group. In contrast, the long-term-therapy group reduces its psychiatric utilization by more than half in the "second year after," but maintains this level in the succeeding 3 years. By adding the outpatient medical visits to the psychiatric visits, it becomes clear that whereas the first two psychotherapy groups have not substituted psychotherapy for medical visits, this does seem to be the case in the long-term psychotherapy group. These results are shown in Table 2.6, and indicate that the *combined* outpatient utilization remains about the same from the "year before" to the "fifth year after" for the third psychotherapy group, while declines are evident for the first two psychotherapy groups. As regards the combined (medical plus psychiatric) utilization, the long-term psychotherapy group is not appreciably different from the control (non-psychiatric) group.

Investigation of inpatient utilization reveals a steady decline in utilization in the three psychotherapy groups from the "year before" to the "second year after," with

Table 2.5 Average Number of Psychotherapy Sessions per Year for 5 Years by Experimental Group

Group	1-A	2-A	3-A	4-A	5-A
One session only	1.00	0.00	0.00	0.02	0.06
Brief therapy	6.22	0.00	0.09	0.57	0.52
Long-term therapy	12.33	5.08	5.56	5.88	5.05

Table 2.6 Combined Averages (Outpatient Medical plus Psychotherapy Visits) of Utilization by Years before and after Psychotherapy for the Experimental Groups, and Total Outpatient Utilization by Corresponding Years for the Control (Non-psychiatric) Group

Group	1-B	1-A	2-A	3-A	4-A	5-A
One session only	11.4	11.2	7.7	6.5	6.1	4.5
Brief therapy	19.0	17.7	8.6	6.4	7.7	6.2
Long-term therapy	11.6	22.7	14.1	14.3	12.4	10.8
All experimental (psychotherapy) groups	13.5	15.3	9.2	8.3	7.9	6.2
Control group	11.4	11.5	11.3	12.4	14.5	12.9

Table 2.7 Number of Days of Hospitalization and Averages by Psychotherapy Group for the Year before and the 5 Years after Psychotherapy, and the Corresponding Period for the Non-psychotherapy Group (Note: Health Plan average is 0.8 per year for patients 20 years old or older.)

Group	1-B	1-A	2-A	3-A	4-A	5-A
One session only, days/year	117	78	52	32	33	31
No. of pts.	80	80	80	57	53	49
Average	1.46	0.98	0.65	0.56	0.62	0.63
Brief therapy, days/year	66	44	31	24	23	23
No. of pts.	41	41	41	32	30	27
Average	1.61	1.07	0.76	0.75	0.77	0.85
Long-term therapy, days/year	153	37	19	18	16	13
No. of pts.	31	31	31	27	24	19
Average	4.94	1.09	0.61	0.67	0.67	0.68
All experimental (psychotherapy) groups, days/year	336	159	102	74	72	67
No. of pts.	152	152	152	116	107	95
Average	2.21	1.05	0.68	0.64	0.67	0.71
Significance		*0.05*	*0.02*	*0.05*	*0.05*	*0.05*
Control (non-psychotherapy) group, days/year	324	307	477	255	208	197
No. of pts.	152	152	152	127	111	98
Average	2.13	2.02	3.07	2.02	1.87	2.01
Significance		*NS*	*0.05*	*NS*	*NS*	*NS*

the 3 remaining "years after" maintaining the level of utilization attained in the "second year after." In contrast, the control sample demonstrated a constant level in number of hospital days throughout the 6 years studied. These results are shown in Table 2.7, which indicates that the approximately 60% decline in number of days of hospitalization between the "year before" and the "second year after" for the first two psychotherapy groups is maintained to the "fifth year after"; this decline is significant at the 0.01 level. The inpatient utilization for the "long-term therapy" group in the "year before" was more than twice that of the non-psychiatric sample, and about three times that of the first two psychotherapy groups. The significant (0.01 level) decline of 88% from the "year before" to the "second year after" is maintained through the "fifth year after," rendering the inpatient utilization of the third psychotherapy group comparable to that of the first two psychotherapy groups.

In terms of decline in the use of inpatient services (days of hospitalization), however, the long-term psychotherapy group and the control group are different, in that the former patients significantly reduce their inpatient utilization from the "year before" to the "fifth year after." However, the small size of the samples limits the conclusions that can be drawn.

Discussion

The original pilot study of which this project is an outgrowth was proposed by the senior author as an aid in planning for psychiatric care as part of comprehensive, prepaid, health-plan coverage. It had long been observed that some of this psychiatric clinic's patients, as well as many patients in the hospital for whom a psychiatric consultation was requested, had very thick medical charts. It was also repeatedly noted that when these patients were treated from a psychiatric point of reference, i.e., as a person who might have primarily emotional distress that was expressed in physical symptoms, they often abandoned their physical complaints. It seemed reasonable to expect that for many of these people, psychiatrically oriented help was a more specific and relevant kind of treatment than the usual medical treatments.

This would be especially true if the effects of psychiatric help were relatively long-lasting, or if a change in the patient affected others in his immediate environment. In the long run, the interruption of the transmission of sick ways of living to succeeding generations would be the most fundamental and efficient kind of preventive medicine. It therefore seemed imperative to test the intuitive impressions that this kind of patient could be treated more effectively by an unstructured psychiatric interview technique than by the more traditional medical routine with its directed history.

The Balints[4,5] have published many valuable case reports that describe the change in quantity and quality in patients' appeals to the general practitioner after the latter learns to listen and understand his patients as people in distress because of current and past life experiences. It would be difficult, however, to design a statistical study of those patients and of a matched control group treated for similar complaints in a more conventional manner.

Psychiatry has been in an ambivalent position in relation to the rest of medicine: welcomed by some, resented by others, often, however, with considerable politeness, which serves to cover up deep-seated fears of and prejudices against "something different." In a medical group associated with a prepaid health plan, conditions are favorable for integrating psychiatry into the medical fraternity as a welcomed and familiar (therefore unthreatening) member specialty. The inherent ease of referral and communication within such a setting would be much further enhanced by the factor of prepayment, which eliminates the financial barrier for all those who can afford health insurance. For many reasons, then, this setting provides both the impetus and the opportunity to attempt an integration of psychiatry into general medical practice and to observe the outcome. In the past 2 decades, medicine has been changing in many significant ways, among which are prepaid health insurance, group practice, increasing specialization, automation, and a focus on the "whole person" rather than on the "pathology."

Forsham[6] and others have suggested that at some not-too-distant date the patient will go through a highly automated process of history, laboratory procedures and physical tests, with the doctor at the end of the line doing a physical examination but occupying mainly the position of a medical psychologist. He will have all the results of the previously completed examinations, which he will interpret for the patient, and he will have time for listening to the patient, if he wishes to do so. The "Multiphasic Health Check,"[7] which has been used for many years in the Northern California region in the Kaiser Foundation medical clinics and which is constantly being expanded, is just such an automated health survey, and Medical Group doctors are in the process of becoming continually better psychologists. Eventually many more of the patients who are now seen in the psychiatric clinic will be expertly treated in the general medical clinics by more "complete physicians."

A study such as this raises more questions than it provides answers. One question alluded to above is whether, with an ongoing training program such as Balint has conducted for general practitioners at Tavistock Clinic, internists might not be just as effective as psychiatric personnel in helping a greater percentage of their patients. A training seminar such as this has been conducted by Dr. Edna Fitch in the Department of Pediatrics of Kaiser Permanente Medical Group in San Francisco for many years and has been effective in helping pediatricians to treat, with more insight and comfort, emotional problems of children and their families and physical disorders that are an expression of emotional distress.

Using a broader perspective than the focus on the clinical pathology, one can wonder what social, economic, or cultural factors are related to choice of symptoms, attitudes toward being "sick" (mentally or physically), attitudes toward and expectations of the doctor, traditions of family illness, superstitions relating to bodily damage, child-raising practices, etc. How often is the understanding of such factors of crucial importance for effective and efficient treatment for the patient? Of special interest in general medical practice and overlooked almost routinely by physicians (and by many in the psychological field) are the "anniversary reactions" in which symptoms appear at an age at which a relative had similar symptoms and/or died.

Health Plan statistics indicate an increase in medical utilization with increasing age in adults. This is consistent with the relatively flat curve seen in the "medical utilization" of the control sample over the 6-year period and is in marked contrast to that of the experimental sample. There is the implication in this that some of the increasing symptoms and disability of advancing years are psychogenic and that psychotherapeutic intervention may in some cases function as preventive medical care for the problems associated with aging as well as preventive medicine in children.

A certain percentage of the long-term psychotherapy group seems to continue without diminution of number of visits to the psychiatric clinic; these patients appear from the data to be interminable or lifelong psychiatric utilizers just as they had been consistently high utilizers of non-psychiatric medical care before. They seem merely to substitute psychiatric visits for some of their medical clinic visits. A further breakdown of the long-term group into three parts, e.g., fewer than 50, 50 to 150, and more than 150 visits, would probably help to sort this population's utilization into several patterns. More precise data on these groups would suggest modifications in classifications and methods of therapy or might suggest alternatives to either traditional medical or traditional psychiatric treatment in favor of some attempt to promote beneficial social changes in the environments of these chronically disturbed people.

Sources of Criticism

(1) One problem in providing a control group comparable to an experimental group in this kind of study is that, although undoubtedly having emotional distress, and in a similar "quantity" according to our yardstick, the control group did not get to the psychiatric clinic by either self- or physician referral. The fact that the control patients had not sought psychiatric help may reflect a more profound difference between this group and the experimental group than is superficially apparent. One cannot assume that the medical utilization of this control group would change if they were seen in the psychiatry clinic. (This objection will be minimized in the "prospective" part of this study, which will be reported in another paper). Although the average inpatient utilization for the three combined psychotherapy groups is the same as that of the control group in the year before (1959), the inpatient utilization of the long-term psychotherapy group is two and a half times that of the control group. If the study were extended to several years before, rather than just 1 year, it would become evident whether this was just a year of crisis for the long-term group or whether this had been a longer pattern of high inpatient utilization.

(2) Patients who visit the psychiatric clinic may, for one reason or another, seek medical help from a physician not associated with the Medical Group so that his medical utilization is not recorded in the clinic record, the source of information about utilization. In the long-term-therapy group the therapist is usually aware if his patient is visiting an outside physician, and although it is an almost negligible factor in that group, there can be no information in this regard for the one-session-only and brief-therapy groups without follow-up investigation.

(3) There is no justification in assuming that decreased utilization means better medical care, necessarily. Criteria of improvement would have to be developed and applied to a significantly large sample to try to answer this important question.

(4) Patients may substitute for physical or emotional symptoms behavioral disturbances that do not bring them to a doctor but may be just as distressing to them or to other people.

(5) The "unit" of utilization cannot be used as a guide in estimating costs, standing as it does for such diverse items. In itself the units are not an exact indicator of severity of illness nor of costs. A person with a minor problem may visit the clinic many times, while a much more severely ill person may visit the clinic infrequently. Even more striking is the variation in the cost of a unit, varying from about $1 for certain laboratory procedures to well more than

$100 for certain hospital days (with admissions procedures, laboratory tests, x-rays, consultations, etc.) each worth one "unit." To arrive at an approximation of costs, the units have to be retabulated in cost-weighted form.

Suggested Further Studies

(1) The question of treatment of patients by nonmedical professional clinicians has been argued for more than a half century. It is generally recognized that there are not enough psychiatrists now and that there will not be enough in the foreseeable future to treat all those persons who have disabling emotional disorders. In the late President Kennedy's program for mental health this lack was recognized; the recommendation for professional staff for community mental health centers included clinical psychologists, psychiatric social workers, and other trained personnel. Having little distinction in our psychiatric clinic between the various disciplines as far as their functions are concerned, it would be feasible and interesting to compare therapeutic results of the disciplines as well as individuals with various types of patients and various types of psychotherapy.

(2) Is length of treatment correlated with diagnostic category, original prognosis by therapist, socioeconomic level of patient, discipline and orientation of therapist, or "severity of pathology"?

(3) What happens to the spouses, parents, and children of the patients seen in psychiatry?

(4) Are there distinguishing patterns of complaints in the three psychotherapy groups?

(5) How do blue-collar patients differ from white-collar or professional patients in number of interviews, diagnostic label, use of medication, recommendation of hospitalization, and type of complaints?

(6) What is the nature of the illness that resulted in hospitalization before the patient came to psychiatry—and after? How often was this a diagnostic work-up because the internist could not find "anything wrong" in the clinic?

Summary

The outpatient and inpatient medical utilization for the year prior to the initial interview in the Department of Psychiatry as well as for the 5 years following were studied for three groups of psychotherapy patients (one interview only, brief therapy with a mean of 6.2 interviews, and long-term therapy with a mean of 33.9 interviews) and a control group of matched patients demonstrating similar criteria of distress but not, in the 6 years under study, seen in psychotherapy. The three psychotherapy groups as well as the control (non-psychotherapy) group were high utilizers of medical facilities, with an average utilization significantly higher than that of the Health Plan average. Results of the study indicated significant declines in medical utilization in the psychotherapy groups when compared to the control group, whose inpatient and outpatient utilization remained relatively constant throughout the 6 years. The most significant declines occurred in the second year after the initial interview, and the one-interview-only and brief-therapy groups did not require additional psychotherapy to maintain the lower utilization level for 5 years. On the other hand, after 2 years, the long-term-psychotherapy group attained a level of psychiatric utilization that remained constant through the remaining 3 years of study.

The combined psychiatric and medical utilization of the long-term-therapy group indicated that for this small group there was no overall decline in outpatient utilization inasmuch as psychotherapy visits seemed to supplant medical visits. On the other hand, there was a significant decline in inpatient utilization, especially in the long-term-therapy group, from an initial utilization of several times that of the Health Plan average, to a level comparable to that of the general adult Health Plan population. This decline in hospitalization rate tended to occur within the first year after the initial interview and remained generally comparable to the Health Plan average for the 5 years.

References

1 Cummings, N. A., Kahn, B. I., & Sparkman, B. (1964). *Psychotherapy and medical utilization.* As cited in Greenfield, Margaret, *Providing for mental illness*. Berkeley: Berkeley Institute of Governmental Studies, University of California.

2 Follette, W. T., & Cummings, N. A. (1962). *Psychiatry and medical utilization.* An unpublished pilot project.

3 Avnet, H. H. (1962). *Psychiatric insurance: Financing short term ambulatory treatment.* New York: Group Health Insurance, Inc.

4 Balint, M. (1957). *The doctor, his patient and the illness.* New York: International Universities Press.

5 Balint, M. & Balint, E. (1961). *Psychotherapeutic techniques in medicine.* London: Tavistock Publications Limited.

6 Forsham, P. H. (1959). *Lecture before the Permanente Medical Group.* Kaiser Permanente Hospital and Medical Center, San Francisco, CA.

7 Collen, M. F., Rubin, L., Neyman, J., Dantzig, G. B., Baer, R. M., & Siegelaub, A. B. (1964). Automated multiphasic screening and diagnosis. *American Journal of Public Health, 54*, 33–77.

3 Psychiatric Services and Medical Utilization in a Prepaid Health Plan Setting II

Nicholas A. Cummings and William T. Follette[*]

Does psychotherapy alter the pattern of medical care? Can emotionally distressed patients who might benefit from psychotherapy be identified by screening a group of patients taking a health checkup? Will an automated psychological test be useful in such a screening process? These are the questions we set out to answer in this study.

The first question has been studied and the results reported by the authors.[1] It was found that psychotherapy patients initially were high "utilizers," but that after psychotherapy their utilization declined significantly. On the other hand, the utilization of the matched "control" group (not receiving psychotherapy) did not decline. The brief-therapy and one-session-only psychotherapy groups had the largest decline in outpatient utilization, which theoretically helped to offset the costs of providing the psychotherapy. The decline in outpatient utilization of the long-term psychotherapy group was not enough to offset the costs of psychiatric and non-psychiatric treatment, being greater than the costs of prior medical utilization alone. However, this group showed considerable decline in days of hospitalization, which helped to make its psychiatric care financially less costly in this setting.

A major criticism of Part I[1] was that, although the psychotherapy and "control" groups were matched socioeconomically and demographically, in medical utilization and in degree of emotional distress, the groups remained different in one crucial respect: the psychotherapy sample, whether self- or physician-referred, voluntarily presented themselves to the psychiatric clinic. In contrast, the matched

* Chief Psychologist and Chief Psychiatrist, respectively, Department of Psychiatry, Kaiser Foundation Hospital and the Permanente Medical Group, San Francisco, Calif.

Presented at a session sponsored by the Group Health Association of America at the 95th annual meeting of the American Public Health Association, Miami Beach, Florida, October 23–27, 1967.

This study was financed by Contract PH 108–66–235, U.S. Public Health Service. The authors gratefully acknowledge the cooperation and assistance of Mrs. Agnes Brewster, chief, Health Economics Branch, and Mr. Royal Crystal, chief, Medical Care Data and Resources Center. The authors also acknowledge their debt to Dr. M. F. Collen, whose research design is reflected in this study, and whose Automated Multiphasic Health Clinic made possible the field tests employed.

This paper is Part II of a two-part series seeking to develop and test methods of assessing the effects of psychiatric services in a comprehensive medical program. Part I involved retrospective methodology, while the present paper reports a prospective study.

group did not come to the psychiatric clinic even if referred by their physicians. The nature of the difference between the two groups made conclusions tentative. The question is crucial, because it may be that the group who did not come to the psychiatric clinic is *unable* to make use of psychiatric services in a meaningful manner, and that psychotherapy would not decrease the medical utilization of this group. The most obvious way to provide a valid control group would be to choose a large sample by uniform criteria and randomly divide it into two parts, then treat the two parts differently and observe the results. The present paper is a report on such a prospective study.

Method

The setting: The Kaiser Foundation Health Plan of Northern California is a group-practice prepayment plan offering comprehensive hospital and professional services on a direct-service basis. Professional services are provided by the Permanente Medical Group—a partnership of physicians. The Medical Group has a contract to provide comprehensive medical care to the members of the Health Plan, of whom there were three quarters of a million at the time of this study. The composition of the Health Plan membership is diverse, encompassing most socioeconomic groups. The Permanente Medical Group comprises all major medical specialties; referral from one specialty clinic to another is facilitated by the organizational features of group practice, geographical proximity, and the use of common medical records. During the years of this study (1965–1966), only 17% of Health Plan members were eligible for psychiatric benefits on a prepaid basis, but in most areas of the Northern California region psychiatric services were available to Health Plan subscribers at reduced rates. The psychiatric staff in the San Francisco Clinic, where the present study took place, consists of psychiatrists, clinical psychologists, psychiatric social workers, and psychology and social work interns. The clinic operates primarily as an outpatient service for adults and children for the evaluation and treatment of emotional disorders, but it also provides consultation for non-psychiatric physicians and consultation in the general hospital and the emergency room. There is no formal "intake" procedure, the first visit with any staff member being considered potentially therapeutic as well as evaluative and dispositional. Regardless of professional discipline, the person who sees the patient initially becomes that patient's therapist unless there is reason for transfer to some other staff member, and he continues to see the patient for the duration of the therapy. An attempt is made to schedule the first interview as soon as possible after the patient calls for an appointment. There is also a "drop-in" or non-appointment service for emergencies so that patients in urgent need of psychiatric help usually can be seen immediately or at least within an hour or two after arrival at the clinic.

One of the unique aspects of this kind of associated health plan and medical group is that it tends to put a premium on health rather than on illness, i.e., it makes preventive medicine economically rewarding, thereby stimulating a constant search for the most effective and specific methods of treatment. Another feature of group practice in this setting is that all medical records for each patient are maintained within the organization.

The subjects: The source of the population for this study was 10,667 patients who voluntarily presented themselves in a 6-month period to the San Francisco Kaiser Permanente Automated Multiphasic Clinic for a health check, part of which includes 19 computerized procedures, ranging from simple body measurements to complex laboratory tests.[2] A routine part of the 3-hour series of examinations is the administration of a psychological test known as the Neuro-Mental Questionnaire, or NMQ.[3] This consists of 155 dichotomous questions that (eventually, when the test is fully developed) will identify approximately 60 psychological categories. Each question is printed on a separate pre-punched card, which the patient must deposit in either the "true" or the "false" section of a divided box. For this study, only the six major psychological categories were used: depression, hysteria, obsession, panic and anxiety attacks, passive-aggressiveness, and schizophrenia. (This probably would identify most of the patients who could be identified by the full test, because 87% of the patients seen in the Department of Psychiatry fall into one or more of these six categories.)

The NMQ was computer-scored, and results were sent to the investigators within 24 hours of the time the patient had the questionnaire. The medical charts of the patients identified by the test were reviewed for evidences of psychological distress in the 12-month period prior to the multiphasic examination.

"Criteria of psychological distress" (developed in Part I[1] and presented in Table 3.1) refer to physicians' notes in the patients' medical charts that indicated emotional distress, whether or not the physicians recognized them as such. These 38 criteria have assigned weights from 1 to 3, a weighted score of 3 within 1 year being accepted as an indication that a patient is in psychological distress. Accordingly, patients for the present study had 1) a "positive NMQ," and 2) a score of 3 or more points in "Criteria of Psychological Distress," for the 12 months prior to taking the multiphasic examination.

Of the 10,667 patients who took the NMQ, 3,682, or 36.4%, yielded a positive score in one or more of the six NMQ categories (depression, hysteria, obsessional, panic-anxiety, passive-aggressive, schizophrenic). Of this group, 822 (7.7%) also scored 3 points or more in "criteria of distress." Of the 6,985 patients who did not score positively on the NMQ, only 56 (0.8%) scored 3 or more points on the "Criteria of Distress." Thus the use of scales in only six categories of the NMQ proved a useful method of eliminating two thirds of the multiphasic population in our search for a group of experimental subjects.

The psychological, socioeconomic, and demographic characteristics of the 822-patient sample are given in Table 3.2. Note that the mean age of 45.1 years is higher than the mean age of 38.1 years for patients generally seen in the Department of Psychiatry. Because the NMQ was administered to only the first 100 patients taking the multiphasic examination each day, rather than the full 130, appreciably more women were tested than men, because men tend to make evening appointments. Consequently, 71% of the sample is composed of women. Note further that in the 822-patient sample, 43% were categorized as neurotic, 32%

Table 3.1 Criteria of Psychological Distress with Assigned Weights

One point	Two points	Three points
1 Tranquilizer or sedative requested.	23 Fear of cancer, brain tumor, venereal disease, heart disease, leukemia, diabetes, etc.	34 Unsubstantiated complaint there is something wrong with genitals.
2 Doctor's statement patient is tense, chronically tired, was reassured, etc.	* 24 Health questionnaire: yes on three or more psych. questions.	35 Psychiatric referral made or requested.
3 Patient's statement as in no. 2.	25 Two or more accidents (bone fractures, etc.) within 1 yr. Pt. may be alcoholic.	36 Suicidal attempt, threat, or preoccupation.
4 Lump in throat.		37 Fear of homosexuals or of homosexuality.
* 5 Health questionnaire: yes on one or two psych. questions.	26 Alcoholism or its complications: delirium tremens, peripheral neuropathy, cirrhosis.	38 Nonorganic delusions and/ or hallucinations; paranoid ideation; psychotic thinking or psychotic behavior.
6 Alopecia areata.	27 Spouse is angry at doctor and demands different treatment for patient.	
7 Vague, unsubstantiated pain.		
8 Tranquilizer or sedative given.	28 Seen by hypnotist or seeks referral to hypnotist.	
9 Vitamin B_{12} shots (except for pernicious anemia).	29 Requests surgery, which is refused.	
10 Negative EEG.	30 Vasectomy: requested or performed.	
11 Migraine or psychogenic headache.	31 Hyperventilation syndrome.	
12 More than four upper respiratory infections per year.	32 Repetitive movements noted by doctor: tics, grimaces, mannerisms, torticollis, hysterical seizures.	
13 Menstrual or premenstrual tension; menopausal sex.	33 Weightlifting and/or health faddism.	
14 Consults doctor about difficulty in childrearing.		
15 Chronic allergic state.		
16 Compulsive eating (or overeating).		
17 Chronic gastrointestinal upset; aereophagia.		
18 Chronic skin disease.		
19 Anal pruritus.		
20 Excessive scratching.		
21 Use of emergency room: two or more visits per year.		
22 Brings written list of symptoms or complaints to doctor.		

* Refers to the last four questions (relating to emotional distress) on a modified Cornell Medical Index—a general medical questionnaire given to patients undergoing the Multiphasic Health Check in the years concerned (1959–1962).

Table 3.2 Psychological, Socioeconomic, and Demographic Characteristics of 822-patient Sample with Positive NMQ and Plus-3 or More on Criteria of Distress

NMQ categories (with category number)		Blue collar			White collar			Totals
		Urban	Suburban	Rural	Urban	Suburban	Rural	
Neurotic								352 (42.8%)
Depressive	30	37	11	2	43	2	1	96
Hysteric	16	12	5	1	2	4	2	26
Obsessional	25	23	6		35	6		70
Obs. hysteric	16, 25	10	3	2	12	3		30
Panic/anxiety	22	25	11		13	7		57
Phobic	24	28	9	2	19	15	1	73
Character disorders								261 (31.8 %)
Anal char.	13, 25	4	2		3	2		11
Depressive	25, 30 (13)	26	7	2	18	3		56
Hysterical	13, 16	15	8	1	14	2	1	41
Phobic	16, 24	21	12	1	20	7	1	62
Passive/aggr.	13	27	5	1	25	13		71
Sadomasoch.	13, 16, 30	6	3	1	8	2		20
Psychotic								209 (25.4%)
Schizophrenic	37	55	19	3	44	20	1	142
Pseudo-neur. Schiz.	37, 25, 30 (plus 1 more)	21	8	2	24	11	1	67
TOTALS		310	109	18	280	97	8	

Mean age:	45.1 yrs.
No. women:	70.1 %
Blue collar:	53.2 %
Urban:	71.8 %
Suburban:	25.0 %
Rural:	3.2 %
Neurotic:	42.8 %
Char. dis.:	31.8 %
Psychotic:	25.4 %

as having character disorders, and 25% as psychotic. There was no difference between the percentages of blue-collar patients and white-collar patients diagnosed as "psychotic."

Experimental condition: All patients with both positive NMQs and 3 or more "distress" points were alternately assigned to either the referred or non-referred ("control") groups. For the referred patients, the computer printed out the following "consider-rule": *Consider referral to psychiatry for emotional problems*. The 411 patients assigned to the control group did not, of course, have such a consider-rule on their printouts.

The physician participants: A few weeks after the multiphasic screening, every patient has a routine follow-up office visit with one of 32 internists. At this time, the physician interviews the patient, completes the physical examination, reviews the clinical information from all sources, and provides appropriate treatment or referral. Prior to conducting the present experiment, the physician coauthor of this paper met with the internists, explained the nature of the study, and solicited their individual cooperation. They were informed that they would be seeing patients whose multiphasic printouts would contain the consider-rule suggesting referral to psychiatry. This was to be regarded as one more item of information to the physician, who would weigh it along with his total knowledge of the patient and make the ultimate decision whether to make such a referral. The internists also were advised that other patients would comprise the control group of the study, would not have the consider-rule in their print-outs, and would be undistinguishable from the other multiphasic patients they would see routinely on follow-up visits.

Thus, "referred" patients (consider-rule) might or might not be referred to psychiatry, and, if referred, might or might not choose to come; or, if not referred by the internist, they might come to the psychiatric clinic through other channels. On the other hand, control patients (no consider-rule) might be referred to psychiatry as the result of the routine practice of medicine in this setting and without regard to the experiment, and, again, might choose to come or not to come to the psychiatric clinic. The various possibilities are shown in Figure 3.1.

Results

No Experimental Generation of a Psychiatric Population

Six months after the last experimental subject consulted with his internist on his multiphasic follow-up visit, only 5 of the 411 patients given the consider-rule had made and kept appointments in the psychiatric clinic! This figure is exactly the same as the number of patients from the control group who made and kept appointments in the psychiatric clinic. Thus, the experimental conditions failed to generate a psychiatric population, and were in no way superior in obtaining early referral to psychiatry than the usual, routine medical practice in this setting (see Fig. 3.1).

Within the referred group, 40 patients were found who had previously been seen in the psychiatric clinic, and 42 in the control group. None of the 82 patients previously seen in psychotherapy returned during the course of the experiment.

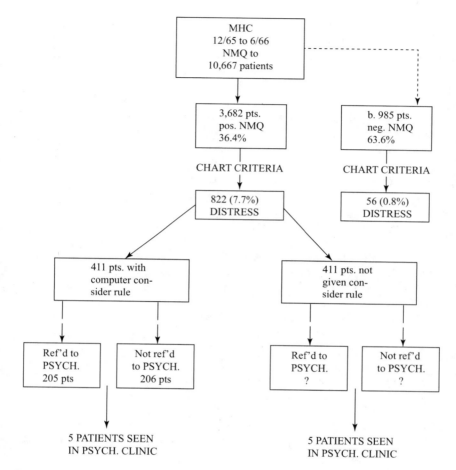

Figure 3.1 Criteria of Psychological Distress with Assigned Weights

Usefulness of Automated Screening

The NMQ, as part of an automated multiphasic screening, proved a useful instrument in identifying a population within which the patients in emotional distress would be found. As seen in Figure 3.1, 36.4% of the patients with positive NMQs also were in emotional distress, while less than 1% of the patients who did not have positive NMQs were in emotional distress.

Degree of Internists' Participation

At the conclusion of the primary phase of this study, and after the last patient had undergone his follow-up visit, 30 of the 32 participating internists were

interviewed individually to determine their reactions to the computerized procedure and why they did or did not refer to psychiatry. As noted in Figure 3.1, about
half the patients given the consider-rule in their computer printouts actually were
referred to psychiatry by their internists, according to notations to that effect in
the patients' charts.

a   Ten (33%) of the internists did not even recall seeing a consider-rule for refer-
     ral to psychiatry; 20 (67%) stated they saw instances of such a consider-rule,
     but the number seen varied from one to 15.
b   Of the 20 internists who saw the consider-rule, 8 made no referrals, 4 referred
     all such patients, and 8 referred half or more.
c   Reasons given for reluctance to refer centered mostly on the physician's feel-
     ings regarding having to deal with an emotional problem when his time with
     the patient was limited. He felt he would open a "Pandora's box" that could
     not appropriately be handled in the 15 minutes allotted for the initial return
     visit. The second most often-mentioned reason for not referring was the phy-
     sician's knowledge of the patient and his circumstances. Typical of this was
     the reply: "I know this patient well. I referred him before and he wouldn't go.
     I had no reason to believe he would go this time." Or, "I know this patient
     has emotional problems, but we have been handling them here because she is
     reluctant to see a psychiatrist." A third type of response by the physician was
     one of antagonism to the procedure. A few internists complained that it was
     "cold" or "impersonal."
d   Internists who made referrals remarked that it made their job somewhat eas-
     ier. They were startled by the accuracy of the consider-rule, for after opening
     up the issue of emotional problems, they found their patients eager to discuss
     them. One physician stated he felt more comfortable referring a patient to
     psychiatry when the patient could blame the computer and not the doctor.
e   Ultimately, the internists' individual procedure regarding referral to psychiatry
     seemed little affected by the consider-rule. Physicians who routinely and easily
     refer to psychiatry continued to do so in the experiment, while physicians who
     usually do not refer to psychiatry essentially ignored the consider-rule. For the
     most part, it was the individual physicians' modes of practice that mattered.

Degree of Outpatient and Inpatient Medical Utilization

Each referred and control patient's utilization of health facilities was investigated
for the full year prior to the patient's having taken the multiphasic screening. This
investigation consisted of a straightforward tabulation of each contact with any
outpatient facility, each laboratory report, and x-ray report. In addition, a tabulation of number of days of hospitalization was made without regard to the type
or quantity of service provided. Each patient's utilization scores consisted of the
total number of separate outpatient tabulations. These results are summarized in
Table 3.3 (outpatient) and Table 3.4 (inpatient). The rural patients were excluded,
inasmuch as their number was too small to contribute significantly to the results.

Table 3.3 Average Utilization of Outpatient Medical Services for the Year Prior to the Multiphasic Screening for Both Referred and Control Groups by Diagnosis, Socioeconomic Status, and Residence (Excluding Rural)

	Blue Collar		White Collar		Totals
	Urban	Suburban	Urban	Suburban	
Neurotic					
No. patients	135	45	124	37	341
Score	2,538	886	2,505	673	6,602
Mean	18.8	19.6	20.2	18.4	19.4
Character disorder					
No. patients	99	37	88	29	253
Score	1,168	396	994	336	2,894
Mean	11.8	10.7	11.3	11.6	11.4
Psychotic					
No. patients	55	19	44	20	138
Score	677	217	480	234	1,608
Mean	12.3	11.4	10.9	11.7	11.6
Pseudo-neurotic					
No. patients	21	8	24	11	64
Score	452	158	571	289	1,470
Mean	21.5	19.7	23.8	26.3	22.9

Table 3.4 Average Utilization of Inpatient Medical Services (Days of Hospitalization) for the Year Prior to the Multiphasic Screening for Both Referred and Control Groups by Diagnosis, Socioeconomic Status, and Residence (Excluding Rural)

	Blue collar		White collar		Totals
	Urban	Suburban	Urban	Suburban	
Neurotic					
No. patients	135	45	124	37	341
Score	170	60	165	48	443
Mean	1.26	1.34	1.33	1.29	1.30
Character disorder					
No. patients	99	37	88	29	253
Score	285	93	239	84	701
Mean	2.88	2.51	2.72	2.91	2.77
Psychotic					
No. patients	55	19	44	20	138
Score	235	94	200	79	608
Mean	4.27	4.95	4.54	3.95	4.41
Pseudo-neurotic					
No. patients	21	8	24	11	64
Score	105	39	122	58	324
Mean	5.00	4.88	5.08	5.27	5.03

* (Note: Health Plan average is 0.8 per year for patients 20 years old or older.)

As expected, no significant differences were found between the experimental and control groups, and both groups are combined (with rural patients excluded) in Tables 3.3 and 3.4.

All 796 patients (26 rural patients excluded) were significantly high utilizers of both outpatient and inpatient medical services.

A $2 \times 3 \times 4$ analysis of variance of the 796 patients indicated no significant difference in terms of blue collar versus white collar, or urban versus suburban conditions, as regards the utilization of both outpatient and inpatient medical services.

There was a significant difference in the degree of utilization of both outpatient and inpatient medical services in terms of diagnostic category. The neurotic patients had the highest outpatient utilization, whereas the psychotic patients had the highest inpatient utilization.

The outpatient utilization of the pseudo-neurotic schizophrenic resembled that of the neurotic, while the inpatient utilization of the pseudo-neurotic schizophrenic is not significantly different than that of the psychotic.

Patients with character disorders utilize outpatient services at the same rate as psychotics, but their inpatient rate is approximately halfway between neurotic and psychotic inpatient rates.

Discussion

Research in human behavior is easy to do, but difficult to do well. A research design may look fine on paper, but may not be feasible in fact. Such was the case with the present experiment: no experimental population was generated. This result can be instructive, however, and we will proceed to search for serendipitous results. Human subjects cannot be manipulated for experimental or therapeutic purposes in the same way animals or machines can. This applies to the doctors in this experiment as well as the patients.

This observation may be timely and relevant now when vast sums of money are being spent in developing mental health programs, many of which are designed on paper from an armchair and have never been proven clinically effective.

A recent paper from the University of California at Los Angeles Alcoholism Research Clinic[4] found the results to be the same in a group of alcoholics randomly assigned by court probation to one of three treatment conditions: (1) a psychiatrically oriented outpatient alcoholic clinic, (2) Alcoholics Anonymous, (3) no treatment. One might conclude that the answer to the problem of alcoholism may not be the provision of a multitude of "alcoholic clinics" across the country. Similarly, it has never been demonstrated that a "suicide prevention center" has lowered the incidence of suicide in any community. We might, on the other hand, expect that such a center would be likely to increase (1) preoccupation with suicide in the community, (2) the number of suicidal threats, and (3) the number of suicidal gestures. In other words, if people volunteer to play dramatic lifesaver, we can confidently expect others to volunteer to threaten self-destruction. Nevertheless, we have suicide prevention centers popping up all over the land.

The question is to what extent psychiatric patients can be "found" in the community and then successfully treated. Is it possible and worthwhile to induce an ever-greater percentage of the population to get some treatment to improve mental health? Are the patients who come to a psychiatric clinic via the common traditional channels (referral by self, relative, friend, family doctor) more or less treatable than those produced by newer "case finding" methods in the community?

The setting in which this study was done is unusual in having had a psychiatric clinic as part of comprehensive healthcare services for about 15 years. For this reason, there was no large reservoir of patients needing and wanting psychiatric services they could not afford. Note that 10% of the patients identified as emotionally disturbed and in acute distress already had been seen in the psychiatric clinic. Many of the others in this group undoubtedly have been referred but will never be seen in psychiatry for a number of reasons, among which may be the following: (1) they have too much invested in their roles of being (physically) sick; (2) they have major physical illnesses they and their doctors use to ignore the emotional illness; (3) they are terrified by the idea of mental illness ("craziness"); (4) there is often a payoff for "real," i.e., physical, illness, but not for emotional disturbance from family, friends, doctors, insurance companies. The fact that 90% of these patients have never gotten to the psychiatric clinic demonstrates that nonpsychiatric physicians have been treating and will continue to treat the bulk of the emotionally disturbed people in the population.

While we have demonstrated that emotionally disturbed patients seen in psychiatry reduce their use of other medical services, we are still unable to determine whether this would hold true for all those patients identified by our double-screening technique as likely candidates for psychotherapy.

One should be cautious in using statistics from mental health clinics when they deviate from the averages reported by most other clinics. It has often been reported that about 1% of a population will seek psychiatric services per year. The Group Health Insurance study[5] showed the pattern of response usually seen when a population is offered low-cost psychiatric services for the first time: increased utilization for the first few months due to an accumulation of need for such services. After that, the demand stabilizes. Active "promotion" of psychiatric benefits did not increase the utilization of psychiatric services in their population.

It is possible to report a much higher rate of utilization, e.g., 5%/year, if one organizes his psychiatric clinic in the following manner: (1) "crisis" orientation; (2) very brief therapy and counselling; (3) representing the psychiatric staff member as "your friendly family counselor"; (4) fostering dependency relationship by encouraging patients to return frequently—whenever they have to make decisions, feel anxious or depressed, etc.; (5) counting each family member as a separate patient when a family is seen together; (6) most of all—by counting each return to the clinic a "new patient." Unfortunately, the higher the percentage, the more effective the service.

Antes muerto que mudado (death rather than change), a Spanish proverb quoted by Lichtenstein[6] in his classic monograph on identity, dramatizes the tremendous dynamic force behind the human being's need to maintain his identity—a force that has priority over all forces motivating a person's behavior and lifestyle. Many otherwise baffling aspects of the behavior of individuals, groups, and nations become clear if this force is recognized. Patients do not want to change, in fact resist change, even though their lives are full of misery and pain. A psychotherapist, then, is relatively helpless unless a patient is highly motivated, i.e., in a great deal of "pain." Getting a patient to the office of a psychotherapist is likely to be a waste of everybody's time unless the patient is "ready" or motivated for some kind of change. It is, of course, the psychotherapist's job to foster and capitalize on every shred of motivation he can find. Many emotionally disturbed people in the community may seem to "need help" but are not at all interested in change. This is certainly true of a high percentage of alcoholics, "hippies," addicts, "psychopaths," criminals and many other types who the community at large thinks "need help."

The assessment of the effectiveness of psychotherapy has always presented great difficulties, conclusions varying from "psychotherapy is worthless"[7] to the behavior therapists' claim of as high as 86–95% effectiveness in 30 interviews or fewer.[8] By far the best investigation of brief psychotherapy was done by the Tavistock group, reported by Malan.[9] We need much more high-quality research of this kind in assessing the value of mental health programs.

It is interesting to note the few differences between blue-collar and white-collar workers (Table 3.2). The blue-collar patients are more apt to be in only 3 (of 14) categories: hysteric; panic and anxiety attacks; and depressive character; and less likely to be obsessional. Otherwise, the two groups are comparable in percentages in the other neurotic and character-disorder categories and in all the psychotic categories. The "pseudo-neurotic schizophrenic" category defines a group of patients who have a wealth of symptoms of many kinds. These patients are the ones who seek professional help constantly, who "never get well," and who may make up a large percentage of those long-term patients in the office of every physician, psychotherapist, and psychoanalyst.

The similar percentages of incidence of psychoses in blue-collar and white-collar groups may reflect the greater impartiality of the computer than the clinician, if we accept the contention of Hollingshead et al.,[7] that middle-class psychotherapists tend to overdiagnose psychosis in patients of lower socioeconomic classes as compared with those of middle or upper classes.

Summary

During a 6-month period, 10,667 patients taking the Automated Multiphasic Screening Examination (Kaiser Permanente Medical Center, San Francisco) were given a computerized psychological test as a routine part of that screening. The tests revealed that 3,682 patients, or one third, had evidence of neurosis, personality disorder, or psychosis. Of these, 822 (or 7.7% of the total multiphasic patients tested) also had high degrees of "emotional distress." The 32 internists conducting the multiphasic follow-up examinations received computer-printed "consider-rules" suggesting referral to psychiatry for half (411) of these patients, while the other half served as a control group and did not have such a "consider-rule."

It was found that attempts at early detection of emotional problems did not generate more psychiatric clinic patients than those generated through routine medical practice in this setting. There was considerable resistance on the part of physicians to the "artificiality" of referral by automated procedures, and there was a comparable rejection by patients of a referral made as a result of such procedures.

The population selected by this automated psychological screening method were high utilizers of medical services. Where neurotics tend to use outpatient medical services, psychotic patients tend to use inpatient medical services. Patients with personality disorders seem to use both. No differences in utilization rates were found in terms of blue collar versus white collar, or urban versus suburban.

The implications of these findings are: (1) attempts at early detection of psychiatric problems will not create as great a demand for psychiatric services as might be expected; (2) whereas many patients seeking outpatient medical treatment may be reflecting neurotic problems, psychotic patients often manifest symptoms that so simulate a variety of baffling problems that they are hospitalized for medical diagnostic workups. Patients with personality disorders seem to require both outpatient and inpatient attention in above-average amounts.

References Notes

1 Follette, W., & Cummings, N. A. (1967). Psychiatric services and medical utilization in a pre-paid health plan setting. *Medical Care, 5,* 5–25.

2 Collen, M. F. (1966). Periodic health examinations using an automated multitest laboratory. *Journal of the American Medical Association, 195,* 8–30.

3 Cummings, N. A., Siegelaub, A., Follette, W., & Collen, M. F. (never published; internally circulated throughout Kaiser Permanente clinics). An automated psychological screening test as part of an automated multiphasic screening.

4 Ditman, K. S., Crawford, G. G., Forgy, E. W., Moskowitz, H., & MacAndrew, C. (1967). A controlled experiment on the use of court probation for drunk arrests. *American Journal of Psychiatry, 124,* 160–182.

5 Avnet, H. H. (1962). *Psychiatric insurance: Financing short term ambulatory treatment.* New York: Group Health Insurance, Inc.

6 Lichtenstein, H. (1961). Identity and sexuality. *Journal of the American Psychoanalytic Association, 9,* 179–184.

7 Hollingshead, A. B., & Redlich, F. C. (1958). *Social class and mental illness.* New York: John Wiley.

8 Wolpe, J., & Lazarus, A. A. (1966). *Behavior therapy techniques.* London: Pergamon Press.

9 Malan, D. H. (1963). *A study of brief psychotherapy.* Springfield, IL: Charles C Thomas.

4   The Anatomy of Psychotherapy under National Health Insurance[1]

Nicholas A. Cummings

As the Carter administration evidences serious concern for the mental and emotional well-being of the American people, there is occurring within the larger context of the pros and cons of national health insurance a heated debate as to whether any national healthcare scheme can feasibly include a mental healthcare component. The dubious experiences of Medicaid, Medicare, and CHAMPUS have left some members of Congress with the conclusion that the inclusion of a mental healthcare provision in whatever national healthcare system is eventually enacted would overinflate what is already contemplated to be a staggering price tag to provide even the basics of national health insurance. Several prominent psychologists, including two past presidents of the American Psychological Association (APA), who have never engaged in the direct delivery of human services (Albee, 1977; Campbell, cited in Humphreys, 1973; Trotter, 1976), have thrown their persuasiveness solidly against the inclusion of psychotherapy in national health insurance. They argue that such a service cannot be financed or monitored, that it is a subsidy of the rich by the poor, and that the insurance benefit would be of doubtful value to the overall health of the American people. Others, principally myself and my colleague (Cummings, 1975; Cummings & Follette, 1976), have taken the opposite stance based on 2 decades of providing mental healthcare services within a comprehensive, prepaid health plan. We have found not only that psychotherapy can be economically included as a prepaid insurance benefit, but also that failure to provide such a benefit jeopardizes the effective functioning of the basic medical services, since 60% or more of the physician visits are made by patients who demonstrate an emotional, rather than an organic, etiology for their physical symptoms.

Despite extensive misquotations to the contrary, Follette and I have never advocated mere across-the-board inclusion of traditional delivery modalities of mental healthcare services into public or third-party payment structures. Rather, we have argued that for psychotherapy to be cost-therapeutically effective, considerable clinical research is necessary before abuses are minimized, therapeutic benefits

1 Reprinted from *American Psychologist*, Vol. 32, No. 9, September 1977.

are maximized, traditionally underserved groups are reached, and deleterious effects are eliminated. It is by addressing the problems confronting the delivery of psychotherapy under public and third-party payment that the anatomy of psychotherapy under national health insurance will be developed and accepted as efficacious by Congress and the consumer. The failure by the mental healthcare professions to take a proactive research stance may result in the elimination of mental healthcare services from national health insurance or, even worse, may result in the provision of an ineffective token benefit that will only underscore the argument that psychotherapy is an unnecessary service. Before proceeding to this basic issue, it is important to examine arguments made by the opponents of psychotherapy's inclusion in national health insurance, inasmuch as they have presented some warnings that have rightfully commanded the attention of consumer groups and Congress.

Warning: The Reverse Robin Hood Phenomenon

The fact that, traditionally, psychotherapy was sought by the more affluent sectors of our society while the underprivileged tended not to utilize such services has prompted some critics, such as Campbell (cited in Trotter, 1976), to view the inclusion of psychotherapy in national health insurance as regressive taxation or, even more harshly, as a "subsidy of the rich by the poor." Simply stated, this view holds that by taxing all of the American people to provide a benefit applicable to a select segment such as the upper-middle class, the benefit is being paid for by the poor, who are least likely to utilize the service and are least able to afford the subsidy. By itself, this position is not totally persuasive, because, as Campbell would be the first to admit, many of our most valued institutions are financed by regressive taxation. The state university system is a case in point. No one would seriously argue the elimination of the state university, but many are striving to make the university more accessible to eligible persons from groups who have traditionally underutilized it. The same would hold true for a mental healthcare benefit if, in fact, it were a valuable service to all of the segments of our population who are at risk.

Since medicine in the United States was originally dispensed under the principle that services to the poor are provided by soaking the rich, it is curious to find mental healthcare subject to a reverse Robin Hood phenomenon. Of the recent rash of so-called abuses that have come to light, two may serve as startling examples of the kind of facts that render Congress uneasy and that ought to serve as warning signs to the profession that restraint and caution are indicated. According to the U.S. Civil Service Commission,[1] under the Blue Cross and Blue Shield Federal Employees Health Benefits Program in the Washington, DC, greater metropolitan area, for the years 1971, 1972, and 1973, 2.3% of those seeking psychotherapy exceeded outpatient costs of $10,000 each per year and accounted for approximately one fourth of the total annual psychotherapy dollar. Furthermore, the same 2.3% of utilizers in the DC area accounted for 66% of the national figure spent by Blue Cross and Blue Shield for the over-$10,000-per-year utilizers in the Federal

Employees Health Benefits Program during this same 3-year period. For psychotherapy to cost more than $10,000 per year, one must visit a psychotherapist no fewer than four times a week for an entire year at $50 per session. One may speculate that Washington, DC, is a fertile area for the young psychiatrist who wants a job for 2 or 3 years so as to complete a training analysis at taxpayer expense and then leave for an originally intended private practice, but this is only speculation. This experience prompted Aetna in 1974 to severely limit its psychotherapy benefit and resulted in Blue Cross/Blue Shield's initiating a troublesome claims review that threatens the confidentiality of the therapist–client relationship, the latter in the interest of determining the variables in the apparent overutilization.

The second example is from an unpublished study by Elpers,[2] available through the Orange County (California) Mental Health Department. As a county health officer, Elpers compared the allocation of Medi-Cal (California's Medicaid program) money to private psychiatrists with a state formula of county needs based on the Medi-Cal caseload. He found that the dollars follow not the need but the number of psychiatrists practicing within a county, since Medi-Cal reimburses the practitioner on the basis of number of patients seen. It comes as no surprise that psychiatrists tend to congregate in urban areas; thus Marin County, an affluent bedroom community for San Francisco, received 470% of its "needed" share in 1975, while that same year, rural Lake County, with virtually no psychiatrists, received only 2%. In counties like Marin and San Francisco, the latter having received 271% of its "needed" share in 1975, there is a large supply of psychiatrists, and the competition for patients results in Medi-Cal patients' having no trouble in finding a psychotherapist. In underserved counties, the practitioners tend to shun the Medi-Cal recipient in favor of the higher-paying, affluent client.

Such problems notwithstanding, California's Medi-Cal figures reveal that 5% of all recipients utilize psychotherapy. This is two and a half times the national average, thus tending to refute the contention by Campbell (cited in Trotter, 1976) and Albee (1977) that the poor do not seek psychotherapy. In fact, there is reason to believe that the poor are at greater risk and will avail themselves of psychotherapy if it is provided in a manner meaningful to the consumer. Such an example is provided by Kaiser Permanente in San Francisco, which has over the past decades taken meticulous care to provide a consumer-oriented, comprehensive health plan. There, psychotherapy is not merely an upper- or middle-class white phenomenon, and subscribers seeking psychotherapy do so in direct proportion to their occupational class numbers in the health plan population. Additionally, black and Chicano clients in psychotherapy are rapidly approaching figures proportional to the numbers of these ethnic groups in the total health plan population. Utilization by Asian Americans lags behind the proportional figures because of the large Chinese population in San Francisco and its traditional resistance to psychotherapy, but the past few years have seen rapid erosion of that resistance, especially in young persons who not only seek services for themselves but bring their parents in when the latter hesitate to come themselves.

Minority and feminist leaders, as well as consumer advocates, have enunciated the limitations of white, middle-class, male psychotherapists, but in attempting to remedy this problem care must be exercised not to substitute a mischief of a different sort. In stressing the indigenous mental health counselor as an alternative, these leaders are not truly expressing the attitudes of their constituents, for the underprivileged resent (and rightly so) receiving care from paraprofessionals while the more affluent have access to journey-level practitioners. The possible exception may be among Native Americans, where the understandable distrust of the white man's "doctor" is pervasive and deeply rooted. Interestingly, when a group practice retains an appropriate balance of minority and female psychotherapists, the consumer demand for a certain kind of therapist tends to disappear. It is almost as if the client senses the awareness of the institution and is confident that his or her problems will receive the appropriate perspective and proper understanding. The poor, the minorities, and women have an inherent right of access to practitioners who are both aware and experienced, and any proposed national healthcare scheme must take this into account.

Warning: The New Mind–Body Dualism

During the past decade, Albee has demonstrated a propensity to anger clinicians, causing them to overlook his contribution as a critic whose consistent illumination of the flaws and foibles of psychotherapy spurs the serious practitioner to strive to improve the state of the art. Perhaps much of the negative reaction stems from the willingness of the semi-popular media to carry Albee's arguments the extra few inches into the realm of absurdity, often beyond his own fondest hopes. Thus, Albee can state that he never advocated suspending all psychotherapy until research can verify the art, that he never pronounced clinical psychology dead, and that he does not believe that all professional societies are conspiracies against the laity, to name only a few excessive positions variously attributed to him in the press. Yet he was the first to point out that psychology does not practice in its own house but in that of medicine. He has tirelessly assailed the medical model and has held steadfastly to the concept that emotional problems are not illnesses but problems in living.

The difficulty with Albee's view is that it would prevent psychology's participation in the treatment process. Interesting, the same arguments he employs to arrive at such a conclusion also make the case for the inclusion of psychological services within the health model as opposed to the medical model, a distinction Albee fails to make. Many, if not most, physical illnesses are the result of problems in living. The way we live, eat, drink, smoke, compete, and pollute relate inevitably to strokes, heart attacks, cancer, obesity, malnutrition, paralysis, cirrhosis, migraine, suicide, and asthma, to list only a few. The attempt to clearly demarcate psychological problems from physical illness by calling them problems in living is a curious form of mind–body dualism that would bring an immediate déjà vu were it not cloaked in this new terminology and sanctified with the struggle against medical domination of the health field. Psychological services are more than health, but they must be a part of health, if not the overriding principle, if the medical model is not to continue to encourage the somatization of emotional problems. The way we live influences our bodies; conversely, chronic illness and intractable pain create a problem in living. Psychotherapy is a viable form of intervention that can alleviate problems in living and lessen disease, and it belongs in any comprehensive healthcare system until that utopian moment when preventive techniques render it unnecessary.

Warning: Research May Be Hazardous to Your Health

Historically, studies of the effectiveness of psychotherapy either have suffered from serious experimental flaws or have yielded negative results. A recent and well-executed review by Olbrisch (1977) appears in another section of this issue. If it were taken completely seriously, every practitioner would lock the office and throw away the key. If taken within the perspective that the flawless experimental design is rarely possible in field research with human subjects, it is a valuable document that can motivate clinical researchers to improve and replicate their work.

In making the valid point that clinical researchers demonstrate greater clinical than experimental sophistication, Olbrisch neglects the fact that the critics of clinical practice and research show a shocking absence of tough clinical experience and a lack of appreciation for the limitations of the clinical method. Needy human beings cannot be denied treatment for the sake of experimental purity, and control groups are seldom more than better or worse approximations. With all of its imperfections, we are dependent on the clinical method, for in spite of the enormous contributions basic research has rendered, the pure experimental method is often helpless in the face of the most pressing human problems. This is not to imply that perfection in design is not the goal of every researcher, but, by and large, the clinical method will continue to be ponderous, inefficient, inaccurate, and vulnerable to severe criticism, but by its sheer persistence and response to pressing demands, the weight of clinical evidence will continue to be the primary vehicle through which the field of healthcare progresses.

So as not to belabor the topic, one example must suffice. To date, the definitive experiment on which the surgeon general's warning on each package of cigarettes might be based has not been forthcoming. Rather, the warning is the result of the preponderance of clinical evidence, any portion of which can and is being refuted by the tobacco industry. In fact, the tobacco industry has produced flawless research that demonstrates that there is no causal link between smoking and lung cancer in humans. Should the American people, as some have done, ignore the weight of 50 years of increasingly sophisticated clinical evidence in favor of the tobacco industry's excellent but unconvincing experiments, such a decision may well be hazardous to their health.

Some patients treated for pneumonia die, while others not treated at all recover. Similarly, the successes and failures of problems in living are not immediately discernible, and clinicians would do well to heed the criticisms of the clinical method and work toward increasing the sophistication of their tools. At no time, however, should a clinician be dismayed that no one research project yields a clear answer, for the clinical method is most persuasive in its preponderance of accumulated evidence, knowledge, and experience.

Proposed Modalities of Delivery under National Health Insurance

No matter how effective it may be demonstrated to be, it is unlikely that psychoanalysis or any other open-ended psychotherapy benefit will be provided under national health insurance. Where it has been attempted on a large scale, such as in the Federal Employees Health Benefits Program and CHAMPUS as previously noted, the costs have been prohibitive. Aetna responded by severely limiting the benefit, Blue Cross and Blue Shield are looking toward significantly redefining the benefit, and only CHAMPUS has made a conscientious effort to find innovative answers to the problem of cost-therapeutic effectiveness. The experiences with Medicare and Medicaid have only increased uneasiness within Congress, and as of this point in time, the proponents of the inclusion of psychotherapy in national health insurance will have to demonstrate its effectiveness.

In response, some segments of organized psychiatry are proposing the "remedicalization" of psychotherapy. Under this ominous plan, national health insurance or any other healthcare system, public or private, would insure only the organic brain syndromes and functional psychoses, excluding the psychoneuroses and character disorders as outside the definition of insurable illness. Under a unique twist to the basic plan, Harrington[3] would refer all persons with emotional distress, but with no organic brain disease or psychosis, to the community colleges for courses in the art of living. This psychiatric proposal may find a not too distant kinship with the concepts of Albee, who may be somewhat embarrassed by his closeness to the new medical model. Such a plan has appeal because it would reduce the cost of providing psychotherapy by drastically restricting the numbers of persons eligible. It would further guarantee income to psychiatrists who, as medical practitioners, would be the only persons eligible to provide what would be defined as a medical service. This obviously leaves psychology in a vulnerable position, but even more important, it deprives the majority of Americans suffering from emotional distress access to treatment.

Of demonstrated effectiveness are the community mental health centers, whose primary limitation is that of cost. Various audits have revealed the cost per unit of service to range from about $60 to a staggering $345 in one center, and a modal cost per unit of service of around $75 to $80 is fairly representative of most centers. Despite the potentially inordinate cost, the National Institute of Mental Health (NIMH) continues to champion the community mental health center concept as the mainstay mental healthcare delivery system under national health insurance. This is understandable, since NIMH spawned the community mental healthcare center movement, but most authorities have retrenched from the overly ambitious goal of the original Kennedy plan that there eventually be a community mental healthcare center in every community. I believe that because of their proven effectiveness, community mental healthcare centers (and their inordinate costs) can still be justified in underserved areas of the nation under national health insurance.

A third delivery approach (Cummings, 1975; Cummings & Follette, 1976) insists that psychological services are a basic ingredient in any truly comprehensive health plan. Such a view holds not only that psychotherapy can be economically included as a prepaid insurance benefit, but also that failure to provide such a benefit jeopardizes the effective functioning of the basic medical services by the 60% or more of the physician visits from patients who demonstrate emotional, rather than organic, etiologies for their physical symptoms.

The Comprehensive Healthcare Model

The Kaiser Permanente Health Plan is recognizable to most readers as the prototype of the modern health maintenance organization (HMO). Founded by Henry J. Kaiser just before World War II as a benefit for his employees, the health plan prospered during the postwar period because it offered the public comprehensive care in its own facilities at moderate cost and without the limitations, deductibles, and co-insurances characteristic of most health plans. At the present time, the health plan serves more than 8 million subscribers in several semiautonomous regions: Northern and Southern California, Portland (Oregon), Hawaii, Cleveland, and Denver. The San Francisco Kaiser Permanente Medical Center is one of a dozen such centers in the Northern California region. It is here, in a setting where the clinical psychologist has been the mainstay practitioner, that 2 decades of pioneering research have been conducted in the delivery of psychological services within a comprehensive health plan. As background, only the briefest summary of several research papers follows.

Beginning with the initial bias that short-term psychotherapy is not as effective as long-term, and burdened with the discovery that providing easily available comprehensive healthcare services as part of a prepaid plan fostered the somatization of emotional problems and the consequent overutilization of medical facilities by patients who had no physical illness, Kaiser Permanente experimented with a number of early attempts to provide long-term therapy for all its subscribers who manifested emotional distress. The problems inherent in most traditional clinics of the time resulted, such as a long waiting list, a high dropout rate, and an only partially successful attempt to reduce the ever-growing waiting list by providing crisis intervention. Following several years on such an unsatisfactory course, a series of evaluative studies was begun that spanned a decade and a half, and during this time an efficient, cost-therapeutically effective treatment system emerged.

In the first of a series of investigations into the relationship between psychological services and medical utilization in a prepaid health plan setting, Follette and Cummings (1967) compared the number, and type of medical services sought before and after the intervention of psychotherapy in a large group of randomly selected patients. The outpatient and inpatient medical utilization for the year immediately prior to the initial interview in the Department of Psychotherapy as well as for the 5 years following were studied for three groups of psychotherapy patients (one interview only, brief therapy with a mean of 6.2 interviews, and long-term therapy with a mean of 33.9 interviews) and a "control" group of matched patients demonstrating similar criteria of distress but not, in the 6 years under study, seen in psychotherapy. The findings indicated that (a) persons in emotional distress were significantly higher users of both inpatient (hospitalization) and outpatient medical facilities as compared to the health plan average; (b) there were significant declines in medical utilization in those emotionally distressed individuals who received psychotherapy, as compared to a "control" group of matched emotionally distressed health plan subscribers who were not accorded psychotherapy; (c) these declines remained constant during the 5 years following the termination of psychotherapy; (d) the most significant declines occurred in the second year after the initial interview, and patients receiving one session only or brief psychotherapy (two to eight sessions) did not require additional psychotherapy to maintain the lower level of utilization for 5 years; and (e) patients seen 2 years or more in continuous psychotherapy demonstrated no overall decline in total outpatient utilization, inasmuch as psychotherapy visits tended to supplant medical visits. However, there was a significant decline in inpatient utilization (hospitalization) in this long-term therapy group from an initial rate several times that of the health plan average, to a level comparable to that of the general, adult, health plan population. The authors criticized their retrospective design in its lack of a true control group, and after considerable difficulty and with the unfortunate necessity of denying treatment to needy individuals, they are currently engaged in replicating their work in a prospective experimental design that is responsive to the criticisms of the previous research.

In a subsequent study, Cummings and Follette (1968) found that intensive efforts to increase the number of referrals to psychotherapy by computerizing psychological screening with early detection and alerting of the attending physicians did not significantly increase the number of patients seeking psychotherapy. The authors concluded that in a prepaid health plan setting already maximally employing educative techniques to both patients and physicians, and already providing a range of prepaid psychological services, the number of subscribers seeking psychotherapy reached an optimal level and remained constant thereafter.

In summarizing nearly 2 decades of prepaid health plan experience, Cummings and Follette (1976) demonstrated that there is no basis for the fear that increased demand for psychotherapy will financially endanger the system, for it is not the number of referrals received that will drive costs up, but the manner in which psychotherapy services are delivered that determines optimal cost-therapeutic effectiveness. The finding that one session only, with no repeat psychological visits, can reduce medical utilization by 60% over the following 5 years was surprising and totally unexpected. Equally surprising was the 75% reduction in medical utilization over a 5-year period in those patients initially receiving two to eight psychotherapy visits (brief therapy).

In a further study, Cummings and Follette (1976) sought to answer in an eighth-year telephone follow-up whether the results described previously were a therapeutic effect, were the consequence of extraneous factors, or were a deleterious effect. It was hypothesized that if better understanding of the problem had occurred in the psychotherapeutic sessions, the patient would recall the actual problem rather than the presenting symptom and would have both lost the presenting symptom and coped more effectively with the real problem. The results suggest that the reduction in medical utilization was the consequence of resolving the emotional distress reflected in the symptoms and in the doctor visits. The modal patient in this eighth-year follow-up may be described as follows: She or he denies ever having consulted a physician for the symptoms for which the referral was originally made. Rather, the actual problem discussed with the psychotherapist is recalled as the reason for the psychotherapy visit, and although the problem is resolved, this resolution is attributed to the patient's own efforts and no credit is given the psychotherapist. This affirms the contention that the reduction in medical utilization reflected the diminution in emotional distress expressed in symptoms presented to the physician.

Demonstrating, as they did in their earlier work, that savings in medical services offset the costs of providing psychotherapy answers the question of cost-effectiveness, but Cummings and Follette insisted that the services provided must also be therapeutic in that they reduce the patient's emotional distress. That both costs *and* therapeutic effectiveness were demonstrated in the Kaiser Permanente studies was attributed by the authors to the therapists' expectations that emotional distress could be alleviated by brief, active psychotherapy that involves the analysis of transference and resistance and the uncovering of unconscious conflicts, and that has all of the characteristics of long-term therapy except length. Given this orientation, it was found over a 5-year period that 84.6% of the patients seen in psychotherapy chose to come for 15 sessions or fewer (with a mean of 8.6). Rather than regarding these patients as "dropouts" from treatment, it was found on follow-up that they achieved a satisfactory state of emotional well-being that continued to the eighth year after termination of therapy. Another 10.1% of the patients were in long-term therapy with a mean of 19.2 sessions, a figure that would probably be regarded as short term in many traditional clinics. Finally, 5.3% of the patients were found to be "interminable," in that once they began psychotherapy they seemingly continued with no indication of termination.

In a recently reported study, Cummings (2001) addressed the problem of the "interminable" patient for whom treatment was neither cost-effective nor therapeutically effective. The concept that some persons may be so emotionally crippled that they might have to be maintained for many years or for life was not satisfactory, for if 5% of the patients entering psychotherapy are in that category, within a few years a program will be hampered by a monolithic case load, which has become a fact in many public clinics where psychotherapy is offered at nominal or no cost. It was hypothesized that these patients required more intensive intervention, and the frequency of psychotherapy visits was doubled for one experimental group, tripled for another experimental group, and held constant for the control group. Surprising, the cost-therapeutic effectiveness ratios deteriorated in direct proportion to the increased intensity; that is, medical utilization increased and the patients manifested greater emotional distress. It was only by reversing the process and seeing these patients at spaced intervals of once every 2 or 3 months that the desired cost-therapeutic effect was obtained. These results are surprising in that they are contrary to traditionally held notions in psychotherapy, but they demonstrate the need for ongoing research, program evaluation, and innovation if psychotherapy is going to be made available to everyone.

The Cost-Therapeutic Effectiveness Ratio (Cummings, 1991) and the 38 Criteria of Distress (Follette & Cummings, 1967) have proven useful evaluation tools at Kaiser Permanente, enabling the San Francisco center to innovate cost-therapeutically effective programs for alcoholism, drug addiction, the "interminable" patient, chronic psychosis, problems of the elderly, severe character disorders, and other conditions many consider too costly and, therefore, uninsurable.

Implications for National Health Insurance

The experiences at Kaiser Permanente demonstrate what has also been found elsewhere: When all barriers are removed from access to medical care, the system will become overloaded with the 60% or more of physician visits by patients manifesting somatized emotional distress. There is every reason to believe this would occur under national health insurance, for the medical model inadvertently encourages somatization. If a patient complains to the physician, "My boss is on my back and it's killing me," a perfunctory, unsympathetic response is most likely. But let the patient unconsciously translate this distress to lower back pain and that patient is immediately rewarded by the physician's attention in the form of x-rays, laboratory tests, medications, and return visits. And even worse, temporary disability may be offered that removes the patient from the presence of the hated boss and renders unconsciously mandatory the continuation of the chronic pain as the only possible solution to what originally was an interpersonal problem.

When psychotherapy is properly provided within a comprehensive healthcare system, the costs of providing the benefit are more than offset by the savings in medical utilization. However, this does not mean that traditional delivery modes of mental healthcare services can be parachuted into the system. Such attempts have proven near disasters in a number of programs. On the other hand, the uses of artificial limitations and co-insurance are only partial answers, for while controlling costs, therapeutic effectiveness is often sacrificed. The experiences over 2 decades at Kaiser Permanente indicate that it is not the provision of a psychotherapy benefit that can bankrupt a system, but the manner in which it is delivered. When active, dynamic, brief therapy is provided early and by psychotherapists who are enthusiastic and proactive regarding such intervention, it is the treatment of choice for about 85% of the patients seeking psychotherapy. Such intervention not only yields a high cost-therapeutic effectiveness ratio, but it is satisfactory to both the patient—in increased emotional well-being—and the patient's physician—in dramatic reduction of somatization and overutilization of medical facilities. Further, providing such brief therapy makes economically feasible the provision of long-term psychotherapy to the approximately 10% of the patients who require it for their treatment to be therapeutically effective.

Finally, cost-therapeutically effective programs can be developed for problems in living traditionally regarded as too resistant and, therefore, too costly to be insurable. This requires constant research, innovation, and program evaluation, but it is important, because if national health insurance is to meet the emotional needs of all Americans, it is untenable to think of excluding one group or another.

Reference Notes

1 U.S. Civil Service Commission. (1976). Unpublished statistics on the Federal Employees Health Benefits Program, Aetna and Blue Cross-Blue Shield. Washington, DC: U.S. Civil Service Commission, Office of the Actuary.
2 Elpers, J. R. (1977). Unpublished report of the Program Chief. Santa Ana, CA: Orange County Department of Mental Health.
3 Harrington, R. (1977). Unpublished report to the executive committee of the Permanente Medical Group. San Jose, CA: Kaiser Permanente Medical Center.

References

Albee, G. W. (1977). Does including psychotherapy in health insurance represent a subsidy to the rich from the poor? *American Psychologist, 32*, 719–721.
Cummings, N. A. (1975). The health model as entree to the human services model in psychotherapy. *The Clinical Psychologist, 29*(1), 19–21.
Cummings, N. A. (1977). Prolonged (ideal) versus short-term (realistic) psychotherapy. *Professional Psychology, 8*, 491–501.
Cummings, N. A. (1991). Arguments for the Financial Efficacy of Psychological Services in Health Care Settings. In J. J. Sweet, R. G. Rozensky, and S. M. Tovian (Eds.), Handbook of clinical psychology in medical settings (pp. 113–126). New York: Plenum.
Cummings, N. A. (2001). Interruption, not Termination. The Model from Focused, Intermittent Psychotherapy Throughout the Life Cycle. Journal of Psychotherapy in Independent Practice, 2, 3–16.
Cummings, N. A., & Follette, W. T. (1968). Psychiatric services and medical utilization in a prepaid health plan setting: Part II. *Medical Care, 6*, 31–41.
Cummings, N. A., & Follette, W. T. (1976). Brief psychotherapy and medical utilization: An eight-year follow-up. In H. Dörken & Associates (Eds.), *The professional psychologist today: New developments in law, health insurance, and health practice* (pp. 211–221). San Francisco, CA: Jossey-Bass.
Follette, W. T., & Cummings, N. A. (1962). Psychiatry and Medical Utilization. An unpublished pilot project.
Follette, W. T., & Cummings, N. A. (1967). Psychiatric services and medical utilization in a prepaid health plan setting. *Medical Care, 5*, 25–35.
Humphreys, L. (1973, September–October). Should psychotherapy be included in national health insurance? No! *APA Monitor, 8.*
Olbrisch, M. E. (1977). Psychotherapeutic interventions in physical health: Effectiveness and economic efficiency. *American Psychologist, 32*, 761–777.
Trotter, S. (1976, November). Insuring psychotherapy: A subsidy to the rich? *APA Monitor, 1*, 16.

5   Turning Bread into Stones

Our Modern Antimiracle

Nicholas A. Cummings

We are told in the New Testament (Matthew 4:3) that while Christ was wandering in the wilderness, the Devil tempted Him by saying, "If indeed thou be the Son of God, cast those stones into bread." That would have been the ancient miracle. Let us move forward in time almost 2,000 years to 1975, the last year for which the National Institute of Alcoholism and Alcohol Abuse (NIAAA) and the National Institute of Drug Abuse (NIDA) have figures.

In 1975, alcoholism, its treatment, and its related problems cost the United States $43 billion (NIAAA).[1] During that same year, drug abuse and drug abuse–related problems cost this country $10.5 billion (NIDA),[2] for a combined total of $53 billion, or 2.5% of the gross national product for that year.

Economists have asked how long our society can support such a price before productivity is affected. Many experts think we have already turned that corner. Startling as it may seem, 1 of every 11 adult Americans suffers from a severe addictive problem. Drug addiction is epidemic among teenagers: One of every 6 teenagers suffers from a severe addictive problem. At any given time on our nation's highways, an average of 1 of every 12 drivers is too drunk to drive. We must not overlook the iatrogenic contribution: At any given time, 1 of every 7 Americans is regularly taking a psychotropic drug prescribed by a physician. Worst of all, the overmedication of our elderly is a national disgrace. Often in clinical practice what appeared to be early senile confusion clears up once the elderly individual is removed from mind-altering prescription drugs that have special side effects for older persons, or from several sometimes incompatible medications prescribed by three or four physicians concurrently.

Our Drug-Oriented Society

We have indeed become a drug-oriented society. I am not making any judgment about that; this may be good or bad, depending on your perspective. It may be that

This article is based on the presidential address delivered at the meeting of the American Psychological Association, New York, September 2, 1979.

The psychotherapeutic techniques described were developed by the author and his colleagues at the Golden Gate Mental Health Center, San Francisco, and the Department of Psychotherapy, Kaiser Permanente, San Francisco, during the past 16 years. I am grateful to William T. Follette for his constant support and encouragement throughout that period.

the mental healthcare movement has promised the American people a freedom from anxiety that is neither possible nor realistic, resulting in an expectation that we have a right to feel good. We may never know to what extent we ourselves have contributed to the steep rise in alcohol consumption and to the almost universal reliance of physicians on the tranquilizer.

What this translates to is that addictive problems are going to take up more and more of our practice. In a recent survey, 23% of a random sample of psychotherapy patients seen in a large metropolitan mental healthcare center were suffering either from addictive problems or from emotional problems substantially exacerbated by alcohol or drug abuse, and only 3.5% of these were so identified by their own therapists (Cummings).[3]

Our drug-oriented society has spawned new industries, and I will only give you three examples. The "free zone" in Miami is the passageway for contraband from Columbia: pounds of cocaine and tons of marijuana come into Miami daily. It is called a free zone because the authorities are totally helpless to stop the drug traffic, and we see entire boatloads of drugs seized and the seamen deported only to show up again within days with another boatload.

In California, where the giant redwoods used to grow but have now been logged, the five most remote northern counties have experienced an economic depression. A new industry is replacing the lumber industry: the growing of marijuana in 7–10-acre plots deep in the forest and hidden from the narcs (narcotics agents). I had the opportunity to visit one of these marijuana-growing communes recently, something you cannot do alone because the foils, traps, and snares created to fool the narc are as complete as the foils, traps, and snares set up in the hills of the rural South where moonshiners are avoiding the revenuer. The marijuana growers even seem to dress and talk the same, but there is one important difference: In the South, you seldom see 5- and 6-year-olds stoned out of their minds, like I did in the northern counties of California.

I will mention only one other new industry you may not have heard of: Chronic cocaine use so degenerates the nasal membranes that in California, plastic surgeons are inserting plastic passages in the nostrils of chronic cocaine users who have destroyed their natural passages. I could list many more new industries resulting from society's drug orientation, not the least of which is our multimillion-dollar drug paraphernalia industry.

A Psychological Model of Addiction

The medical profession is totally unprepared to deal with addiction. The medical model treats addiction to one substance by substituting another substance. In this way we used heroin to cure morphine addiction. We now use methadone to cure heroin addiction, Valium to cure alcoholism, amphetamines to cure carbohydrate and sugar addiction. I would suggest to you that the medical model, which plays a kind of addictive musical chairs, is a total failure because it actually escalates the problem in severity. Attempts to educate physicians about the dangers of substitute addiction or overmedication are difficult, if not often futile. The prescription pad is the number one item in the physician's armamentarium and is one of the very few truly licensable medical activities.

I would like to present to you a psychological model that has its roots 16 years ago in San Francisco in the treatment of the runaways to the Haight-Ashbury district of San Francisco and the Telegraph Avenue area of Berkeley. At that time I was co-director of the Golden Gate Mental Health Center, a privately financed community mental healthcare agency. I was treating these runaways under California law, which allows teenagers to receive treatment for addiction or sex problems without parental consent, something that could not be obtained in these cases.

In one way I was fortunate to be in San Francisco, because we felt the shock waves of a drug-oriented society fully 10 years before the rest of the nation. You may laugh at what happens in California, but whether you talk about the patio, the barbeque pit, the divorce rate, the hot tub, the cocaine party, or Levis, today's California fad becomes commonplace throughout the nation within 5–15 years. The drug cult and the waves of drug taking we saw in San Francisco in the mid-1960s are now commonplace across the land.

What I would like to do is describe a treatment approach that began some 16 years ago and introduce it by some formal comments about the causes of addiction. We just do not know what they are. We know a lot about addiction, none of which satisfactorily explains causality, but the interesting thing is that one does not need to know cause in order to intervene. There is a growing body of evidence that indicates that some people are born with a genetic predisposition to become addicted (Kandel, 1976). For others it is congenital and in utero; for example, very small amounts of alcohol imbibed by the mother during certain months of pregnancy predispose a child to alcoholism (Julien, 1978). So compelling is this evidence that a couple of years ago, the Food and Drug Administration considered requiring a label on bottles of alcohol stating that even small amounts of alcohol are dangerous to pregnancy. This would have been a very unpopular move, and I think that is why it was dropped. There is alcohol and drug addiction that is acquired (Blum et al., 1972; Peele & Brodsky, 1975). These causes are difficult to demonstrate, and the bottom line has yet to be written in any of them. Apparently, some people must have had a genetic predisposition, because the first time they took a glass of beer at the age of 11, they were alcoholics. Others seem to acquire the addiction. There is no question that the frequent ingestion of any addictive substance is sufficiently reinforcing so that everyone takes the risk of addiction. Yet not everyone becomes addicted, even children born of women who are heroin addicts. Although 92% of these infants show severe withdrawal upon birth, 8% do not, and the presence or absence of withdrawal has nothing to do with the amount of heroin the mother has taken. These are all questions for which we do not have the answers, so in treating my clients, I tell them the answers don't matter. In our program, we stress the concept that addiction is something for which the individual can and has to take responsibility. I give the following example to my clients: We do not know what causes diabetes. We know it is a failure of the isles of Langerhans in the pancreas to produce insulin, but why one person's isles of Langerhans fail and another's do not is irrelevant to treatment. Some families seem predisposed to the disease, and others do not; in many cases, individuals seem to acquire it through prolonged obesity. In either situation, the answer is abstinence from sugar. The first, first, first thing one must do when confronted with an addict is convince that person that the prerequisite intervention in the addiction is abstinence from the chemical to which one is addicted.

In our program, we stress that the concept of addiction as a disease is useless because it implies that one is helpless and cannot do anything about it. We say that least important of all is the debate over what is habitual and what is addictive. The medical definition of an addictive substance has to do with whether or not physical withdrawal occurs when a person is deprived of that chemical. I submit to you that the physical withdrawal from heroin is 72–90 hours. The psychological withdrawal is the rest of your life. The same thing is true with alcohol, amphetamine, tranquilizer, or barbiturate abuse: The psychological reinforcement is the crucial factor. An excellent example is the history of thousands of heroin-addicted combat troops in Vietnam who readily gave up their narcotics use once they were back home and the psychological factors encouraging their addiction were removed (Peele, 1978). I say to my clients, "Do not ask whether a chemical is addictive or habituating," and they understand when I point out that although cocaine is regarded in medicine as not addictive, it is so highly reinforcing that cocaine dependency will not be abated even though the drug costs $2,500–$3,000 an ounce, will burn out your nasal passages, and produces such behavioral side effects as paranoia and grandiosity.

I would like to give a fascinating example of "addiction" in a hospital during the days when alcoholics were placed in locked wards. In this instance, the hospitalized moved their cots into the bathroom while the staff looked on, baffled. After several days it was found that these alcoholics had substituted water for alcohol. If one drinks 8 gallons or more of water per day, the pH level of the blood is altered and one becomes intoxicated. The consequence of this was that the patients had to move their cots to the bathroom to be near the spout and the toilet, because 8 gallons of water per day results in constant drinking and urinating. So I say to my clients, "Do not ask me about what is addictive and what is not. If you are an addictive personality, you can even get addicted to water."

So it is irrelevant whether addicts lack endorphins, the natural substances in the brain that mitigate against pain and help us survive unpleasantness, and whether this is genetic, in utero; or acquired. I now want to describe to you how we treat addiction, a method that after several years of trial at the Golden Gate Mental Health Center became the backbone of the addiction treatment program at Kaiser Permanente in San Francisco, and one that is used in several other programs throughout the United States (Cummings).[4,5]

I tell my clients that addiction is not merely popping something into one's mouth but a constellation of behaviors that constitute a way of life. An addict can be likened to an unfinished house that has only an attic and a basement. When one falls out of the attic, one falls all the way down to the basement because there are no intervening floors to stop the fall. My addicts know exactly what I mean, because they know only two moods: elation and depression. They do not know what normal is. They do not experience the limited, normal mood swings common to other persons, because when they start to fall out of the attic, they run quickly to the bottle, the pill, the needle, anything to prevent falling clear down to the basement. So, indeed, the first thing we have to teach them is how to build a floor in that house, because you cannot live just in elation or depression. As one philosopher put it, those who are chronically depressed are damned to pursue pleasure constantly for the rest of their lives.

I remember that during the early days in the Haight-Ashbury, adolescent runaways came to me because they did not want to go to the city clinics, which were required to report addiction. Many got their money from Philadelphia, or Atlanta, or wherever their parents would send the money on the promise they would not come back home and embarrass the family. Others, both girls and boys, sold their bodies on the street to make their bread; still others stole or sold dope. At that time I realized what it costs to keep a habit going, and this is where the title of my address comes from. Using the vernacular I learned from my teenage runaways 15 or 16 years ago, it takes an awful lot of bread to make a stone. This is our modern antimiracle.

In the beginning, I treated addiction in the traditional, ineffective fashion, using the premise that one need not confront and prohibit the addictive behavior; through insight and understanding the client will come to lose the compulsive craving. This was before I recognized that addicts are extremely adept at playing this psychotherapy game and do not need the collaboration of an incompetent therapist to perpetuate their addiction under the guise of seeking help. I will never forget the time a young man in one group said to me, "Nick, you are never going to help us as long as we are hitting." I asked what he meant and he wisely indicated that "whether we see you once a week, twice a week, three times a week, or every day, hitting is so pleasurable, we can wipe out all the psychotherapy you give us with one pill or a touch of the needle." He was right, and for the first time in my professional career I learned that all insight is soluble in alcohol or drugs. So in that group we made a commitment to total abstinence for a period of 3 months. They all agreed, but came in the following week and tried to talk me out of it. I said no, that we had made a commitment and I insisted we honor it. They did, and it was the first group of teenage runaways that I was able to help not only to give up drugs, but also to become reconnected to life. After that I began to develop with these and other teenagers a system of treatment wherein the client earns his or her way into the treatment situation and continues to earn a place in that treatment situation by making gradual steps agreed on in advance. Failure to meet agreed-on standards results in various degrees of exclusion, and finally one may be thrown completely out of the program. This is why Wolfgang Lederer, seeing a demonstration, named it *exclusion therapy*. I did not like the name at first, but I have since come to regard it as a proper title based on truth in packaging. We anticipated therapeutic contracts before these became popular or standard, and today I make a detailed contract with every client very early in our sessions. As I show later, the technique is a combination of (a) therapeutic contracts, (b) reality therapy, (c) operant conditioning, (d) insight therapy,

(e) brief psychotherapy, (f) communication theory employing the double-bind and paradoxical intention, and (g) group therapy, all melded into a system of "psycho-judo," wherein the addict's own massive resistance is used to propel him or her toward giving up the addictive lifestyle. Although individual sessions are used to establish a transference and to motivate the client toward health, the job really gets done in the group sessions. Group therapy is essential for these persons who, as teenage or adult addicts, are fixated at the adolescent level of rebelliousness and acting out. At this level, peer pressure has its greatest impact, and the newfound peer pressure toward health of the group is the ultimate ingredient in solidifying a determination to clean up.

Intervention Phase 1: Withdrawal

Addicts do not come to us to be helped for their addiction. They come to us because they are about to lose something or have lost something. It may be a spouse, a job, a driver's license, freedom (threat of jail), or health (e.g., cirrhosis of the liver, esophageal hemorrhaging). Essentially, they come wanting the therapist to bring back the halcyon days when drugs worked and made them feel mellow. The therapist must start with the full realization that the client does not really intend to give up either drugs or the way of life. During the first half of the first session the therapist must listen very intently. Then, somewhere in midsession, using all of his or her rigorous training, therapeutic acumen, and the third, fourth, fifth, and sixth years, the therapist discerns some unresolved wish, some long-gone dream still residing deep in that human being, and then the therapist pulls it out and ignites the client with a desire to somehow look at that dream again. This is not easy, because if the right nerve is not touched, the therapist loses the client. Some readers will erroneously regard our approach to treating addiction as harsh or punitive in its stark sense of reality. Whitaker's[6] admonition is important here: Because the therapist's distance can be destructive in psychotherapy, we tend to emphasize closeness too much. A good therapist is one who can commingle closeness and distance as is appropriate at the moment. An inept therapist is one who has only one approach, either closeness or distance. Because addictive persons have character disorders, they behave in infuriating ways. To become angry (even unconsciously) at someone with a character disorder results in the forfeiture of the therapist's ability to help. Exclusion therapy provides a time-limited microcosm of the real world that enables the therapist to be close when needed, but distant enough to avoid anger when the client behaves in an infuriating manner.

Some will also erroneously prejudge exclusion therapy as manipulative. Haley (1976) pointed out that all good psychotherapists manipulate. The inept therapist is often the one who cannot admit this, so that manipulation is to the benefit of the therapist rather than of the client. As I show later, game playing is a cardinal feature of addicts, whose negative or destructive games must be countered with positive or healthy games.

Once the client is motivated to continue in the first session, I advise my client, to his or her amazement, that I will not make a second appointment until he or she is clean. For the heroin addict, this mean 3 days; for the alcoholic, it means 14 days; for the barbiturate addict it, means 10 days; for the amphetamine addict, it means 7 days. Most clients today are what I call cafeteria addicts; they take anything placed before them, and while remaining constantly stoned, they pride themselves that they are not really addicted to any one substance. The cafeteria addict is required to stay clean for 10 days, and the withdrawal really drives home the fact that he or she has become dependent on being stoned. I say to them, "I will not even give you a second appointment until you call me up and say to me, 'Nick, I'm clean.'" Because of the addicts' negativism, the refusal to see them sets up a challenge they cannot ignore. They become determined to go clean in order to foil the therapist, who expresses out loud doubts that they can really do it. Heroin addicts are amazed that I will not put them in the hospital. What I do is find a friend who has never been on drugs, and I give that person a crash course in taking care of somebody going through withdrawal. Then I call the client and the sitter every 2 hours, day and night, for 3 days. On each call, I have the client tell me what is being experienced, and I tell them exactly what they will feel during the next 2 hours. This removes the terror from the unknown. Then there comes a point somewhere around the 60th or 70th hour when I am able to report to the client that he or she has crested: "From now on, every time we talk you are going to feel a little better. You won't be out of the woods for a couple of more days, but you will feel better every time we talk."

When I am asked why I do not hospitalize patients who are withdrawing, I answer with an axiom: "Degree of pain is directly proportional to the proximity of the sympathetic physician. In other words, the hospital is where all the drugs are, and if you scream enough and hurt enough, at 3:00 in the morning some intern or nurse will not be able to resist giving you the needle, and that means if you are on your second day you may have to start at Square 1 again." I say to them, "It hurts more in the hospital because the drugs are there." They hear me.

Addicts use what I call the street-paver syndrome. Have you noticed that when a street is torn up to replace underground utilities, the street pavers put the pavement back, but never at quite the same height? It is either half an inch too low or half an inch too high, so passing cars hit a bump. Similarly, addicts will always comply, but not quite. The heroin addict will demand an appointment 1 hour before the 72 hours are up. The alcoholic will call 1 day before the 14 days are up. When the heroin addict calls, I say, "Don't call me now, I can't give you another appointment. You call me in an hour." When the alcoholic calls, I say, "Your time is up at 3:30 tomorrow afternoon." They reply that I am the craziest doctor they have ever encountered, and they slam down the telephone vowing never to call again. One hour or 24 hours later to the moment, they telephone. No matter what the therapist is doing, it is imperative that the client be seen that day. I am often scheduled as late as 10:00 or 11:00 at night and must see them after that. The client recognizes the commitment of the therapist and never forgets it. I have clients all over California who shake their heads and say, "My second appointment with that guy was at 1:30 in the morning. How do you turn down a guy like that?"

Our treatment has been devised into a set of easily appreciated and understood axioms that reduce the "analgesic experience," as Peele (1978) has called the lifestyle of the addict, into easily understood phrases that may seem simplistic but that, to the addict, are like words of wisdom. The addict uses what has been called "the cutoff," a form of denial in which the addict tunes out anything that touches on his or her addiction. These simple axioms have a propensity to break through the cutoff. Scare tactics are counterproductive. Telling an alcoholic that cirrhosis will kill is enough to drive him or her to drink.

When addicts first come in, they are determined not to see you. They are there because their spouse, their boss, their probation officer, their doctor, somebody has said, "You've got to do something about this addiction." They come in determined to convince the therapist that they do not need to be seen. During the course of the first interview, after having ascertained the precious deeply buried wish, I say, "It's a shame that you have this dream, but you are not ready to give up your addiction and I can't see you." The first response from this person who came in determined not to continue is rage and a demand to be seen. Addicts are determined to do the opposite of whatever you tell them, and here is where the double bind is useful. When you tell them you won't see them, they get furious. One must start with whatever the client brings to the first session, so the therapist takes seriously the need to get out of trouble. But the client must be helped to see the long-term problem and that the future under the present lifestyle is bleak. This is done not by reasoning, which will be tuned out, but by outmaneuvering the negativism. With every intent of helping the client, the therapist suggests possible solutions that can be provided but makes these contingent on fulfilling the required number of days of abstinence. The client is thus placed in another double bind. The therapist states unabashedly that he or she will do everything possible to help the client out of trouble once the addict is truly a client, a status that is not attained until the client has been clean for the requisite number of days and has earned a second appointment.

During this phase, the therapist will be confronted with two related games addicts play. The first of these is, "I can quit any time, but I don't want to." The therapist agrees that the client is indeed not ready and would not be able to quit even if he or she wanted to, for if the person were truly not an addict, quitting for the prescribed period would be easy. The client digests this as a challenge or counters with a related game: "I cannot quit." The first game is, "I am not really addicted," and the second is, "I am no longer responsible." Using psycho-judo again, the therapist agrees with the client, sighs that the client seems hopelessly addicted or unmotivated, and urges him or her not to really try because it would be an exercise in futility. At this point, the client needs an assurance, and the therapist cites one or two examples of successful cases that were similar to the present client but again sighs that this would not seem to apply to him or her.

In the 16 years we have been using this technique, four of five addicts so challenged will respond by meeting the requisite number of days of total abstinence. Of the remainder, about half will call 6 months to a year later to announce they have fulfilled their required period of withdrawal. We have even had addicts return triumphantly as much as 2 years later, having carried the therapist's telephone number with them for that entire period.

Once the client returns for the second interview, the successful withdrawal is lorded over the therapist, who immediately concedes having been wrong about the client, congratulates the client on the victory, and admits how delighted he or she is to have miscalculated the strength and determination of the client. At this point, the client has had the first experience in self-mastery and has put the first plank in the floor that is to be eventually built between the attic and basement, as discussed earlier.

On the second appointment the therapist is able to build on the client's feeling of self-mastery and to agree on a contract wherein each succeeding session is dependent on the client's continuing to remain clean. Each session is begun by asking if the client is clean. If not, there is no session that day, and the client returns the following week at the scheduled time. The client is not permitted to telephone, admitting he or she has had a fall, and then not come in. It is part of the necessary procedure that the client take responsibility for the fall and experience the therapist's reaction: The therapist does not disapprove; he or she merely complies with the agreed-on terms. Interesting things happen during this period: The client attempts unsuccessfully to draw the therapist into the kind of struggles he or she has carried on with co-addicts (parents, spouse, boss, lover, friends).

The next task is to motivate the client for the group program of 24 sessions. This requires 4–12 sessions, depending on the individual. The therapeutic contract for the group program involves an agreement to attend all 24 sessions, to be excluded for any sessions prior to which the client has had a fall, and to be permanently excluded on the fourth fall. Furthermore, the client must pay for all subsequent sessions after permanent exclusion. Because of insurance, this will often mean no money or as little as $1, but the weekly bill is a regular reminder that the client is a member in exclusion. This has very frequently motivated the client to return and try again, something the excluded addict can do after the 24 sessions have been completed and the group disbands.

At this point, a note of caution is important. Some addicts, though the minority, require hospitalization for withdrawal, and it is a matter of considerable expertise to differentiate these. The close collaboration with an internist skilled in the treatment of severe withdrawal is essential. Some alcoholics are on the verge of delirium tremens when first seen. Other alcoholics, as well as barbiturate and Valium addicts, are subject to convulsions on withdrawal. Most of these can be treated without hospitalization by providing the sitter with a "hummer," a dose of the chemical from which the client is withdrawing, to be administered when the client demonstrates signs of impending convulsion. It is important that the existence of the hummer be kept a secret from the withdrawing client, because knowledge of it will surely trigger a convulsion as a means of legitimately obtaining the chemical.

It is interesting that heroin withdrawal, with its severe chills, cramps, and other symptoms, does not present these medical complications. Special mention must be made of Valium withdrawal, which persists for as long as 6 weeks, with recurring waves of severity during which the individual may wander or have convulsions that he or she will not remember. Another drug with a prolonged withdrawal period is methadone, which is given to heroin addicts presumably as an alternative to the isolation and criminal behavior that become so important in the addictive lifestyle. I have seen the bone aches in methadone withdrawal persist well into the second month.

Intervention Phase 2: The Games

The 10 members in each group all start at once. There is enough flow that new groups are starting at regular intervals. Once the clients have been motivated to come in, the therapist must bear in mind that they have made a 6-month commitment only, after which it is their fond hope that they will become social drinkers or weekend joy poppers. There is an interesting thing about addiction, and it takes the 24 sessions before these clients realize it. Once addicted, no matter how long one remains clean, the addiction remains at the highest achieved level of tolerance for the rest of one's life. This is very easily demonstrated with "foodaholics." A foodaholic may take 20 years to get to 400 pounds. Once a fat cell is formed, it never disappears. Losing weight makes it empty, but it sits there like a flat plastic bag, waiting to be replenished. The foodaholic can shrink back to 175 pounds, but if he or she begins overeating again, it is only a matter of a couple of months before the body reaches its greatest attained weight of 400 pounds, because new fat cells do not have to be created. Something similar seems to happen with the addictions to chemicals. This is most easily demonstrated by a heroin addict who took years to build up a $300-a-day habit. That addict can be clean for 5 or 10 years, but if he or she starts to shoot up again, the $300-a-day habit will resume within a brief time. An alcoholic can build up to a quart a day of bourbon over many years. If that person quits and then starts to drink again, the result will be a quart-a-day craving within 2 weeks. The more you drink, the more you can because your tolerance goes up, except for Valium. Valium has no overdose level. It is the most commonly prescribed drug in America, with 11 billion tablets consumed in the United States in 1975. The only ways one can die on Valium are to swallow enough pills to choke or to mix Valium with alcohol. Valium is usually prescribed in 5 mg pills. Those addicted to Valium (another so-called non-addictive drug) get 20 or 30 physicians to prescribe these 5 mg pills, and they take 700–900 mg per day. A nurse I worked with was taking 1,100 mg of Valium per day, and it was difficult to believe she could work. On one hand, she was a zombie, and on the other hand, all she was doing all day was swallowing pills. Debbie has now been clean for 7 years.

Once in the group program, the phase called "the games" begins. All addicts play games. The major game played is "the rescue game." All addicts become the focal point of everybody who has a problem. They are called on the phone day and night by friends who tell them their troubles. They play the rescue game, no matter how undeserving the person. They attempt to rescue them because when they themselves mess up and are undeserving, they can then feel entitled to be rescued.

Alcoholics Anonymous (AA) turns a destructive rescue game that enables the person to continue to drink into a positive rescue game called sobriety. I have great respect for AA. In our program, however, our goal is to end the rescue game once and for all and free the alcoholic from having to spend the rest of his or her life going to AA meetings or to a psychotherapist. Addicts play games, and they cannot go from destructive games directly to no games. We spend this phase, Phase 2, in teaching them constructive games.

What are some of the games they play? "The rubber ruler" is one of the most frequent and can take many forms. It can consist of telling the bartender to leave the olive out of the martini, with all kinds of jokes about how many cubic centimeters of gin the olive displaces. The real reason is that after seven martinis, the alcoholic does not want to look at an ashtray and see seven toothpicks, because he or she wants to walk out of the bar and say that only three martinis were consumed.

The foodaholic will believe that the giant-sized bag of potato chips he or she just demolished was only one quarter full, when it was really seven eighths full. The rubber ruler can be either stretched or compressed. An addict will often be convinced he or she has been clean for 1.5 months when it has only been about 10 days.

"The vending machine" is an interesting game alcoholics play. It says, "I have been a good boy; I have been a good girl. Why isn't life making it easy for me?" It begins in childhood, when our parents forgive our F in spelling because we did so well in Sunday School 2 days earlier, even though the two are totally unrelated. Alcoholics continue such childish expectations and demand miracles after having been dry for 2 or 3 weeks. Because they have been good, addicts expect life to open up and give them all they want: a better job, a better lover, freedom from their probation officers, instant health.

Another common game is self-pity, and no addicts will resume their addiction until they first get themselves into the vortex of self-pity that makes the thing possible. Self-pity can be justified by a cross word from a boss, a nagging spouse, or a so-called sick society. All of these become excuses to resume drug activity. In fact, addicts quite frequently precipitate crises in order to justify their addiction, a common ploy being to incite a previously nagging spouse to begin nagging again as an excuse to end a period of sobriety.

In all of these games, one sees the addict's careful point-counterpoint in which guilt, justification, absolution, and punishment abound in complex acting-out patterns that assure the continuation of the addictive lifestyle. From morning-after remorse to contrition when arrested for drunk driving, the addict not only is full of good intentions, but manages to suffer in such a way that he or she can continue to view himself or herself as blameless and misunderstood. So the addict settles for what Peele (1978) called "comfortable discomfort." He or she becomes a kind of successful loser who alternates between elation at having fooled the world and depression at the discovery of his or her low self-esteem and lack of self-confidence.

The addict is adroit at playing "the feeling game," so the unwary therapist may be fooled into accepting the counterfeit feelings as genuine insight, just as the addict's friends have been fooled for years. In fact, everyone has had the experience of being shocked to learn that a friend or neighbor known for sincerity, concern, and honest feeling turned out to be an addict who had neglected his or her family for years. The therapist would do well to employ only positive changes in behavior over suitable periods of time as the real yardstick to insight or understanding.

"The file card" is an important game because it is an unconscious determination to resume drinking at a certain point in time, or once certain conditions have been fulfilled. In *While Rome Burns*, Alexander Woollcott has one of his characters telephone his hostess of the night before to apologize for missing her dinner party, saying, "On the way to your home I was taken unexpectedly drunk." No one is taken unexpectedly drunk. Rather, one plants a decision in the back of one's mind to the effect that if my wife nags me the 20th time or if my boss makes me work weekends, I deserve a drink. So once the event happens, the addict begins to drink, or pop pills, without having to arrive at any further conscious decision, in such a way that the file card, once filed, is automatic although forgotten.

Alcoholics are perfectionists. If I were an unscrupulous employer, I would hire nobody but primary alcoholics. I would expect them not to work on Mondays because they would be recovering from their hangovers, and they would miss work on Fridays because they could not hold off for the weekend and would begin drinking on Thursday nights. But on Tuesdays, Wednesdays, and Thursdays, I would get 2 weeks' worth of work out of them. They are perfectionists, but their perfectionism is part of the game that feeds their lifestyle and justifies addiction.

Intervention Phase 3: The Working Through

With the mastery of the destructive games and before the substitution of positive or healthy games, the group members suddenly become zealots. This is "the holier-than-thou stage" out of which many reformed drunks never emerge. It is important that this highly authoritarian outlook be understood and ameliorated, for during this phase the addict becomes merciless toward a fellow group member who may have a fall. Such an outlook toward the world can lead only to new kinds of problems in living.

Once this is worked through, and about halfway through the 24 group sessions, the group members become depressed. They realize there is no shortcut, only hard work ahead. The fanaticism disappears, but so does the enthusiasm that carried the client thus far. It is as if the energy goes out of the group, and each group member settles into a profound depression that places him or her at risk. It is interesting that few clients have falls during this period; most of the falls have occurred in Phase 2, when most of the testing of the limits is being acted out. Furthermore, the therapist's vigilance is alerted at this period, and the group members who have now been working together for several months accept the assurance that once this depression is weathered, better days are coming.

Intervention Phase 4: Self-Responsibility

In the final phase, the client seems to finally accept responsibility. This is in the form of a conviction, heretofore aggressively resisted, which concludes that abstinence is for life, not the 6 months of the group program. With the acceptance of this fact comes a kind of peaceful resolution with oneself and a sense of mastery.

This phase appears just at the point when the addict despairs that he or she will never emerge from the profound depression. It happens suddenly, and clients describe it as an experience similar to learning to type or mastering a foreign language: Proficiency is preceded by a seemingly interminable period of more or less mechanical struggling. Then one day, one is typing or speaking the language. In our case, the intervening floor in the house has been built and the client is no longer subject to panicky mood swings that send him or her scurrying for the bottle, the needle, or the pill.

A key ingredient has been the therapist, whose unrelenting firmness, fairness, and honesty have provided a role model and whose deep commitment and concern have ameliorated the client's chronically low self-esteem and interpersonal distrust, so aptly described by Chein et al. (1964).

Special Cases

Exclusion therapy is applicable to foodaholics as well as to therapy addicts and compulsive gamblers. These require special therapeutic contracts, but space limitations permit only brief mention of them. Exclusion therapy is not applicable to tobacco addiction.

There are two types of foodaholics: carbohydrate addicts and sugar addicts. The two types of addiction are often mixed in one person, but it is surprising how frequently the pure forms of addiction are found. Since the therapist cannot insist on total abstinence (one has to eat), the client is required to lose 5 pounds for a second appointment and 2 pounds per week to qualify for the subsequent sessions. Foodaholics usually insist on losing more than the required amount, a sure sign they will fail, so the therapist must point out, "Even when you are losing weight, you insist on gluttony in reverse."

Foodaholics will reach what has been termed in the group a "sound barrier," the weight that the client will seemingly be unable to go below. It was so named because once beyond the barrier, it is difficult to recall why it was so difficult, somewhat analogous to what the field of aviation experienced with supersonic flight. The sound barrier is mostly psychological, for the client changes from the psychological outlook of a fat person trying to lose weight to that of a thin person who is still somewhat overweight.

The temporary bouts of hypoglycemia foodaholics experience as they lose weight are not restricted to them. All withdrawal results in recurring periods of hypoglycemia, not only because the alcoholic is used to a high quantity of alcohol or sugar in the blood, but also because the glycogen function of the liver has been disrupted by prolonged use of a chemical. In fact, the so-called rush in drug taking is essentially the result of drugs triggering the sudden discharge of stored glycogen.

It is important that the therapist never recommend a diet to the foodaholic, stressing instead that the client understands his or her body a lot better than the therapist does and has long ago learned what will lead to weight loss. This prevents the game foodaholics play with their physicians, getting them to prescribe a diet that the patient will effectively sabotage.

In the United States, we have unfortunately created a legion of therapy addicts who constantly pursue psychotherapy, individual growth, and every new fad that emerges, in the firm belief, somewhat analogous to the Santa Claus fantasy, that the next encounter will produce the desired insight and state of narcissistic peace. We call these persons couch freaks, growth grogs, or woe-is-me artists. Exclusion therapy is very successful in helping these heretofore repressed individuals realize that the cure for constipation is not diarrhea. Space does not permit an adequate description of the special technique required in these cases.

Conclusion

Exclusion therapy is not an elegant theory of the addictive personality or a hypothesis about the cause of addiction. It is a viable system of intervention that has proven successful in a variety of settings in the United States during the past 16 years.

With our own clients at the Kaiser Permanente Center in San Francisco, we have followed a randomly selected sample over the years and have maintained active follow-up. Of this sample of 639 clients who have been in the program, 73% are living drug-free lives. Of these, 472 have been clean for 5 years, and 123 have been clean for more than 10 years. Almost half of the total sample experienced at least one fall, for which they came to the clinic for several individual sessions. Occasionally, someone requests that he or she repeat the entire group program, and this is granted. Others have entered traditional therapy and gained the kind of insight that was not possible as long as they were drunk or stoned.

If the estimate is correct that 23% of clients seen in psychotherapy are suffering from either addictive problems or emotional problems exacerbated by alcohol or drug abuse, then psychotherapists must be prepared to discover, confront, and intervene in these conditions. Medicine has not been successful in meeting the wave of addiction and problems exacerbated by drug abuse because the very nature of the medical model inadvertently encourages either iatrogenic addiction or the substitution of one addictive substance for another. Like the efforts of most workers in the field of alcohol and drug abuse, traditional therapy, based on the assumption that insight must precede abstinence, is even worse than no intervention inasmuch as it kindles the addict's fantasy that something will happen for him or her.

In mental health clinics in the San Francisco area, 40% of those seeking psychotherapy are manifesting or hiding alcohol or drug abuse problems, and my own estimates indicate that within a decade, a figure of 40% for the nation as a whole is not to be unexpected. Professional psychology must be prepared to meet this epidemic. The psychological model of intervention remains the most viable, and I hope I have done something in this address to enable psychology to meet the challenge these problems will continue to present in even greater degree in the future.

Reference Notes

1 National Institute of Alcoholism and Alcohol Abuse. (1978). *1975 statistical report*. Washington, DC: Alcohol, Drug Abuse, and Mental Health Administration Clearinghouse.

2 National Institute of Drug Abuse. (1978). *1975 statistical report*. Washington, DC: Alcohol, Drug Abuse, and Mental Health Administration Clearinghouse.

3 Cummings, N. A. (1975). *Survey of addictive characteristics of a random sampling of patients presenting themselves for psychotherapy* (In-House Paper). San Francisco, CA: Kaiser Permanente.

4 Cummings, N. A. (1969). *Exclusion therapy: An alternative to going after the drug cult adolescent*. Paper presented at the meeting of the American Psychological Association, Washington, DC, September 4.

5 Cummings, N. A. (1970). *Exclusion therapy II*. Paper presented at the meeting of the American Psychological Association, Miami, September 7.

6 Whitaker, C. (1979). *The present imperfect*. Paper presented at the Fourth Don D. Jackson Memorial Workshop (sponsored by the Mental Research Institute, Palo Alto, CA), San Francisco, August 3–4.

References

Blum, R. H. et al. (1972). *Horatio Alger's children*. San Francisco, CA: Jossey-Bass.

Chein, I., Gerard, D., Lee, R., & Rosenfeld, E. (1964). *The road to H*. New York: Basic Books.

Haley, J. (1976). *Problem solving therapy*. San Francisco, CA: Jossey-Bass.

Julien, R. M. (1978). *A primer of drug action* (2nd ed.). San Francisco, CA: Freeman.

Kandel, E. R. (1976). *Cellular basis of behavior*. San Francisco, CA: Freeman.

Peele, S. (1978, September). Addiction: The analgesic experience. *Human Nature*.

Peele, S., & Brodsky, A. (1975). *Love and addiction*. New York: Taplinger.

6 Arguments for the Financial Efficacy of Psychological Services in Healthcare Settings[1]

Nicholas A. Cummings

Introduction

By the beginning of the 1980s, it was generally conceded that psychologists had won their hard-fought struggle for inclusion in third-party payment for mental healthcare services. The notable exception was in Medicare and Medicaid, where the inclusion of psychological services was, at best, sparse and spotty and indicated a job yet to be concluded. The history of this movement, which began in the late 1950s, was detailed by Cummings (1979) in an article that fell just short of signaling victory.

The effort to achieve parity with psychiatry in the recognition of psychology by the insurance industry and the government is a case history in the struggle for the autonomy of the psychological profession, most often bitter, sometimes comical, but always colorful. Professional psychologists had to overcome the resistance not only of the insurance industry, which was reluctant to add another class of practitioners, but also of their own American Psychological Association (APA), which was then academically dominated and was indifferent to the professional psychologists' struggle for survival. This phase of the fight concluded with psychology's recognition along with psychiatry as one of the dominant practitioner forces in the field of mental healthcare. It also concluded with a thoroughly professionalized APA, which, in contrast to the prior era, now spends a very significant portion of its resources on professional issues.

Now all of this is rapidly changing. Those who would plead for the financial efficacy of psychological services in healthcare settings are once again on the defensive. This threat has been brought about by what has been termed the *healthcare revolution* (Kiesler & Morton, 1988; Kramon, 1989), which has created an array of new healthcare and mental healthcare delivery systems to which psychology must adapt in its effort to be included. In the original struggle for the inclusion of psychologists in third-party reimbursement in private practice, failure to be included would have spelled economic extinction. Again, in the present situation,

1 From *Handbook of Clinical Psychology in Medical Settings*, edited by Jerry J. Sweet, Ronald G. Rozensky, & Steven M. Tovian, Plenum Publishing Corporation, 1991.

failure to be included in the new delivery systems may result in the demise of professional psychology. The arguments for the financial efficacy of psychological services in healthcare settings have never been more crucial.

This article delineates the original arguments for the inclusion of psychology in third-party payment, for they are as valid now as they were then. Second, the healthcare revolution, with its implied threat to professional psychology as it is now constituted, is described. Finally, this article addresses how the arguments for the financial efficacy of the inclusion of psychologists in healthcare must be modified in the face of the healthcare revolution.

The Historical Perspective

Immediately following World War II, the Kaiser Permanente Health Plan on the West Coast began offering total healthcare benefits to millions of enrollees without the usual limitations, copayments, first-dollar deductibles, and other such restrictions that were customary in all other health plans at that time. In that era, mental healthcare and substance abuse benefits were totally excluded, as they were also at Kaiser Permanente. The research that led Kaiser Permanente to include mental healthcare and substance abuse as covered services became the basis of more than two dozen research replications and constituted the arguments for the inclusion of psychologists in healthcare. The 20-year experience at Kaiser Permanente, which demonstrated the financial efficacy of psychological services and the public policy implications in favor of the inclusion of psychologists, was summarized by Cummings and VandenBos (1981).

The Beginning of the Kaiser Permanente Mental Healthcare Benefit

Kaiser Permanente soon found, to its dismay, that, once a healthcare system makes it easy and free to see a physician, there occurs an alarming inundation of medical utilization by seemingly physically healthy persons. In private practice, the physician's fee has served as a partial deterrent to overutilization, until the recent growth of third-party payment for healthcare services. The financial base at Kaiser Permanente is one of capitation, and neither the physician nor the health plan derives an additional fee for seeing the patient. Rather than becoming wealthy from imagined physical illnesses, the system could have been bankrupted by what was regarded as abuse by the hypochondriac.

Early in its history, Kaiser Permanente added psychotherapy to its list of services, first on a courtesy reduced fee of $5 per visit and eventually as a prepaid benefit. This addition was initially motivated not by a belief in the efficacy of psychotherapy, but by the urgent need to get the so-called hypochondriac out of the physician's office. From this initial perception of mental healthcare as a dumping ground for bothersome patients, 25 years of research has led to the conclusion that no comprehensive prepaid healthcare system can survive if it does not provide a psychotherapy benefit.

The Patient with "No Significant Abnormality"

Early investigations (Follette & Cummings, 1967) confirmed physicians' fears they were being inundated, for they found that 60% of all visits were by patients who had nothing physically wrong with them. Add to this the medical visits by patients whose physical illnesses were stress-related (e.g., peptic ulcer ulcerative colitis, and hypertension), and the total approached a staggering 80% to 90% of all physician visits. Surprising as these findings were 30 years ago, nationally accepted estimates today of stress-related visits range from 50% to 80% (Shapiro, 1971). Interesting, more than 2,000 years ago, Galen pointed out that 60% of all persons visiting a doctor suffered from symptoms caused emotionally, rather than physically (Shapiro, 1971).

The experience at Kaiser Permanente subsequently demonstrated that it is not merely the removal of all access barriers to physicians that fosters somatization. The customary manner in which healthcare is delivered inadvertently promotes somatization (Cummings & VandenBos, 1979). When a patient who has not been feeling up to par attempts to discuss a problem in living (e.g., job stress or marital difficulty) during the course of a consultation with a physician, that patient is usually either politely dismissed by an overworked physician or given a tranquilizer. This reaction unintentionally implies criticism of the patient, which, when repeated on subsequent visits, fosters the translation of this emotional problem into something toward which the physician will respond. For example, in a purely psychogenic pain patient, the complaint that "My boss is on my back" may become at some point a lower back pain, and neither the patient nor the physician may associate the symptom with the original complaint. Suddenly, the patient is "rewarded" with x-rays, laboratory tests, return visits, referrals to specialists, and, finally, even temporary disability, which removes the patient from the original job stress and tends to reinforce protraction and even permanence of the disability.

Estimates of stress-related physical illness are subjectively determined, whereas the number of physician visits by persons demonstrating no physical illness can be objectively verified through random samplings of all visits to the doctor. After more-or-less exhaustive examination, the physician arrives at a diagnosis of "no significant abnormality," noted by the simple entry of *NSA* in the patient's medical chart. Repeated tabulations of the NSA entries, along with such straightforward notations as "tension syndrome" and similar designations, consistently yielded the average figure of 60%. This figure is now generally recognized in the medical profession, which refers to these patients as *somaticizers*, and in behavioral healthcare, which has named them the *worried well*.

During the early years of Kaiser Permanente, there was considerable resistance to accepting such estimates because it was reasoned that if 60% to 90% of physician visits reflected emotional distress, 60% to 90% of the doctors should be psychotherapists! This concern, as will be demonstrated later, was unfounded because subsequent research indicated that a relatively small number of psychotherapists can effectively treat these patients.

In an effort to help the physician recognize and cope with the distress-somatization cycle, Follette and Cummings (1967) developed a scale of 38

Criteria of Distress. These criteria do not use psychological jargon; rather, they are derived from typical physicians' entries in the medical charts of their patients. The researchers worked back from patients seen in psychotherapy to their medical charts, on which the diagnosis NSA had been made. They gathered extensive samplings of typical entries that connoted distress and validated these into the 38 criteria shown in Table 6.1. Physicians were urged to refer patients for

Table 6.1 Criteria of Psychological Distress with Assigned Weights

One point	Two points	Three points
1 Tranquilizer or sedative requested	23 Fear of cancer, brain tumor, venereal disease, heart disease, leukemia, diabetes, etc.	34 Unsubstantiated complaint that there is something wrong with genitals
2 Doctor's statement patient is tense, chronically tired, was reassured, etc.	24 Health questionnaire: yes on three or more psychological questions	35 Psychiatric referral made or requested
3 Patient's statement as in no. 2	25 Two or more accidents (bone fractures, etc.) within 1 year. Patient may be alcoholic	36 Suicidal attempt, threat, or preoccupation
4 Lump in throat		37 Fear of homosexuals or of homosexuality
5 Health questionnaire: yes on one or two psychological questions[a]	26 Alcoholism or its complications: delirium tremens, peripheral neuropathy, cirrhosis	38 Nonorganic delusions and or hallucinations; paranoid ideation; psychotic thinking or psychotic behavior
6 Alopecia areata		
7 Vague, unsubstantiated pain	27 Spouse is angry at doctor and demands different treatment for patient	
8 Tranquilizer or sedative given		
9 Vitamin B_{12} shots (except for pernicious anemia)	28 Seen by hypnotist or seeks referral to hypnotist	
10 Negative EEG	29 Requests surgery, which is refused.	
11 Migraine or psychogenic headache	30 Vasectomy: requested or performed.	
12 More than four upper-respiratory infections per year	31 Hyperventilation syndrome	
13 Menstrual or premenstrual tension; menopausal sex	32 Repetitive movements noted by doctor: tics, grimaces, mannerisms, torticollis, hysterical seizures	
14 Consults doctor about difficulty in childrearing		
15 Chronic allergic state		
16 Compulsive eating (or overeating)	33 Weightlifting and/or health faddism.	
17 Chronic gastrointestinal upset; aereophagia		
18 Chronic skin disease		
19 Anal pruritus		
20 Excessive scratching		
21 Use of emergency room; two or more visits per year		
22 Brings written list of symptoms or complaints to doctor		

[a] Refers to the last four questions (relating to emotional distress) on a modified Cornell Medical Questionnaire given to patients undergoing the Multiphasic Health Check in the years 1962–1964.

psychotherapy who scored 3 points or more on this scale as attested by the physicians' own medical chart entries.

After expending considerable effort and time validating this scale, it was discovered that emotional distress could be just as effectively predicted by weighing the patient's medical chart. The reason is that patients with chronic illness (or those involved in prenatal care) tend to see a physician at more-or-less scheduled appointments, whereas a patient suffering from emotional distress tends to use drop-in services, night visits, and the emergency room. In the instance of the chronically ill patient, the physician makes each entry in the chart immediately under the one bearing the date of the previous visit; thus, several visits are recorded on one sheet, front and back, in the medical chart. By comparison, when emotionally distressed persons make nonscheduled visits, the medical chart is not available, and the physician makes the entry on a new and separate sheet, which is later filed in the chart by medical records librarians. Repeating this practice through months and years builds up enormous medical charts, sometimes into the second and third volume.

Once the patient enters the somatization cycle, there is an ever-burgeoning symptomatology because the original stress problem still exists in spite of all the physician's good efforts to treat the physical complaints. The patient's investment in his or her own symptom is only temporarily threatened by the physician's eventual exasperation, often accompanied by that unfortunate phrase, "It's all in your head." A new physician within the care system is found, one whose sympathy and eagerness to determine the physical basis for the symptom have not been worn down by this particular patient. The inadvertent reward system continues, as does the growth of the medical chart. In a similar fashion, stress can impact an existing physical illness, exacerbating its symptomatology and increasing its duration. The baffled and frustrated physician uses such terminology as "failure to respond" to account for the ineffectiveness of the treatment and often silently suspects noncompliance or malingering.

The Effect of Psychotherapy on Medical Utilization

In the first of a series of investigations into the relationship between psychological services and medical utilization in a prepaid health plan setting, Follette and Cummings (1967) compared the number and type of medical services sought before and after the intervention of psychotherapy for a large group of randomly selected patients. The outpatient and inpatient medical utilization by these patients for the year immediately before their initial interview in the Kaiser Permanente Department of Psychotherapy, as well as for the 5 years following that intervention, was studied for three groups of psychotherapy patients (one interview only, brief therapy with a mean of 6.2 interviews, and long-term therapy with a mean of 33.9 interviews) and a control group of matched patients who demonstrated similar criteria of distress but who were not, in the 6 years under study, seen in psychotherapy.

The findings indicated that (1) persons in emotional distress were significantly higher users of both inpatient facilities (hospitalization) and outpatient medical facilities than the health plan average; (2) there were significant declines in medical utilization by those emotionally distressed individuals who received psychotherapy, compared to that of the control group of matched patients; (3) these declines remained constant during the 5 years following the termination of psychotherapy; (4) the most significant declines occurred in the second year after the initial interview, and those patients receiving one session only or brief psychotherapy (two to eight sessions) did not require additional psychotherapy to maintain the lower level of medical utilization for 5 years; and (5) patients seen 2 years or more in continuous psychotherapy demonstrated no overall decline in total outpatient utilization (inasmuch as psychotherapy visits tended to supplant medical visits). However, even for this group of long-term therapy patients, there was a significant decline in inpatient utilization (hospitalization), from an initial rate several times that of the health plan average to a level comparable to that of the general adult health plan population. Thus, even long-term therapy is cost-effective in reducing medical utilization if it is applied only to those patients who need and should receive long-term therapy.

In a subsequent study, Cummings and Follette (1968) found that intensive efforts to increase the number of referrals to psychotherapy by computerizing psychological screening with early detection and alerting the attending physicians did not significantly increase the number of patients seeking psychotherapy. The authors concluded that, in a prepaid health plan that already maximally uses educative techniques for both patients and physicians and that provides a range of psychological services, the number of subscribers seeking psychotherapy at any given time reaches an optimal level and remains constant thereafter.

In another study, Cummings and Follette (1976) sought to answer, in an eighth-year tele-phone follow-up, whether the results described previously were a therapeutic effect, were the consequences of extraneous factors, or were a deleterious effect. It was hypothesized that, if better understanding of the problem had occurred in the psychotherapeutic sessions, the patient would recall the actual problem rather than the presenting symptom and would have lost the presenting symptom and coped more effectively with the real problem. The results suggest that the reduction in medical utilization was the consequence of resolving the emotional distress reflected in the symptoms and in the doctor's visits. The modal patient in this eighth-year follow-up may be described as follows: She or he denied ever having consulted a physician for the symptoms for which the referral was originally made. Rather, the actual problem discussed with the psychotherapist was recalled as the reason for the psychotherapy visit, and although the problem had been resolved, this resolution was attributed to the patient's own efforts, and no credit was given the psychotherapist. These results confirm that the reduction in medical utilization reflected a diminution in the emotional distress expressed in symptoms presented to the physician.

Although they demonstrated in this study as they did in their earlier work, that savings in medical services do offset the costs of providing psychotherapy, Cummings and Follette insisted that the services provided must also be therapeutic in that they reduce the patient's emotional distress. Both the cost savings and the therapeutic effectiveness demonstrated in the Kaiser Permanente studies were attributed by the authors to the therapists' expectations that emotional distress could be alleviated by brief, active psychotherapy. Such therapy, as Malan (1976) pointed out, involves the analysis of transference and resistance and the uncovering of unconscious conflicts and has all the characteristics of long-term therapy, except length. Given this orientation, it was found over a 5-year period that 84.6% of the patients seen in psychotherapy chose to come for 15 sessions or fewer (with a mean of 8.6). Rather than regarding these patients as "dropouts" from treatment, it was found on follow-up that they had achieved a satisfactory state of emotional well-being that had continued into the eighth year after the termination of therapy. Another 10.1% of the patients were in moderate-term therapy with a mean of 19.2 sessions, a figure that would probably be regarded as short-term in many traditional climes. Finally, 5.3% of the patients were found to be "interminable," in that, once they had begun psychotherapy, they had continued, seemingly with no indication of termination.

In another study, Cummings (1977) addressed the problem of the "interminable" patient, for whom treatment is neither cost-effective nor therapeutically effective. The concept that some persons are so emotionally crippled that they may have to be maintained for many years or for life was not satisfactory, for if 5% of all patients entering psychotherapy are "interminable," within a few years a program will be hampered by a monolithic caseload, a possibility that has become a fact in many public clinics where psychotherapy is offered at nominal or no cost. It was originally hypothesized that these patients required more intensive intervention, and the frequency of psychotherapy visits was doubled for one experimental group, tripled for another experimental group, and held constant for the control group. Surprising, the cost-therapeutic-effectiveness ratios deteriorated in direct proportion to the increased intensity; that is, medical utilization increased, and the patients manifested greater emotional distress. It was only by reversing the process and seeing these patients at spaced intervals of once every 2 or 3 months that the desired cost-therapeutic effect was obtained. These results are surprising in that they are contrary to traditionally held notions that more therapy is better, but they demonstrate the need for ongoing research, program evaluation, and innovation if psychotherapy is going to be made available to everyone as needed.

The Kaiser Permanente findings regarding the offsetting of medical-cost savings by providing psychological services have been replicated by others (Goldberg et al., 1970; Rosen & Wiens, 1979). In fact, such findings have been replicated in more than 20 widely varied healthcare delivery systems (Jones & Vischi, 1978). Even in the most methodologically rigorous review of the literature on the relationship between the provision of psychotherapy and medical utilization (Mumford et al., 1978), the "best estimate" of cost savings is seen to range between 0% and 24%, with the cost savings increasing as the interventions are tailored to the effective treatment of stress.

The Effects of Behavioral Medicine on Medical Utilization

The foregoing addresses interventions with the patients who comprise 60% of all physician visits: somaticizers who have no physical disease but are replicating physical symptoms as a result of stress, and who are commonly referred to as the worried well. There is also the worried sick patient whose physical illness is a source of stress (secondary stress attendant on physical illness, e.g., fear of death following a myocardial infarct), or whose stress has contributed to succumbing to a physical illness or complicates a physical illness (e.g., tension-induced peptic ulcers or ulcerative colitis, failure-to-thrive syndrome). Finally, there is the asymptomatically sick patient who experiences no discomfort and for whom a medical evaluation is necessary to establish the existence of the disease (e.g., essential hypertension). Mechanic (1966) estimated that, if one looks at all three of the preceding categories, 95% of all medical-surgical patients could profit from psychotherapy or behavioral medicine interventions. Even with many supposedly biologically based physical health disorders, psychotherapy and behavioral medicine work and are cost-effective in that they reduce medical utilization (Yates, 1984; VandenBos & DeLeon, 1988).

Although physicians are becoming increasingly cognizant of the somaticizer, there still is resistance to referring to a mental health professional in cases of actual illness. This resistance prompted an editorial in *Newsweek* by a journalist with breast cancer:

> Curiously, while I was advised to see an internist, a surgeon, [a] cosmetic surgeon, an oncologist and [a] radiation therapist, at no point did anyone in the medical fraternity recommend that I see a mental health professional to help me cope with the emotional impact of breast cancer. Perhaps they didn't realize that breast cancer had an emotional impact. But I did. So, I went to see a psychologist, ironically the one specialist not covered by my insurance. It was worth the cash out of pocket. (Kaufman, 1989, p. 32)

Patients like this journalist report beneficial effects from counseling and behavioral medicine. That this benefit translates into a medical offset for the physically ill is demonstrated by a growing body of research, a few studies of which will serve as examples.

Schlesinger et al. (1980) found that the greatest medical offset was obtained in the chronic diseases of diabetes, ischemic heart disease, airways diseases (e.g., emphysema), and hypertension. This finding was corroborated by Shellenberger et al. (1986), who reported a 70% reduction in physician visits in a chronically ill population following a 10-week biofeedback and stress management program. Fahrion et al. (1987) were able to alter dramatically, through behavioral medicine interventions, including biofeedback, a group of hypertensives' reliance on medication. A 33-month follow-up revealed that 51% had been well controlled off medication, an additional 41% had been partially controlled, and only 8% had been unsuccessful in lowering their blood pressure without medication. Assuming a 5-year medication cost of $1,338, the authors demonstrated significant cost savings.

Olbrisch (1981) found a savings of 1.2 hospital days on average in surgical patients who received preoperative interventions. Similarly, Jacobs (1988), using biofeedback training before surgery, reduced hospital days by 72% and postoperative outpatient visits by 63%. Friedman et al. (1974) found that they could predict through an automated screening the recovery rate following myocardial infarct and could influence that recovery rate through behavioral medicine interventions. This recovery period varied more than 6 months, which reflects high potential savings through behavioral medicine. Flor et al. (1983) reported a significant reduction in physician visits and medication rates in rheumatological back pain patients after EMG biofeedback.

Impressive as the savings to the medical system can be through behavioral medicine, the potential savings in workers' compensation costs can even be greater. Steig and Williams (1983) calculated, for both treatment costs and disability payments, the estimated lifetime medical savings per patient as a result of a behavioral outpatient pain treatment program. Gonick et al. (1981) studied hospital costs 5 years pre- and post-treatment for 235 consecutive patients referred to behavioral medicine. The costs of providing the behavioral interventions, related to the savings in medical offset, yielded a cost–benefit ratio of $5 to $1.

Cummings and VandenBos (1981) described in detail the public policy implications that resulted in the eventual inclusion of psychologists as mental healthcare providers in healthcare settings, as did DeLeon et al. (1983). These conclusions indicated that any comprehensive healthcare system that did not include a mental healthcare or behavioral healthcare benefit would pay for that lack of benefit in its medical-surgical benefit. Also, that cost would amount to far more than the costs of providing a psychological benefit. Insurers became convinced. Then came a whole new ballgame (Duhl & Cummings, 1987).

The Healthcare Revolution

Actually, the healthcare revolution has been occurring since the early 1980s (Bevan, 1982), but it did not impact the field of mental health until a few years ago because the initial cost containment efforts focused largely on reducing medical and surgical costs. An early alert was sounded by Cummings and Fernandez (1985) and 3 years later by Cummings (1986). By the time Duhl and Cummings (1987) described it extensively and Kiesler and Morton (1988) sought to inform all of psychology, the mental healthcare part of the healthcare revolution was well under way, with more than 31 million Americans covered under *managed* mental healthcare rather than traditional fee-for-service. The figure is growing at 25% a year, and it is predicted that, by 1995, at least half of all Americans will receive their mental healthcare benefits under managed mental healthcare and that 50% of all present fee-for-service mental healthcare practitioners will be out of business (Cummings, 1986; Cummings & Duhl, 1986, 1987). At the same time, psychiatry is undergoing what it terms *remedicalization*, a euphemism for the position that only the medical aspects of mental healthcare should be covered, and is fiercely opposing the extension of hospital privileges to psychologists ("Supreme Court to Review," 1988; see Chapter 5). In the absence of such privileges, psychiatry would have no competitors, as it is the only mental healthcare profession licensed to perform medical services. Because federally chartered health maintenance organizations (HMOs; to be described further later) are largely exempt from state statutes, they are under no duress to recognize and employ psychologists. Many are seduced into "going on the cheap" in mental healthcare and employing less-expensive providers, not only social workers who are qualified, but also mental healthcare "counselors" with as little as 1 or 2 years of community college psychology training (Cummings & Duhl, 1987). This is a crisis for psychology of enormous proportions.

The fuel for the healthcare revolution came from spiraling healthcare costs, which were exceeding twice the rate of inflation for the rest of the economy, and the thrust came from the entry into the healthcare arena of the new heavy hitters: American corporations. Where, in the previous struggle, professional psychologists had to persuade the insurance industry and their own APA, now they are confronted by those who pay the bills and who have cried. "Enough!" The new drive for healthcare cost containment not only has produced such unlikely bedfellows as industry and labor but has been joined by farmers and consumers as well. In 1965, healthcare accounted for 6% of the gross national product (GNP). The projections made from the accelerating costs in 1979 predicted a doubling to 12% of the GNP. The beginning of 1989 saw it at just over 11% of the GNP, attesting to the success of cost containment efforts to slow it down. The exception has been the cost of mental healthcare, which is running away.

Whereas the current inflation in the healthcare field is about 9% a year, in 1988 mental healthcare was increasing at almost twice that rate, at 16.5% per year (Mullen, 1988). Aside from the fact that the healthcare industry was not confronting mental healthcare costs because of the overriding priority of medical and surgical costs, how did this happen? The efforts to control healthcare costs caused mental healthcare to balloon like an aneurism in a blocked artery. Primary among these efforts was the introduction of diagnosis-related groups (DRGs) by Medicare and Medicaid. DRGs imposed on hospitals lengths of stay limited by the diagnosis for each patient (or category of patients, more than 300 in all). This limitation resulted in thousands of empty hospital beds throughout the nation, threatening the financial stability of the American hospital system. Hospitals were quick to note that DRGs did not apply to psychiatry and substance abuse, and they began a rapid conversion of their excess beds to adult psychiatry, substance abuse, and the new phenomenon of adolescent psychiatric hospitalization. They embraced huckstering and marketed these beds in slick television commercials guaranteed to frighten any spouse or parent into hospitalizing a husband, wife, or child. General hospitals, which never had psychiatric beds, soon had 50% of their beds converted to mental healthcare and substance abuse. Something that was never predicted became commonplace. Psychiatrists were lured into lucrative hospital-based practices and began to fill these beds. In 1986, the last year for which statistics are now available, psychiatric hospital beds increased by 37%, and expenditures for psychiatric hospitalization increased by 44% in the United States (Mullen, 1988). Preliminary data for 1988 and 1989 suggest similar increases for each of those years (Mullen, 1989). There is now a saying in the psychiatric units of private hospitals: "A built bed is a billed bed."

Outpatient psychotherapy still accounts for a relatively small portion of the increase in mental healthcare costs, and hospitalization is responsible for the runaway costs. Nonetheless, the healthcare industry is turning its attention to aggressively reducing the cost of mental healthcare. Some insurers, regarding mental healthcare services as unimportant, are severely reducing this benefit. Others are aggressively turning to managed mental healthcare. This reaction has created an industry where none existed before, with companies such as American Biodyne, American PsychManagement, Metropolitan Clinics of Counseling (MCC), Preferred Healthcare, Plymouth, United Clinics of Counseling (UCC), and U.S. Behavioral Health, to name only a few, are suddenly having an impact on the way mental healthcare is dispensed.

Necessary Modifications

Any healthcare system that does not include a comprehensive mental healthcare service will pay for stress-related conditions through the overutilization of its medical services. This fact was learned by the insurance industry in the 1980s, and resulted in the inclusion of mental healthcare services (and the subsequent inclusion of psychologists as providers). Now there is an entirely new set of players who have to be persuaded: the giant health corporations that are rapidly gaining control of our healthcare system and instituting managed care. The foregoing arguments are all still valid, but they will have to be reiterated.

There is an array of new delivery systems, sometimes called the alphabet soup of healthcare, which psychologists and other mental healthcare practitioners must learn (Cummings & Duhl, 1987). These managed-care systems include the HMO (health maintenance organization, which is capitated and closed-panel), the PPO (the preferred provider organization, the purpose of which is to compete with existing providers), the EPO (the exclusive provider organization, in which all health enrollees must seek the benefit services), and the IPA (the independent provider association, where capitated providers practice in their own office), to name only the dominant few. Psychologists will have to adapt to and be willing to assume the risk for mental healthcare services, which means that, if a prospective reimbursement is not sufficient because of provider inefficiencies, the provider sustains the financial loss. Psychologists will need a great deal of training, as well as encouragement from the APA and the leadership of the profession. Unfortunately, most of our resources at the present time are expended in attempting to preserve the status quo and to stave off the rapid emergence of managed care.

Psychologists are in an excellent position to innovate delivery systems. Psychiatry has all but abandoned psychotherapy, and because the psychologist cannot prescribe medication, our profession has developed an impressive number of targeted, brief interventions. These targeted interventions, focused on specific psychological conditions, can bring rapid relief from pain, anxiety, and depression that is a change of behavior, rather than the masking of behavior accomplished by most chemotherapies (Cummings, 1985, 1988a). The managed healthcare industry must be made aware of our expertise in this regard.

We must abandon the concept of cure (Cummings & VandenBos, 1979). This concept has held back psychotherapy more than any other. First of all, we are dealing with psychological conditions, not an illness. Furthermore, behavioral healthcare has shown that stress derives from the way we live: what we eat or do not eat; how we eschew exercise; how we smoke, drink, and pollute; and an array of other lifestyle variables. Psychologists have developed wellness programs and need to demonstrate their importance in any comprehensive healthcare system. We are on the defensive here, because many in the healthcare industry remember psychologists as those ethereal beings who were committed, for all their patients, to the nirvana of self-actualization and human potential, the so-called happiness variables that no one has ever been able to measure adequately in psychotherapy outcome studies. Psychology has innovated brief, intermittent therapy throughout the life cycle, which is focused, problem-solving therapy at stress points in a person's life (Cummings & VandenBos, 1979; Cummings, 1986, 1988b). The ultimate cure of anxiety is never the focus, as anxiety is a normal accompaniment of life. Rather, the person is encouraged to seek brief therapy at various stress points throughout the life cycle.

Because most increases in mental healthcare expenditures in the past several years have resulted from unnecessary psychiatric hospitalization, psychology is in an excellent position to demonstrate that it has proven outpatient alternatives to the over-hospitalization of emotionally disturbed adults and adolescents, as well as of substance abusers. The average for non-managed mental healthcare plans currently exceeds 100 hospital days per year per 1,000 enrollees, and we have seen it approach 300. Contrast these numbers with those for a well-run HMO, which average between 40 and 50 hospital days per year per 1,000 enrollees. American Biodyne, a psychology-driven mental health maintenance organization (MHMO) using a wide array of aggressive psychotherapy protocols, has achieved what is regarded as the lowest psychiatric and substance abuse hospitalization in the nation. On its entering one market, the 178,000 enrollees averaged 114 days of hospitalization per year per 1,000 enrollees. Within 60 days, American Biodyne reduced the yearly hospital days to 4 per 1,000 enrollees per year and demonstrated what can be accomplished with the appropriate application of current psychological services.

Psychology is now engaged in a national struggle to obtain hospital privileges for psychologists. It will one day succeed, but at that time, it would be a tragedy if psychologists were to succumb to the temptation of the temporary, lucrative, hospital-filling practices that have attracted many psychiatrists. Rather, psychologists need to continue to demonstrate that outpatient psychotherapy can reduce unnecessary psychiatric hospitalization. Care outside the mental hospital is likely to be the wave of the future because it is more effective and can be less expensive (Kiesler, 1982; Kiesler & Sibulkin, 1987).

Finally, psychologists are uniquely prepared to render program evaluation and outcome measures of the effectiveness of all of healthcare, not just mental healthcare. In an era of healthcare rationing, public policy concerns center on the adequate distribution of our healthcare resources, the elimination of waste and duplication, quality assurance, and the strengthening of our limited resources through efficacy of treatment and efficiency of delivery (Reinhardt, 1987). The profession of psychology, with its scientific base, is integral to the design, delivery, and outcome evaluation of *all* healthcare (Cummings, 1987).

Outreach: Physician Cooperation and Consumer Education

It has been demonstrated that physician referral is the most effective way to triage a patient into a behavioral healthcare system (Friedman et al., 1974). Patients respect their physicians and will generally accept such a referral. Unfortunately, in the case of the somaticizer, the exasperated physician often refers in a manner not conducive to compliance: "It's all in your head." Various methods have been used to help the physician identify and refer the somaticizer early in the cycle, by far the most frequent of which has been screening through computer-based test instruments (CBTI). Cummings (1985) issued a note of caution. In a study of the practice patterns over a 2-year period of 34 primary-care physicians who received regular CBTI printouts identifying somaticizing patients, it was found that the rate of missed diagnoses of actual physical illness increased dramatically. The physicians began to rely overly on the results of CBTI screening and did not look further into the symptomatology of patients identified as somaticizers, thus failing to heed the age-old adage, "Hypochondriacs can get sick, too."

The economics of practice influence whether a physician will refer a somaticizing patient. Capitated physicians readily refer such patients, as there is no economic incentive to hang on to them, whereas fee-for-service physicians regard the high-utilizing patient as a source of revenue (Rand Corporation, 1987). It becomes useful, in such a setting, to access the somaticizer directly through outreach and consumer education.

One of the most successful triaging methods to directly address the overutilizer has been in operation for several years at American Biodyne and was reported on by Cummings and Bragman (1988). Founded in 1985, American Biodyne is a for-profit behavioral health maintenance organization (BHMO) that services the mental healthcare and behavioral healthcare needs of 2.1 million enrollees of several health insurers (e.g., Blue Cross and Blue Shield, CIGNA, Humana, and Select-Care) in eight states. Where its triage is in operation, American Biodyne receives a monthly computer printout of the 10% highest utilizers of medical facilities and resources as identified by frequency of service, not cost. The somaticizer is characterized by excessive visits to a physician, whereas high dollar amounts identify super-costly interventions such as open-heart surgery, organ transplants, and other medical heroics. Of these 10%, more than half are either somaticizers or persons suffering from physical illness whose treatment may be enhanced by behavioral healthcare intervention. The outreach program is directed toward getting that 5%–6% of the patients into mental health or behavioral health treatment.

Because of their extensive knowledge of physical illness, and their ability to be conversant with patients about physical illness, coupled with their psychotherapeutic skills, psychiatric nurses are usually employed by American Biodyne to conduct the telephone outreach. A medical social worker having similar knowl-edge and skills is an acceptable substitute for the psychiatric nurse. However, as a new center is being implemented, our procedure is to use the initial free time of psychologists, at least until the therapeutic load builds to the level where their time is not available. Therefore, it is necessary for each therapist on the staff to learn the outreach procedure.

The nurse, the social worker, or the psychologist is responsible for calling a pre-determined number of these high utilizers. From the outset, it is important that the patient's belief in the somatic nature of his or her complaints not be challenged, even to the slightest degree. The patient's interest can usually be aroused by the statement, "Someone who has had as much illness as you have had certainly must be upset about it." This statement usually elicits an immediate reaction, ranging from an exposition of symptoms to the complaint that physicians don't seem to understand or to be sympathetic to the patient's plight. After the patient has been heard out sufficiently to permit the development of some initial trust, the patient is invited to come in to explore how American Biodyne can investigate the pos-sibilities of an alternative to the treatments that have not worked, or perhaps, the patient, once the difficulty is better appraised, may be put in touch with a more sympathetic physician. Then, an initial appointment for psychotherapy is made. If the psychologist is doing the outreach, there is the immediate advantage that an appointment can be made with that therapist.

The telephone outreach is only one method used in an attempt to bring somati-cizing patients into therapy. At American Biodyne, there are periodic mailings of brochures or newsletters to remind these high medical utilizers of the services offered. In addition, each issue of the monthly newsletter features an article about a specific somatic complaint. The condition is discussed, and suggestions for change are made, along with the suggestion that an appointment at American Bio-dyne may be appropriate. Psychologists and outreach personnel are also encour-aged to take part in community presentations and presentations to local industries, in an attempt to further identify the high utilizers and to encourage their participa-tion in psychotherapy.

Once the patient comes to American Biodyne, it is vital that the therapist continue meticulously not to challenge the somaticization. The therapist's inter-viewing skills are marshaled to detect the problem being somaticized. Once this problem or set of problems is determined, the therapist treats these without ever relating them to the physical symptoms. In fact, most patients conclude rather brief therapy with a relief of somatic symptoms without every consciously relat-ing psychological discoveries to the previous physical complaints.

It is important to note that the American Biodyne model of triaging somaticiz-ers out of the medical system and into a psychological system was not developed as a cost-containment procedure. Rather, it was developed first to bring thera-peutic effectiveness and relief of pain, anxiety, and depression to the patient in psychological distress. The model became an integral part of a therapeutically effective, comprehensive mental health treatment system, and only then was it discovered that it was also cost-effective.

In cases of actual physical illness, the psychologist accepts the illness as a given. At that point, the therapist concentrates on the patient's reaction to the condition (e.g., depression, rage, or despair), and also to any neurotic conflicts that may be impeding or slowing recovery. These issues are then addressed in the course of the psychotherapy or the behavioral health intervention with the patient.

Perhaps one of the most effective methods developed for triaging the worried well into a behavioral healthcare system and the asymptomatic sick into the medical system has been automated multiphasic health screening, which includes psychological screening (Friedman et al., 1974). In the early 1980s, it was by far the approach of choice in most comprehensive prepaid health plans, and some had as many as 30 to 35 laboratory and other health checks online, and all within a 2-hour period. Eventually, such elaborate automated systems proved too costly, and they have given way to smaller, less ambitious health-screening systems, most of which can be quite effective when there is an awareness of physicians' propensity to miss physical diagnoses (as noted earlier).

Summary

Like all healthcare disciplines, clinical psychology is increasingly confronted with the need to prove not only its clinical effectiveness, but also its *cost*-effectiveness. Numerous powerful forces, whether in the form of DRGs or HMOs or some new form that has yet to appear on the healthcare scene, will continue to require accountability and justification for the expenditure of healthcare dollars. In part because of the scientific motivation of clinical psychologists to study what they do, data relevant to the clinical *and* the financial efficacy of services in healthcare settings are available to address these issues. The evidence thus far suggests that psychological services can reduce the inappropriate utilization of expensive medical care among the "worried well" and can improve medical management and behavioral outcomes among the chronically ill.

References

Bevan, W. (1982). Human welfare and national policy: A conversation with Stuart Eizenstat. *American Psychologist, 37*, 1128–1135.

Cummings, N. A. (1977). Prolonged or "ideal" verses short-term or "realistic" psychotherapy. *Professional Psychology, 8*, 491–501.

Cummings, N. A. (1979). Mental health and national health insurance: A case study of the struggle for professional autonomy. In C. A. Kiesler, N. A. Cummings, & G. R. VandenBos (Eds.), *Psychology and national health insurance: A sourcebook* (pp. 5–16). Washington, DC: American Psychological Association.

Cummings, N. A. (1985). Assessing the computer's impact: Professional concerns. *Computers in Human Behavior, 1*, 293–300.

Cummings, N. A. (1986). The dismantling of our health system: Strategies for the survival of psychological practice. *American Psychologist, 41*, 426–431.

Cummings, N. A. (1987). The future of psychotherapy: One psychologist's perspective. *American Journal of Psychotherapy, 61*, 349–360.

Cummings, N. A. (1988a). Brief, intermittent psychotherapy throughout the life cycle. *News from EFPPA (European Federation of Professional Psychologists Association), 2*(3), 4–11.

Cummings, N. A. (1988b). Emergence of the mental health complex: Adaptive and maladaptive responses. *Professional Psychology: Research and Practice, 19*(3), 308–315.

Cummings, N. A., & Bragman, J. I. (1988). Triaging the "somaticizer" out of the medical system into a psychological system. In E. M. Stern & V. F. Stern (Eds.), *The psychotherapy patient* (pp. 109–112). Binghamton, NY: Syracuse University Press.

Cummings, N. A., & Duhl, L. J. (1986). Mental health: A whole new ballgame. *Psychiatric Annals, 16*, 93–100.

Cummings, N. A., & Duhl, L. J. (1987). The new delivery system. In L. J. Duhl & N. A. Cummings (Eds.), *The future of mental health services: Coping with crisis* (pp. 85–88). New York: Springer.

Cummings, N. A., & Fernandez, L. E. (1985, March). Exciting future possibilities for psychologists in the marketplace. *Independent Practitioner, 3*, 38–42.

Cummings, N. A., & Follette, W. T. (1968). Psychiatric services and medical utilization in a prepaid health plan setting: Part 2. *Medical Care, 6*, 31–41.

Cummings, N. A., & Follette, W. T. (1976). Psychotherapy and medical utilization: An eight-year follow-up. In H. Dörken (Ed.), *Professional psychology today* (pp. 176–197). San Francisco, CA: Jossey-Bass.

Cummings, N. A., & VandenBos, G. R. (1979). The general practice of psychology. *Professional Psychology, 10*, 430–440.

Cummings, N. A., & VandenBos, G. R. (1981). The twenty year Kaiser Permanente experience with psychotherapy and medical utilization: Implications for national health policy and National Health Insurance. *Health Policy Quarterly, 1*(2), 159–175.

DeLeon, P. H., VandenBos, G. R., & Cummings, N. A. (1983). Psychotherapy—Is it safe, effective and appropriate? The beginning of an evolutionary dialogue. *American Psychologist, 38*, 907–911.

Duhl, L. J., & Cummings, N. A. (1987). The emergence of the mental health complex. In L. J. Duhl & N. A. Cummings (Eds.), *The future of mental health services: Coping with crisis* (pp. 1–13). New York: Springer.

Fahrion, S., Norris, P., Green, E., & Schnar, R. (1987). Behavioral treatment of hypertension: A group outcome study. *Biofeedback and Self-Regulation, 11*, 257–278.

Flor, H., Haag, G., Turk, D., & Koehler, H. (1983). Efficacy of biofeedback, pseudotherapy, and conventional medical treatment for chronic rheumatic back pain. *Pain, 17*, 21–31.

Follette, W. T., & Cummings, N. A. (1967). Psychiatric services and medical utilization in a prepaid health plan setting. *Medical Care, 5*, 25–35.

Friedman, G. D., Ury, H. K., Klatsky, A. L., & Siegelaub, A. B. (1974). A psychological questionnaire predictive of myocardial infarction: Results of the Kaiser Permanente epidemiologic study of myocardial infarction. *Psychosomatic Medicine, 36*, 71–97.

Goldberg, I. D., Krantz, G., & Locke, B. Z. (1970). Effect of a short-term outpatient psychiatric therapy benefit on the utilization of medical services in a prepaid group practice medical program. *Medical Care, 8*, 419–428.

Gonick, U., Farrow, I., Meier, M., Ostmand, G., & Frolick. L. (1981). Cost effectiveness of behavioral medicine procedures in the treatment of stress-related disorders. *American Journal of Clinical Biofeedback, 4*, 16–24.

Jacobs, D. (1988). Cost-effectiveness of specialized psychological programs for reducing hospital stays and outpatient visits. *Journal of Clinical Psychology, 21,* 23–49.

Kaufman, M. (1989, April 24). Cancer: Facts vs. feelings. *Newsweek*, 10.

Kiesler, C. A. (1982). Mental hospitals and alternative care: Non-institutionalization as potential public policy for mental patients. *American Psychologist, 37,* 349–360.

Kiesler, C. A., & Morton, T. L. (1988). Psychology and public policy in the "healthcare revolution." *America: Psychologist, 43*(12), 993–1003.

Kiesler, C. A., & Sibulkin, A. (1987). *Mental hospitalization: Myths and facts about a national crisis.* Newbury Park, CA: Sage.

Kramon, G. (1989, January 8). Taking a scalpel to health costs. *New York Times*, sect. 3, pp. 1, 9–10.

Malan, D. H. (1976). *The frontier of brief psychotherapy.* New York: Plenum.

Mechanic, D. (1966). Response factors in illness: The study of illness behavior. *Social Psychiatry, 1,* 106–115.

Mullen, P. (1988, December 27). Big increases in health premiums. *Healthweek, 2*(25), 1, 26.

Mullen, P. (1989, November). Increases in health premiums continue. *Healthweek, 3*(22).

Mumford, E., Schlesinger, H. J., & Glass, G. V. (1978). *A critical review and indexed bibliography of the literature up to 1978 on the effects of psychotherapy on medical utilization* (NIMH: Report to NIMH under Contract No. 278–77–0049-M.H).

Olbrisch, M. (1981). Evaluation of a stress management program. *Medical Care, 19,* 153–159.

Rand Corporation. (1987, July). *A report on the changing practice patterns of primary care physicians in geographical areas with too many physicians.* Santa Monica, CA: Author.

Reinhardt, U. E. (1987). Resource allocation in healthcare: The allocation of lifestyles to providers. *The Milbank Quarterly, 65,* 153–176.

Rosen, J. C., & Wiens, A. N. (1979). Changes in medical problems and use of medical services following psychological intervention. *American Psychologist, 34,* 420–431.

Schlesinger, H. J., Mumford, E., & Glass, G. V. (1980). Mental health services and medical utilization. In G. R. VandenBos (Ed.), *Psychotherapy: Practice, research, policy* (pp. 422–429). Beverly Hills, CA: Sage.

Shapiro, A. K. (1971). Placebo effects in medicine, psychotherapy and psychoanalysis. In S. L. Garfield & A. E. Bergin (Eds.), *Handbook of psychotherapy and behavioral change: An empirical analysis* (pp. 66–83). New York: Wiley.

Shellenberger, R., Turner, J., Green, J., & Cooney, J. (1986). Health changes in a biofeedback and stress management program. *Clinical Biofeedback and Health, 9,* 23–24.

Steig, R., & Williams, P. (1983). Cost effectiveness study of multidisciplinary pain treatment of industrial-injured workers. *Seminars in Neurology, 3,* 375.

Supreme Court to review psychology's arguments in CAPP v. Rank Case. (1988, December 1). *California Psychologist.* Special Edition: CAPP v. Rank.

VandenBos, G. R., & DeLeon, P. H. (1988). The use of psychotherapy to improve physical health. *Psychotherapy, 25*(3), 335–342.

Yates, B. T. (1984). How psychology can improve effectiveness and reduce costs of health services. *Psychotherapy, 21*(3), 439–451.

7 A Collaborative Primary Care/ Behavioral Healthcare Model for the Use of Psychotropic Medication with Children and Adolescents

The Report of a National Retrospective Study

Nicholas A. Cummings and Jack G. Wiggins

The current professional, government, and public concern over the increased psychotropic medication of preschool children and the continuing increases in such medication of children and adolescents is in part a result of the dearth of research data, particularly in the interaction of combined treatment use of psychotherapy and pharmacology. A collaborative model involving both primary care physicians and behavioral specialists addressed this concern in the retrospective study of a large, national sample of children and adolescents. The model also involved the participation of parent-figures and the community.

The growing concern among a number of healthcare professionals with the increased use of psychotropic medications with children and adolescents culminated in a high level of public awareness when Zito et al. (2000) sounded an alarm regarding the newer and seemingly widespread use of such medications with preschool children. Several television newscasters echoed the warning (e.g., Brokaw, 2000; Rather, 2000), and the matter gained the rapid attention of the White House, which convened two special conferences headed by the First Lady that same year to address the issue (Rabasca, 2000). The public debate grew more strident as researchers at the University of Michigan (Rushton et al., 2000) insisted that the furor over psychotropic drugs with children is overblown. The apparently sudden increase in public concern may be partially due to the attention given the subject by the media, but it may also reflect congressional debates in a presidential election year (2000) and thereafter regarding the cost of prescriptions, as well as a drug benefit in Medicare and Medicaid. Regardless of how this public concern came about, this does not detract from the importance of appropriate prescribing. The possibility of the misuse of medications, or the overmedicating of children and adolescents whose health is vulnerable to the control of others, remains a concern. Whatever the eventual outcome of the debate, the controversy is no longer limited to the healthcare community as it has commanded the ongoing attention of both the public and the federal government.

The importance of the issue prompted the authors to search the data warehouse of the Foundation for Behavioral Health for pertinent information. They were rewarded with data regarding 168,113 episodes of children and adolescents who received intensive behavioral interventions following their having been prescribed psychotropic medications in an organized national health plan over a 4-year period from 1988 to 1992. These data unfortunately are not only retrospective but are summary in nature and lack much of the specificity desired. Nonetheless, the large number of children and adolescents involved, along with the nationwide, but community-based, multidimensional method of data collection, has the potential of adding to our knowledge or at least to strongly suggest areas of needed future research. This is a report of those recently retrieved data.

The Mixed Results of Research with Psychotropic Medications: A Brief Review

Antidepressant medication has become the most popular treatment for depression, and antidepressants have become among the most prescribed psychotropic drugs in America (Antonuccio et al., 1999). Almost all controlled placebo studies favor antidepressants as more effective than a placebo (e.g., Van Praag, 1996; Schatzberg, 1998; Staley et al., 1998; Pearlson, 1999; Munoz, 2000), although Antonuccio and his colleagues (Antonuccio et al., 1995; DeRubeis et al., 1999) challenge these results. The latter contend that in so-called double-blind studies, the presence of side effects tips off the participants that the drug is present, increasing the placebo effect over that of the plain placebo. This position follows the well-known treatise, "Listening to Prozac and Hearing Placebo" (Kirsch & Saperstein, 1998). Furthermore, Antonuccio et al. (1995) quote studies that would demonstrate that most acute depressions, even those that are severe, respond to behavioral interventions with results that are more lasting. They also contend that behavioral interventions are more effective in the prevention of depression, and indeed, some studies suggest antidepressants render the patient more vulnerable to relapse (Hollon et al., 1991; Segal et al., 1999).

Munoz (2000) regards the debate as to which is more efficacious, medication or behavioral intervention, as irrelevant because a large body of research demonstrates the two in combination are superior to one alone. The American Psychiatric Association Guidelines (1999) would support such a conclusion in spite of some very recent research that suggests, for panic disorder at least, that either medication or behavioral intervention alone is superior to the two in combination (Tech, 2001). These considerations are of importance because not only are healthcare systems spending more dollars on psychotropic medications than on behavioral care, but psychopharmacology has escalated dramatically in costs during recent years, creating a significant financial burden. Consequently, the expanding use of psychotropic medications raises questions of efficacy. Beardsley et al. (1988) point out that 70% of prescriptions are written by non-psychiatric physicians, often in inadequate doses and for too short a length of treatment. These physicians prescribe conservatively because the tendency is to prescribe medication to all depressed patients, even the mild cases that might do better with behavioral interventions, whereas the more severe cases, which require greater dosage and length, receive the same inadequate prescription. Pincus et al. (1998) document the increasing use of medications, especially Selective Serotonin Reuptake Inhibitor (SSRI) antidepressants, over less invasive (behavioral) approaches, a concern echoed by an impressive number of authorities (Fisher & Greenberg, 1989; Fisher & Fisher, 1996; Greenhill, 1998; Emslie et al., 1999, with commentary on his article by Safer et al., 1996; Traversa et al., 1996; Zito et al., 1997; Jensen, 1998; Minde, 1998; Olfson et al., 1998; Zito et al., 1998, 2000).

Kaplan (1999) provides an excellent summary of the current status of the medication-prescribing practices for children, which has increased in use for both stimulants and antidepressants. Jensen (1998) reported that stimulants were the leading pediatric use of medications, accounting for 2 million office visits in 1995. SSRI antidepressants were the next most often prescribed, accounting for 358,616 office visits. Some researchers have expressed skepticism about the effectiveness of antidepressants (e.g., Fisher & Greenberg, 1989, 1997), while Fisher and Fisher (1996) evaluated 13 double-blind controlled placebo studies of the use of antidepressants with children and adolescents. They challenged the use of antidepressants with children, especially very young children, in the face of a consistent failure to demonstrate an advantage over placebo in this vulnerable population. Johnson and Fruehling (1994) found little or no evidence for the usefulness of antidepressants with children, yet recommended their use anyway. Pelligrino (1996), however, continued to caution physicians about the ethics of prescribing antidepressants for children in the absence of scientific data, whereas Vitiello (1998) warned of serious side effects in the use of antidepressants with children that may damage the developing brains of preschoolers. Although a growing number of studies challenged the use of these medications with children (Safer et al., 1996; Zito et al., 1997, 1998), these concerns crested with the publication of the warnings that attracted widespread public and government attention (Zito et al., 2000).

The Collaborative Model

The model was based on a collegial, collaborative relationship between primary care physicians treating children and adolescents (both pediatricians and family medical practitioners) who simply relied on referral to a closed panel of behavioral healthcare specialists (psychiatric nurse practitioners, psychologists, and social workers on a ratio of 1:5:3) of all children and adolescents for whom psychotropic medications were prescribed. The primary care physicians and behavioral healthcare specialists consulted regularly on each case until the episode of treatment was concluded. This collaboration took place within a national behavioral healthcare delivery system that was a "carve-out" to a number of national health plans as described in the next section.

The behavioral healthcare specialists, several hundred in number, all had received 130 hours of intensive training, 10 hours a day for 2 consecutive weeks, in groups of 25 participants, in what has come to be known in the behavioral healthcare industry as the "Biodyne boot camp." The training was in Focused, Intermittent Psychotherapy throughout the Life Cycle (see Cummings & Sayama, 1995), and in the 68 American Biodyne protocols that were empirically based and developed over a 25-year period at Kaiser Permanente and fine-tuned in the Health Care Financing Administration's (HCFA) extensive 7-year Hawaii Medicaid Project conducted by the Foundation for Behavioral Health. In addition, all behavioral healthcare specialists thereafter devoted 15% of their work time to quality assurance, which included weekly clinical case conferencing (3 hours) and weekly individual and group supervision. Thus, there was assurance that there was both adherence to the protocols and flexibility to deviate from those protocols in accordance with guidelines and individual patient exigencies. For those children and adolescents who lacked a significant male role model in their lives, or who were subjected to a series of negative male role models (about two thirds of the patients of both genders), a special effort was made to (a) assign them to a male therapist and (b) arrange for ongoing contact with surrogate father figures in their lives such as grandfathers, male teachers and coaches, Big Brothers, Boy Scout leaders, Sunday School teachers, or whoever might be available.

The behavioral treatment also required that at least one parent (biological, step, adoptee, foster, significant other, or caregiver), and hopefully two, participate in the counseling. In cases of divorce, or even in intact families where the mother and father, by virtue of employment, had two different health plans, the rules were bent for the non-eligible parental figure so that he (in most cases) or she (in rare cases) could be seen. Because of the predominance of single-parent families in our child and adolescent patient populations, only in 18% of the cases were both biological or stepparents involved in the treatment.

The Setting and the Population

The study took place at American Biodyne, the nation's first and only psychology-driven national behavioral healthcare carve-out, during the 4 years of July 1, 1988, to July 1, 1992. During that time, American Biodyne grew to 14.5 million covered lives in 39 states. Cohesive data are not available before July 1, 1988, as the company was growing too rapidly to engage in extensive research. The company was sold to Medco/Merck in the latter part of 1992. It subsequently was spun off as Merit Behavioral Care and is now part of Magellan Health Care, the largest behavioral carve-out with more than 60 million covered lives. During the years of this study, American Biodyne was the behavioral healthcare carve-out for a number of health plans, such as several Blue Cross/Blue Shield plans, Humana, U.S. Healthcare, and so on. In all instances, the collaborative model between primary care and behavioral care as just described was a basic part of the service delivery contract.

During these 4 years, 168,113 child/adolescent treatment episodes took place, defined as a series of sessions, including those of parental figures, that constituted the entire treatment for one child/adolescent. These were discrete episodes (i.e., no repeat treatment of the same child/adolescent). The child/adolescent population was a subset of the adult population of 1.6 million episodes as previously

Table 7.1 Number of Covered Lives, and Adult Versus Child/Adolescent Treatment Episodes, by Year

Year	Number Covered Lives	Adult Tx Episodes	Child/Adolescent Tx Episodes
1988–1989	3,483,000	174,149	18,046
1989–1990	5,753,000	287,648	29,114
1990–1991	9,038,000	451,391	47,036
1991–1992	14,532,000	726,614	73,917
Totals		1,639,802	168,113

reported by the authors (Wiggins & Cummings, 1998) and which report did not include the pre-adult patients. The number of covered lives for each of the afore-mentioned 4 years, along with the adult treatment episodes versus child/adolescent treatment episodes for each of those 4 years, is shown in Table 7.1.

The average number of sessions for parent figures (as defined earlier) was 8.3 sessions per episode. For each child/adolescent seen, 1.3 parent figures received counseling regarding the behaviors of these young patients. Thus, for each child/adolescent there was an average treatment sequence of 172 sessions (6.3 for the child/adolescent and 10.9 for the parent figure). The total utilization (penetration) rate of 3.24%, though less than the rate for adults, required three times the resources expended for the usual adults (6.2 sessions per episode), who were seen for problems not related to their children or adolescents.

The data available in the Foundation for Behavioral Health warehouse are unfortunately unrefined for comparison of medications, site by site, year by year, and employed versus Medicaid, making analyses of these variables impossible. However, the diverse population scattered throughout 39 states was in the era before the large-scale assignment of Medicaid patients to managed care. Therefore, it can be said that the vast majority of patients seen (as much as 85%, according to estimates for the period received from HCFA) were from employed families. Furthermore, this was an era when children and adolescents were infrequently prescribed antidepressants and/or neuroleptic medications (Jensen, 1998). The exception to the latter was the use of Imipramine for nocturnal enuresis (Foxman et al., 1986). Most of the psychotropic medications were for stimulants, predominantly methylphenidate (Ritalin) and pemoline (Cylert), prescribed for Attention Deficit Disorder and Attention Deficit Hyperactivity Disorder (ADD/ADHD). This period also preceded the advent of the newer medications for ADD/ADHD. Although other medications (such as Dilantin for convulsive disorders and Imipramine for nocturnal enuresis) were also prescribed to this population, these were infrequent when compared to the preponderance of stimulants administered.

Findings

Again with reference to Table 7.1, it can be seen that the child/adolescent treatment episodes constitute a little more than 10% of the total number of treatment episodes for all patients. This approximates the national incidence of child/adolescent disorders reported to be 7.7% of the total number of psychiatric disorders (Pincus et al., 1998). The difference between the expected 7.7% and the obtained 10% can easily be the increase due to intensive outreach and referral in the model used. The steady increases in covered lives for each of the 4 years reflect the rapid growth of American Biodyne.

The distribution by age of children and adolescents on psychotropic medications at the time they entered behavioral treatment, as well as on discharge, is shown in Table 7.2. The percentage of patients receiving medication when referred for behavioral treatment increases somewhat from age 5 to 8 (6.2% to 8.5%), but it more than triples to 29.3% by age 10. Thereafter the percentage of patients prescribed medication at the time of referral to American Biodyne increases strongly and steadily at each age interval so that by age 18 the percentage of 66.9% is almost the expected rate (68.0%) for adults referred for behavioral treatment.

The impact of behavioral interventions is demonstrated by the dramatic reduction in the use of medications at the conclusion of treatment. This ranges from a 95% reduction for the 5- to 6-year-old group, to a 92% reduction for the 17- to 18-year-old group. The prescribing patterns were the sole discretion of the primary care physician (PCP), but in this model, the PCPs made the decision after feedback during regular collaborative meetings with each young patient's behavioral therapist. The criteria used to assess the patient's progress, with the eventual conclusion, "the patient is no longer in need of medication," are given in the next section.

Since the preponderance of medications prescribed were for ADD/ADHD, it is important to note the percentage of children/adolescents with these diagnoses at the beginning of behavioral treatment, versus the percentage who retained these diagnoses after the conclusion of the behavioral interventions with these children/adolescents as well as their parental figures. Table 7.3 indicates that on entering treatment, 61% of the boys and 23% of the girls had been diagnosed with

Table 7.2 Percentage of Children/Adolescents by Age on Medication Versus Adults on Medication on Entering Treatment (Tx) and after Conclusion of Treatment

Age on Entering Tx	Percentage on Medications on Entering Tx	Percentage on Medications Concluding Tx
5–6	6.2	0.3
7–8	8.5	0.5
9–10	29.3	2.1
11–12	36.8	3.7
13–14	42.1	3.9
15–16	57.4	5.2
17–18	66.9	5.8
19+ (adults)	68.0	13.1

Note: Episodes of treatments averaged 6.3 sessions for children/adolescents, 8.2 for their parents, and 6.2 for other adults.

Table 7.3 Percentage of Children/Adolescents by Gender Entering and Concluding Treatment (Tx) with the Diagnosis of Attention Deficit Disorder and Attention Deficit Hyperactivity Disorder

	On Entering Tx	On Concluding Tx
Male participants	61	11
Female participants	23	2

ADD/ADHD by their PCPs and had been prescribed medication accordingly. At the conclusion of the behavioral interventions with the children/adolescents and their parental figures, only 11% of the boys and 2% of the girls retained these diagnoses. That only one fifth of the originally diagnosed male participants and only one tenth of the originally diagnosed female participants at the conclusion of relatively brief therapy demonstrated behaviors consistent with the diagnoses of ADD/ADHD raises questions discussed later.

The notable decline from entrance to outcome in the use of psychotropic medications for children/adolescents parallels the American Biodyne experience with adults on medication (Wiggins & Cummings, 1998). The decline in the entering/concluding treatment ratio (E/C ratio) for those on medication at the beginning of behavioral treatment versus those remaining on medication at the conclusion of behavioral treatment was the steepest in the younger age groups, and stable in the older age groups. Extrapolating the data in Table 7.2, the E/C ratio was 20:7 and 17:0 in the 5 to 6 and the 7 to 8 age groups, respectively, whereas it stabilized in the range of 9:9 to 11:5 in the 9- to 18-year-old groupings. The sharp increase in the E/C ratio in the 9 to 10 age group does not seem to correspond with any developmental or biological changes, such as puberty, and raises additional questions.

Criteria for Medication Discontinuation

Most children and adolescents referred with behavioral problems are in friction with certain aspects of the environment: teachers, juvenile authorities, peers, parents, or usually a combination of these. The pressure on both parents and PCPs from teachers demanding medication for their disruptive students can often be intense, and the threat of having to go back to juvenile jail increases the pleas to the doctor by parents as well as juvenile probation officers. The discontinuance of medication, therefore, is seldom a benign matter. In the model used in this study, the behavioral therapists sought feedback from teachers, parents, or juvenile authorities as to the child's or adolescent's progress and obtained (sometimes with hesitation and reservation) the concurrence to interrupt the medication regimen. Following the discontinuation, continuing feedback was actively solicited. This close collaboration among PCPs, behavioral specialists, parents, teachers, and other sectors of the relevant community doubtlessly contributed to the stabilization of the patients' behaviors without medication or further intensive behavioral interventions. In this population of more than 168,311 episodes, only 4,684 (or less than 3%) of the children and adolescents had to resume medication following its discontinuance once the behavioral criteria had been met.

Discussion

Because the summary data available to us lack sufficient specificity, these findings cannot provide definitive answers to the public debate sparked by Zito and her colleagues (Zito et al., 2000). Nonetheless, the magnitude of our sample, its unique behavioral and collaborative approach, and its national scope over a 4-year period suggest important directions for future research. From our data the following questions are pertinent and remain unanswered: (a) Are PCPs overdiagnosing ADD/ADHD? (b) Are PCPs, under pressure for an immediate fix, overprescribing to children and adolescents? (c) Are ADD/ADHD more amenable to behavioral interventions than previously thought? (d) Are behavioral interventions a viable alternative to prolonged use of psychotropic drugs with children and adolescents even if the original diagnosis is correct?

The dramatic reduction in reliance on medication in this large population of children/adolescents suggests that psychological interventions can be an effective alternative to prolonged or continual medication in many children and adolescents. This does not mean that medication is not important for even these young patients, for the initial prescriptions given them may well have rendered them more accessible and amenable to the subsequent behavioral interventions, leading to the eventual discontinuation of medication.

The possibility of the overdiagnosis of ADD/ADHD was addressed early by Ahmann et al. (1993), who noted that such overdiagnosis could be corrected if the positive and negative side effects of Ritalin emerging in each individual were made a part of the routine evaluation of the child or adolescent. It has long been noted that non-ADD/ADHD children/adolescents do not experience the sought-for sedating effect with Ritalin, but rather experience the more usual stimulating effect inasmuch as Ritalin is, after all, a stimulant. Since then, the recently published guidelines for the diagnosis of ADD/ADHD by the American Academy of Pediatrics (AAP, 2000) has been helpful in clarifying some of Ahmann's concerns. The AAP took note of the considerable documented research on the sustained useful effect in appropriately diagnosed ADD/ADHD (e.g., Gillberg et al., 1997; Firestone et al., 1998). During the time of this report, Ritalin was the predominant, but not exclusive, medication listed when requesting child/adolescent behavioral services from American Biodyne. Beyond this observation, our data are unrefined for types and frequency of medications.

The authors' tentative interpretation of the E/C ratio is that the higher the ratio, the greater the likelihood the patient group has been overmedicated. From this standpoint, the frequency of use of medication at the onset of treatment was not necessarily a satisfactory baseline indicator of the need for medication in that age group. E/C ratios for the use of medication with children and adolescents range from 20:7 to 9:9 and are higher than the adult population of 5:2. It is difficult to generalize from one population to another, even within the same delivery system, inasmuch as different classes of medication were prescribed for adults than for children. Furthermore, adults are more likely to be seen for counseling or psychotherapy, suggesting that children/adolescents seen might reflect a selectivity resulting in a narrower band of presenting problems. In spite of the difficulties, however, our data would suggest that the more frequent use of psychotropic drugs with children and adolescents would warrant the kinds of outcome studies called for by Zito et al. (2000). Even without these, our limited findings suggest a trend toward medicating younger and younger patients instead of understanding their needs and managing their behavior.

The more than three-and-a-half-fold increase in the use of medications in the 9 to 10 age group remains unexplained by any biological factors in the maturation process of these children. It is possible that psychosocial factors are operative inasmuch as this is the age in which more "mature" behavior is expected by adults than the previous group of 7 to 8 years of age. Again, our data lack specificity, but is usual childhood behavior suddenly less tolerated by our society when the child reaches age 10? This might especially be true for boys, who are known for seemingly troublesome, but nonetheless innocent "roughhousing" at that age.

A New Controversy and a Caveat

Role modeling has long been an important part of the psychological treatment of adults and adolescents. The decision to make male role modeling an integral part of the behavioral interventions with children and adolescents was prompted by the significant absence of fathers in the population being referred. A 1-year pilot study conducted the year before the period of the current report strongly indicated that positive male role modeling in a population where fathers were significantly absent in the child's or adolescent's life augmented substantially the array of other behavioral interventions. Recently, two books purportedly ascribing most, if not all behavioral problems in children and adolescents to the absence of involvement by fathers in their lives (Pollock, 2000; Sommers, 2000) have commanded considerable public attention. The authors wish to proffer a note of caution, as our limited data cannot contribute answers to the frequent and sweeping generalizations made by these authors and should not be used to bolster their unsubstantiated contentions.

Our findings are limited to a population (albeit a large one) where the absence of fathers was a significant factor, and we know nothing of the children and adolescents without fathers in the general population who are doing well and are not considered for either medication or psychotherapy. With the children/adolescents in this study, addressing the lack of fathering as part of a more comprehensive psychotherapeutic approach that dealt with a multitude of other problems was beneficial. The provision of father substitutes and the attention paid to the child's or adolescent's needs for such, reflected certain focal issues. These included (a) the absence of a consistent father or positive male role model, especially in the lives of boys; (b) the effects of a weak, abusive, or irresponsible father, or a succession of males brought into the home by a single mother, with consequent inconsistency and often abuse (the negative male role model); (c) the lack of appreciation by otherwise well-meaning single mothers of what constitutes typical boyish behavior; (d) the difficulty experienced in the current school setting that finds itself in a rapidly changing society attempting to differentiate aberrant behavior from that of boys who are characteristically struggling at this age with their emerging manhood.

The treatment protocol used revealed almost immediately how quickly troublesome boys would accept direction from a male they came to admire, while the same direction might well be resented and rejected if proffered by a female or a male the boy had not come to admire. These are clinical observations only, and cannot be regarded as conclusive inasmuch as role modeling was only one of many behavioral interventions. Furthermore, in our non-controlled, retrospective study, the finding that attending to these issues in the treatment of this patient population had a stabilizing effect cannot be extrapolated to the general population. In this nonrepresentative sample, nonetheless, follow-up study of the clinicians' notes revealed reported increases in school performance as well as observable increases in attention and motivation. Furthermore, the homes, the schools, and the courts reported what was to them satisfying diminution of troublesome behavior.

Operations statistics at American Biodyne revealed an elevated incidence of ADD/ADHD in three widely separated metropolitan communities. There were also aggressive ADHD treatment centers in these three communities. It could be argued that the elevated incidence was due to clinical acumen and vigilance in diagnosis, were it not for the fact that in one of these three centers over several years not a single child or adolescent was examined who did not receive the diagnosis of ADD/ADHD. In the other two centers, the diagnosis applied was almost, but not quite, 100% of the children and adolescents seen. In the first community, the aggressive treatment center had surveyed and diagnosed 60% of the boys in one middle school as suffering from ADD/ADHD. One cannot help but ask the question: If 60% of a population exhibits a certain behavioral constellation, why would it be considered a psychiatric syndrome rather than typical behavior?

Summary and Conclusions

A large national sample of children and adolescents studied by the Foundation for Behavioral Health illustrates that a psychological model of treatment, in a collegial and collaborative working relationship with primary care physicians (pediatricians and family medical practitioners), can result in the prompt stabilization of child/adolescent patients and a consequent rapid reduction in the use of psychotropic medications, particularly in the use of stimulants. The model also involved the relevant sectors of the community that initially brought the child/adolescent to the attention of the primary care physician. The treatment necessary for stabilizing the behavior of these children and adolescents consumed significantly more professional resources than those needed for the treatment of adults in the same setting. Nonetheless, these expenditures were less than the resources that would have been necessary in ongoing psychotropic medication of these patients over extended time.

The size of the sample and the rapid stabilization of previously troublesome behavior suggest either the overdiagnosis of children/adolescents into syndromes that require psychotropic medication, or that these diagnoses are correct and are more amenable to behavioral intervention than previously thought so that a collaborative model with initial medication and rapid follow-up with behavioral interventions may be a viable alternative to long-term administration of medication. Perhaps even both are operative. The data are limited by their non-controlled, retrospective nature, but they raise several important questions that future controlled, prospective investigations should address.

References

Ahmann, P. A., Waltonen, S. J., Olson, K. A., Theye, F. W., Van Erem, A. J., & La Plant, R. J. (1993). Placebo-controlled evaluation of Ritalin side effects. *Pediatrics, 91*, 1101–1106.

American Academy of Pediatrics. (2000). Clinical guidelines: Diagnosis and evaluation of the child with attention-deficit/hyperactivity disorder. *Pediatrics, 105*(5), 1158–1170.

American Psychiatric Association. (1999). *APA practice guideline for the treatment of patients with major depressive disorder*. Washington, DC: Author.

Antonuccio, D. O., Danton, W. G., & DeNelsky, G. Y. (1995). Psychotherapy versus medication for depression: Challenging the conventional wisdom with data. *Professional Psychology: Research and Practice, 26*(6), 574–585.

Antonuccio, D. O., Danton, W. G., & DeNelsky, G. Y. (1999). Raising questions about antidepressants. *Psychotherapy and Psychosomatic Medicine, 68*(1), 3–14.

Beardsley, R. S., Gaidocki, G. J., Larson, D. B., & Hildalgo, J. (1988). Prescribing of psychotropic medication by primary care physicians and psychiatrists. *Archives of General Psychiatry, 45*, 1117–1119.

Brokaw, T. (2000, May 4). In-depth: Attention deficit/hyperactivity disorder. *NBC Nightly News*. New York: NBC.

Cummings, N., & Sayama, M. (1995). *Focused psychotherapy: A casebook of brief, intermittent psychotherapy throughout the life cycle*. Madison, CT: Psychosocial Press.

DeRubeis, R. J., Gelland, L. A., Tang, T. Z., & Simons, A. D. (1999). Medications versus cognitive behavior therapy for severely depressed outpatients: Mega-analysis of four randomized comparisons. *American Journal of Psychiatry, 156*(7), 1007–1113.

Emslie, G. J., Walkup, J. T., Pliska, S. R., & Ernst, M. (1999). Nontricyclic antidepressants: Current trends in children and adolescents. *Journal of the American Academy of Child and Adolescent Psychiatry, 38*, 517–528.

Firestone, P., Musten, L. M., Pisterman, S., Mercer, J., & Bennett, S. (1998). Short-term side effects of stimulant medication are increased in pre-school children with attention-deficit/hyperactivity disorder: A double-blind placebo-controlled study. *Journal of Child and Adolescent Psychopharmacology, 8*, 13–25.

Fisher, R. L., & Fisher, S. (1996). Anti-depressants for children: Is scientific support necessary? *Journal of Nervous and Mental Disease, 184*, 99–102.

Fisher, S., & Greenberg, R. P. (1989). *The limits of biological treatments for psychological distress*. Hillside, NJ: Lawrence Erlbaum.

Fisher, S., & Greenberg, R. P. (1997). *From placebo to panacea: Putting psychiatric drugs to the test.* New York: John Wiley.

Foxman, B., Valdez, R. B., & Brook, R. B. (1986). Childhood enuresis: Prevalence, perceived impact, and prescribed treatments. *Pediatrics, 77,* 482–487.

Gillberg, C., Melander, H., von Knorring, A. L., Janois, L. O., Thenlund, G, Hagglof, B., Eidevall-Wallin, L., Gustafsson, P., & Kopp, S. (1997). Long-term stimulant treatment of children with attention-deficit/hyperactivity disorder symptoms. *Archives of General Psychiatry, 54,* 587–664.

Greenhill, L. L. (1998). The use of psychotropic medication in preschoolers: Indications, safety, and efficacy. *Canadian Journal of Psychiatry, 43,* 576–581.

Hollon, S. D., Shelton, R. C., & Loosen, P. T. (1991). Cognitive therapy and pharmacotherapy for depression. *Journal of Consulting and Clinical Psychology, 59*(1), 88–99.

Jensen, P. S. (1998). Ethical and pragmatic issues in the use of psychotropic agents in young children. *Canadian Journal of Psychiatry, 43,* 585–588.

Johnson, H. F., & Fruehling, J. J. (1994). Pharmacological therapy for depression in children and adolescents. In W. M. Reynolds & H. F. Johnson (Eds.), *Handbook of depression in children and adolescents* (pp. 122–131). New York: Plenum.

Kaplan, A. (1999, September). Medication prescribing practices for children and adolescents. *Psychiatric Times, 9,* 5, 11.

Kirsch, I., & Saperstein, G. (1998). Listening to Prozac and hearing placebo: A meta-analysis of antidepressant medication. *Prevention and Treatment* [Online]. http://psychrights.org/research/Digest/CriticalThinkRxCites/KirschandSapirstein1998.pdf

Minde, K. (1998). The use of psychotropic medication in preschoolers: Some recent developments. *Canadian Journal of Psychiatry, 43,* 571–575.

Munoz, R. A. (2000, August). Pharmacologic nihilism. *Psychiatric Times,* 25–26.

Olfson, M., Marcus, S. C., Pincus, H. A., Zito, J. M., Thompson, J. W., & Zarin, D. A. (1998). Antidepressant prescribing practices of outpatient psychiatrists. *Archives of General Psychiatry, 55,* 310–316.

Pearlson, G. D. (1999). Structural and functional brain changes in bipolar disorder: A selective review. *Schizophrenia Research, 39*(2), 133–140.

Pelligrino, E. D. (1996). Clinical judgment, scientific data, and ethics: Antidepressant therapy in adolescents and children. *Journal of Nervous and Mental Disease, 184,* 106–108.

Pincus, H. A., Tanielian, T. L., Marcus, S. C., Olfson, M., Zarin, D. A., Thompson, J., & Zito, J. M. (1998). Prescribing trends in psychotropic medication: Primary care, psychiatry, and other medical specialties. *Journal of the American Medical Association, 279,* 526–531.

Pollock, W. (2000). *Real boys' voices.* New York: Random House.

Rabasca, L. (2000). APA participates in White House meeting that questions psychotropic drug use among preschoolers. *Monitor on Psychology, 31*(5), 10.

Rather, D. (2000, May 9). Eye on America: Attention-deficit/hyperactivity disorder. *CBS Evening News.* New York: CBS.

Rushton, J. L., Clark, S. J., & Freed, G. L. (2000). Primary care role in management of childhood depression: A comparison of pediatricians and family physicians. *Pediatrics, 105,* 957–962.

Safer, D. J., Zito, J. M., & Fine, E. M. (1996). Increased methylphenidate usage for attention deficit disorder in the 1990s. *Pediatrics, 98,* 1084–1088.

Schatzberg, A. F. (1998). Noradrenergic versus serotonergic antidepressants: Predictors of treatment response. *Journal of Clinical Psychiatry, 59*(suppl. 14), 15–18.

Segal, Z. V., Gemar, M., & Williams, S. (1999). Differential cognitive response to a mood challenge following successful cognitive therapy or pharmacotherapy for unipolar depression. *Journal of Abnormal Psychology, 108*(1), 3–10.

Sommers, C. F. (2000). *The war against boys*. New York: Simon and Schuster.

Staley, J. K., Madison, R. T., & Inns, R. B. (1998). Imaging of the serotonergic system: Interactions of neuroanatomical and functional abnormalities of depression. *Biological Psychiatry, 44*(7), 534–549.

Tech, M. (2001, January 19–20). *Nature and treatment of anxiety disorders: Implications for medical utilization and costs.* Proceedings of the University of Nevada, Reno Conference on Medical Cost Offset, Foundation for Behavioral Health, Reno, NV.

Traversa, G., Spila-Alegriana, S., Arpina, C., & Ferrara, M. (1996). Prescription of neuroleptics for children and adolescents in Italy. *Journal of Child and Adolescent Psychopharmacology, 8,* 175–180.

Van Praag, H. M. (1996). Faulty cortisol/serotonin interplay: Psychological and biological characterization of a new, hypothetical depression subtype (SeCa depression). *Psychiatry Research, 65*(3), 143–157.

Vitiello, B. (1998). Pediatric psychopharmacology and the interaction between drugs and the developing brain. *Canadian Journal of Psychiatry, 43,* 582–584.

Wiggins, J. G., & Cummings, N. A. (1998). National study of the experiences of psychologists with psychotropic medication and psychotherapy. *Professional Psychology: Research and Practice, 29,* 549–552.

Zito, J. M., Safer, D. J., dosReis, S., Gardner, J. F., Boles, M., & Lynch, F. (2000). Trends in prescribing of psychotropic medications to preschoolers. *Journal of the American Medical Association, 283,* 1025–1030.

Zito, J. M., Safer, D. J., dosReis, S., Magdder, L. S., & Riddle, M. A. (1997). Methylphenidate patients among Medicaid youths. *Psychopharmacology Bulletin, 33,* 143–147.

Zito, J. M., Safer. D. J., Riddle, M. A., Johnson, R. E., Speedle, S. M., & Fox, M. (1998). Prevalence variations in psychotropic treatment of children. *Journal of Child and Adolescent Psychopharmacology, 8,* 99–105.

8   The Next Phase in the Evolution of Behavioral Care and Its Re-empowerment of the Practitioner

Nicholas A. Cummings

> Making predictions is difficult,
> especially if it involves the future.
> Yogi Berra

The past decade has been the most difficult in the 50-year history of professional psychology. Essentially born in its present form after World War II, psychology in its first 30 years saw hard-fought gains as chronicled in the saga of the Dirty Dozen (Martin, 1999; Saeman, 1999), culminating in psychology becoming the nation's preeminent psychotherapy profession. This status was brief, lasting only about 10 years before the industrialization of healthcare, and professional psychology's own inability to adapt to the new marketplace rendered it a beleaguered profession. The earlier warnings of the dire impact of industrialization were we not to be in control of the process went unheeded, and soon the decimation of psychological practice unfortunately exceeded even our greatest fears (Cummings & Fernandez, 1985; Cummings, 1986). We have seen healthcare become the province of business interests, with practitioners losing control of how psychotherapy is dispensed. Competition has become so keen that the economic base of independent practice is severely eroded. We have seen managed behavioral care grow from essentially zero to where it encompasses 75% of insured Americans (more than 175 million lives). Furthermore, the period of consolidation we foresaw has far surpassed our worst expectations, largely because of the so-called mega-mergers whose magnitude could not be imagined 2 decades ago, but which have become typical in all sectors of our booming economy. These have resulted in 50% of managed behavioral care controlled by just three companies (Magellan, ValueOptions, and United), while 10 companies control more than 90% of the industry. We are now engulfed in the chaos we predicted would prevail as we made the transition from the old to the new system. In short, the industrialization of healthcare (i.e., managed care) is following the exact course that every previous industrialization had to traverse (manufacturing, transportation, retailing).

A particularly painful aspect of that inevitable transition is the friction between the industrialized interests and their labor force, in our case the psychotherapists. As competition heats up, in an attempt to offer the marketplace the most competitive product, industry squeezes its own labor force as a means of further lowering costs. In previous industrialized sectors, this resulted in a strong labor movement, with Walter Reuther being able to shut down the automotive industry with one phone call, and with Harry Bridges and John L. Lewis being able to do the same in shipping and mining, respectively. Today the professional societies are similarly at war with managed care, and the history of industrialization would predict that compromises are in the offing. These would be hastened if: (1) the professional organizations were not restricted by federal law from activities that could be construed in the courts as a health boycott, and (2) would permit themselves to enter into constructive engagement with managed care. This latter approach has resulted in an enlightened era between management and labor in the industries that have gone before us. At the present time the climate between the managed care organizations (MCOs) and the American Psychological Association (APA) can only be described as open warfare. Psychiatry is in a similar stance, and only social work has learned constructive engagement and is prospering from it.

Whatever the outcome of either approach, constructive engagement or the continuation of aggressive activities (e.g., lawsuits, legislative thrusts), practice will never go back to its previous cottage industry. History has taught us that once industrialization occurs, it never regresses to the previous state. For example, once Henry Ford invented the assembly line, no matter what gains autoworkers made at the bargaining table, the way they worked and built cars was changed forever.

Industrialization is never static; rather, it is constantly evolving. So it is with behavioral healthcare, and we are about to witness the next wave. It is our prediction that the current health maintenance organizations (HMOs) and MCOs bear little resemblance to the industry of the future. By illustration, when society was making the transition from the horse to the automobile, the automobile looked like a carriage without the horse, earning the appellation "horseless carriage." One day it was asked, "Why does the automobile have to look like the carriage?" It was then that the auto began to take on its own morphology. In a similar vein and at a time when we have all but forgotten the typewriter, someone will ask, "Why does the computer have to look like a typewriter?" and just as inevitably, the question will arise, "Why does healthcare have to look like either solo practice or the HMO?" When these questions are asked, it is because dramatic changes have either begun or are about to begin. Let us look at the morphology these changes will bring to behavioral care and what impact this will have on our profession.

Behavioral Healthcare Reform: The Era of Regulation

An industry does not go from zero to the overwhelming majority of the market in just 1 decade without incurring regulation. Such a virtual stampede is bound to leave the consumer (in our case, the patient) with considerable dissatisfaction and trepidation. However, the wide publicity given horror stories by the media belie the data from independent surveys (e.g., Arizona State University, the Rand

Corporation) that show most Americans are generally satisfied with their health plans. It is clear, however, that the era of regulatory reform in managed care has begun, with some states outpacing the federal government in this regard.

A note of caution is indicated here. As psychologists we tend to elect leaders and hire staff that will reinforce our fond hope that somehow the industrialization of behavioral care will be reversed. We have been doing this for more than a decade, and all we have seen is the continuing devaluation of independent practice. Our elected public officials also reinforce this wishful thinking. It is important to be aware that it is easy for a politician seeking reelection to decry managed care, but once elected, every member of Congress knows that the healthcare industry must be part of any solution. Regulation has limits, and we can expect important changes in behavioral care akin to the airbags, sturdier frames, catalytic converters, and seat belts in the automobile that fall far short of reversing any industrialization.

In our zeal to recapture the halcyon days of truly independent practice, we overlook history's important lesson that once a sector of our economy has industrialized, it never goes back to its former cottage industry. Psychologists often ask why healthcare had to industrialize at all. The real question is the opposite one: Why did a sector that comprises one sixth of our gross national product (GNP) take so long to industrialize? This was not only inevitable, but once it began it would be accomplished in a fraction of the time required in previous instances of industrialization. Our concern should be what morphology the evolution of behavioral healthcare will take in the future. In this regard there is both good and bad news, and it is imperative for the survival of our profession that we prepare to meet the challenges and seize the opportunities. To these we now turn.

The Integration of Behavioral Healthcare with Primary Care

A growing body of research has demonstrated the advantages to patient care of having behavioral healthcare an integral part of primary care, with health psychologists on location with primary care physicians, and with teams delivering population- and disease-based care. At the present time, there is enormous cultural resistance in both medicine and psychology to this integration, and the huge behavioral carve-out industry that separates the mind and the body not only in treatment, but also into separate companies, has strong economic incentives to perpetuate the dualism. All of the fat has been wrung out of behavioral care, but a vast overutilization of medicine and surgery remains due to psychological problems that stay inaccessible to medical cost offset research in the present divided system. In spite of resistance, at the point in which the financial advantage is established, integrated care will soar as rapidly as did managed care in the face of all the entrenched forces that opposed it in 1985.

There are several important integration projects in healthcare throughout the United States, the most important of which is that of Kaiser Permanente in Northern California. Under the leadership of Robin Dea, a psychiatrist who heads mental healthcare services, and Kirk Strosahl, a psychologist hired specifically for this project, the world's largest HMO is embarked on a major retooling of its 2.3 million subscriber base in this one region (Rollins, 1999). There will be teams of physicians, behavioral health specialists, nurses, health educators, and other personnel, one such team for every 20,000 covered lives. This team will be responsible for the healthcare, medical and behavioral, of all the patients from its cohort of 20,000. This retooling combines the advantages of the close patient care inherent in smallness with the financial, research, and other strengths of large market share. It is much easier to accomplish such drastic integration in a staff model such as Kaiser, but soon some economic genius will demonstrate how it can also be done in a network model. For the psychologist, it will mean equality with the physician, as both will be integral parts of the primary care team. Those who qualify will see the restoration of the dignity and self-respect that come with being in control of one's expertise and practice.

The Emerging New Psychologist

The doctoral behavioral care specialist of the future will be much different than today's practitioner inasmuch as master's-level therapists will continue to do most of the treatment, using empirically derived protocols and supervised by doctoral psychologists. These will have training in medical psychology, program planning, outcomes research, and finally in business because never again will we be able to practice without being cognizant of costs. With the forthcoming integration, behavioral healthcare will have true parity with physical care for the first time, and it follows that in this system the psychologist will be of equal stature and importance with the physician.

To produce this markedly different psychologist, the doctoral professional training programs will be drastically different than that those represented by today's clinical psychology training programs. An early example of a markedly different training track is found at the University of Nevada, Reno. Here has been established the first endowed professorship dedicated to the emerging model: the Nicholas Cummings Chair in Organized Behavioral Healthcare Delivery. This new training track leads not only to the PhD in clinical psychology, but also to a certificate in behavioral healthcare delivery. Interesting, all of the necessary technology is already available in the research literature. The integrated delivery system of the future will espouse the public health model of primary prevention, and again this technology is also awaiting implementation. Finally, because of the trend in our society to push knowledge downward, doctoral-level psychologists will very likely gain prescription authority, thus strengthening further their contributions to the integrated primary care team. This author is excited about the forthcoming integrated model that will see the re-empowerment of the professional psychologist as the behavioral care specialist of the future.

The Impact of the Information Age

While psychologists still struggle to accommodate the industrialization of healthcare, the remainder of our economy is rapidly moving from industrialization to the new information era. This failure to adapt even to what is already becoming obsolete places the traditional practitioner even farther behind.

In the information age, specialty care will be determined in specialty centers that may be a considerable distance from the locale in which the primary care is delivered. These specialty centers will be staffed not only with some of the finest specialists in each field, but they will have the most sophisticated of diagnostic and information systems. Primary care teams will transmit data to the appropriate specialty center and receive back expert advice as to appropriate care. These specialty centers will eliminate redundancy and thus will be able to pick and choose the finest minds in each specialty, including those of the new professional psychology. These specialty centers will further reflect two distinct trends: the national emphasis on the importance of hands-on primary care, and the reduction of the over-production of specialists.

Downsizing

No specialty field in healthcare has greater over-production than psychotherapy, making future downsizing inevitable. How large our field will ultimately be will be determined by the needs of the marketplace. In the long run this is economically healthy, but in the short term there will be much pain as many struggling in independent practice today fall by the wayside. Those who survive will be the new genre of professional psychologists.

Do not be dismayed that current doctoral training programs are resisting change. For the past 4 years, applications to APA-approved clinical training programs have steadily declined, and will continue to decline as prospective students realize the field is overcrowded with traditional professional psychologists. As graduate student bodies begin to dry up and academic jobs are threatened because applicants are looking for relevant training, suddenly academia will see the light and will rush to emulate those first new programs that are flourishing. And as the APA finds itself for the first time in history also downsizing, changes will spread rapidly within our national organization.

Enter the Human Services Model

There will exist to one side a smaller mental healthcare system that will reflect the more traditional model of longer-term psychotherapy than that offered within healthcare delivery. At some near point in this parallel system, the time will be right for the emergence of a full-fledged human services model that is independent of the existing health benefits. All that remains is the appearance of an economic genius who will design the financial basis for the non-healthcare financed model that at the present time is limited to fee-for-service that is also out of pocket. Unfortunately, most humanistic and psychodynamic psychologists disdain business and finance, so the absence of an economic vehicle continues. Some advocates of this model erroneously believe that clients will pay for these services, overlooking the fact there is a limit to how large a sector of any society will pay for services covered in prepaid healthcare. Experience in countries with universal healthcare demonstrates this is about 5–7%, making it a sort of carriage trade. With the formulation of an economic base, this figure could be much higher, enabling psychologists who wish to practice longer-term therapy to do so. However, there will never be enough such clients to support the continuation of the overcrowded field of traditional psychotherapy.

Healthcare and the Genetic Revolution

As part of the information age, the decoding of the human genome will be completed within the next several years. This will drastically change everything. Not only will maladaptive behaviors be found to have a genetic constellation that interacts with learning, but the development of new classes of drugs with far fewer side effects, coupled with the infusion of stem cells and other forms of genetic therapy, will amazingly transform healthcare. In behavioral healthcare, the initial impact will be on our most troublesome condition, bipolar disorder and schizophrenia, with alcoholism, other addictions, and borderline personality disorder coming closely behind. The need for the training of psychologists who are knowledgeable and comfortable working within the genetic revolution opens an entire new field. At the present time, only a handful of psychologists have concurrent expertise in cellular biology and genetics, but this will change with demand and opportunity. Many of the behavioral interventions of the future will complement the finding of genetics.

Reason for Optimism

In the past decade, our profession has been beaten up and has left us professionally depressed. It is time we stop lamenting what has happened and look to the challenges and opportunities, the even more dramatic changes, the future certainly will bring. For too long, many psychologists, including many of our leaders, have looked upon these changes as temporary and reversible. It is time we faced up to the fact that industrialization is here to stay, and then prepare for the coming second wave of industrialization that will merge with the information age. I see in this new era the disappearance of managed care as we now know it, the integration of behavioral healthcare with primary care, and the consequent reempowerment of the professional psychologist who has prepared for these events.

The healthcare we predicted 20 years or more ago was upon us before we realized it. By forsaking our professional biases and our wish-fulfilling fantasies, we can prepare for the even greater challenges of the future with the out-of-the-box thinking needed to transform many of the troublesome changes into opportunities. We know the term; it is called *adaptation*. If only a relatively few professional psychologists do so, our profession will evolve and prosper. The alternative would be too unfortunate for consideration.

References

Cummings, N. A. (1986). The dismantling of our health system: Strategies for the survival of psychological practice. *American Psychologist, 41*, 426–431.

Cummings, N. A., & Fernandez, L. (1985, March). Exciting new opportunities for psychologists in the marketplace. *Independent Practitioner, 5*, 38–42.

Martin, S. (1999, October). Kudos to the "Dirty Dozen." *APA Monitor*, 7.

Rollins, G. (1999, June). Integrating behavioral health and primary care pays off. *Healthcare Management*, 10–12.

Saeman, H. (1999, November/December). "Dirty Dozen" transformed psychology from academic to practice profession. *National Psychologist, 1*, 3–4.

9 A New Vision of Healthcare for America

Nicholas A. Cummings

Once again behavioral healthcare is about to experience dramatic changes that will rival those of the mid-1980s. The behavioral healthcare professions failed then to recognize the impending industrialization of healthcare, and thus found themselves left out of the subsequent decision-making process. Although the next leap forward will be evolutionary rather than revolutionary as was the period we are experiencing, the mental healthcare professions will have the first real opportunity in several years to participate in the future of behavioral healthcare. In the previous decade, the professional guilds ignored the trend toward industrialization, and remained oblivious to the disturbing fact that insurers were rapidly dropping mental healthcare as a benefit. Within a short time, the hard-fought psychotherapy benefits of health insurance would have disappeared if the early managed behavioral care companies (American Biodyne, American Psych Management, MCC, and Preferred Health) had not demonstrated to the industry that they could roll back costs and cap them for 3 years, all the while expanding the mental healthcare benefit. The immediate losers were the psychiatric hospitals and the solo practitioners of long-term psychotherapy, for it was by reducing these overly utilized services that stability was quickly acquired. The beneficiaries were those who pay the costs and the patients who now had a new continuum of care. Managed behavioral care has resulted in an expansion of services as well as a substitution of services, with increases in psychiatric rehabilitation, day treatment, consumer-run peer support, residential treatment, and crisis programs in lieu of psychiatric hospitalization and private practice psychotherapy, both of which declined and have never recovered (Ross, 1998; Cummings, 1999).

Finally the Trend Is Our Friend

The previous decade may well be known as the point in history that demonstrated that the introduction of business principles into the heretofore undisciplined healthcare system could not only tether costs, but expand the range of services available to the patient. Especially was this true in behavioral care, where previously those who paid the bills were intimidated by a psychobabble given credibility only because of the general lack of data. It also demonstrated that industrialization can proceed in spite of the fierce opposition of practitioners.

After 15 years, the so-called carve-out industry, named because the companies delivering behavioral healthcare were separate from those delivering general healthcare, has outlived its usefulness. It has saved the mental healthcare benefit, and it is time to "carve-in" with primary care, where behavioral care belongs. This integration of primary care and behavioral healthcare, which involves behavioral healthcare specialists being on site in the medical setting, is gaining momentum among primary care physicians, even though mental health practitioners show continued reluctance to leave the tradition of their private offices. Again, the next evolutionary step in healthcare will occur with or without the concurrence of the professional guilds. Far too many practitioners are once again ready to break ranks with their respective societies, and seize the unprecedented opportunity that will accompany the new era of practitioner-dominated behavioral healthcare. These practitioners have learned to predict and control costs, and are prepared to participate in the future of integrated healthcare. The new era will be dependent on data, which gives scientifically trained professional psychologists an unprecedented advantage. Future behavioral care will be evidence-based, and the mantra was enunciated by Yank Coble, addressing the industry on behalf of the American Medical Association: "In God we trust. All others must have data" (as quoted in *Time*, November 24, 1998, p. 69). Before proceeding to what the new integrated healthcare delivery system may look like, it may be important to review the medical cost offset research that has attracted the attention of the healthcare industry, especially employers and other third-party payers, and is contributing to the trend toward the integration of behavioral healthcare with primary care.

Medical Cost Offset: The Value Added

At the Kaiser Permanente Health System, the nation's prototype of the modern health maintenance organization (HMO), in the early 1960s it was discovered that 60% of all physician visits were by patients who were somaticizing stress, or whose stress was exacerbating physical illness. It was further discovered that brief psychotherapeutic interventions had a surprising impact in that they reduced this overutilization by addressing the patient's stress (Cummings et al.et al., 1962; Follette & Cummings, 1967; Cummings & Follette, 1968). Somatization was defined differently than the Somatization Disorder found in DSM-IV, and was seen simply as the translation of emotional problems into physical symptoms, or the exacerbation of a disease by emotional factors or stress. This somatization inevitably results in overutilization of healthcare, overloading the system. The typical effect Cummings and Follette discovered is portrayed in Figure 9.1, which demonstrates a steady reduction in the 5 years following behavioral healthcare intervention. A leveling off at 62.5% reduction takes place in the fifth year, which represents average utilization for a "healthy" population, and where on an eighth-year follow-up (Cummings & Follette, 1976) it remained with no further somatization.

It is important to note that medical cost offset is not just about money. It is about appropriate treatment. Addressing the patient's emotional distress has the value-added of reducing healthcare costs even after paying for the effective psychotherapy. More important, it spares the patient years of having to suffer painful physical symptoms in that the treatment of choice (psychotherapy rather than medical treatment) has been provided. But this body of research has not been without its methodological difficulties, many of which have been overcome during its 3 decades.

The medical cost offset literature can be divided into three generations. The first generation (1965–1979) saw the discovery that 60% of physician visits were by somaticizers. The National Institute of Mental Health (NIMH) sponsored a number of replications, and published a summary of these (Jones & Vischi, 1979), which revealed a medical cost offset of 30% to 65%. That same year NIMH convened the Bethesda Consensus Conference in an effort to ascertain why some studies yielded impressive savings in medical/surgical costs, while others did not produce enough offset to pay for the behavioral care interventions. All of the investigators in medical cost offset were invited to a 3-day session during which the studies to that date, 28 in all, were evaluated. A consensus emerged (Jones & Vischi, 1980) that included the following: (1) Medical cost offset is feasible only in organized settings where commitment, capability, and incentive exist, and where somaticizers can be identified, appropriately treated, and traced through sophisticated informatics. (2) The more traditional the behavioral interventions, the less the medical cost offset. The cost offset increases to the degree in which primary care and behavioral care are coordinated, collaborative, or integrated.

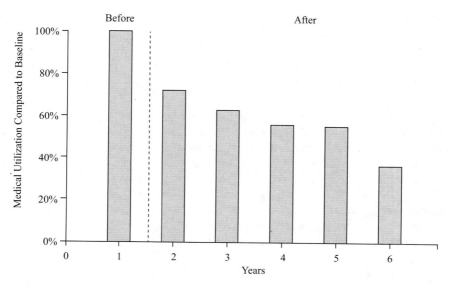

Figure 9.1   Reduction in medical utilization from the year before behavioral care interventions and through the succeeding 5 years following these interventions to an eventual reduction of 62.5% from the first year. Data are from Follette & Cummings (1967).

(3) Medical cost offset increases to the degree that somatization is addressed through focused interventions, targeted to specific populations.

The Bethesda Consensus Conference enumerated a number of methodological issues and recommended that a way be found to conduct randomized (prospective) studies rather than retrospective studies. The difficulty had been the contractual relationship with insured patients that prevented research in which those in the control group would be denied the treatment accorded to those in the experimental group. In an insured environment, the denial of a contracted treatment to some patients, even for research purposes, is both illegal and unethical. The conclusions of the Bethesda Consensus Conference were not widely disseminated in that just 2 months later the government scientists who convened it were swept out of office when the Carter administration lost the election.

The second generation (1980–1990) saw the emergence of national organized settings when the managed behavioral care industry came of age and captured most of the insured market. Unfortunately, with the carve-out arrangement, it was not possible to conduct medical cost offset research between two companies that did not share informatics. Nonetheless, during this decade, the role of stress, which was not adequately understood in the 1960s, was clarified in both somatization and unhealthy lifestyles (Ford, 1983, 1986; Pellitier, 1993; Sobel, 1995). The Health Care Financing Administration (HCFA), in conjunction with the State of Hawaii, sponsored the Hawaii Medicaid Project as the first comprehensive prospective study. Since this was a 7-year investigation, the results did not emerge until the following generation.

In the third generation (1990–1999), a number of organized settings attained the capability of conducting medical cost offset research, and managed behavioral care made a commitment to ongoing outcomes research. Not only were the new studies of a prospective (randomized) design, but they were of such a nature that they could be used in program planning and implementation (Cummings, 1994). The Hawaii Medicaid Project became the prototype of this new generation of studies, which surprisingly confirmed the medical cost offset findings of previous, but retrospective research. It compared the impact of targeted, focused interventions, with the liberal 52-session annual Hawaii Medicaid psychotherapy benefit that could be obtained through any licensed privately practicing psychiatrist or psychologist of the patient's choice, and finally with those who received no treatment. Therefore, there were two experimental groups and one control group, all randomized. The Medicaid groups served 36,000 beneficiaries, to which were added in each of the conditions the 91,000 federal employees in Honolulu. The subjects were further identified between those who had no physical disease and those who had a chronic physical condition (asthma, diabetes, emphysema, hypertension, ischemic heart disease, and rheumatoid arthritis, which together account for 40% of the medical dollars in the ages 21 to 60 population). The results of the Hawaii Medicaid Project are found in Figures 9.2 and 9.3, which reveal that targeted, focused interventions impressively reduced medical overutilization, while the privately practicing psychotherapists increased costs. The difference is the greatest in the chronic disease groups (Figure 9.3). Targeted, focused interventions

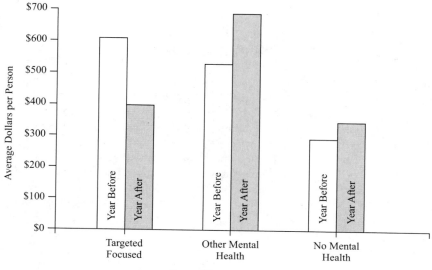

Figure 9.2 Average medical utilization in constant dollars for the Hawaii Medicaid Project non-chronic group for the year before (white columns) and the year after (black columns) receiving targeted and focused treatment, other mental health treatment in the private practice community, or no treatment. Data are from Cummings (1993).

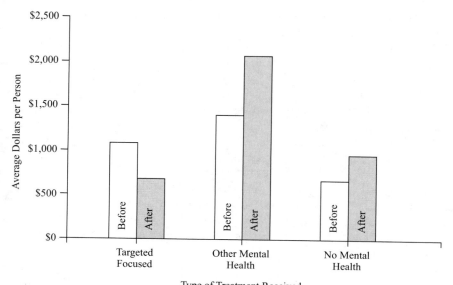

Figure 9.3 Average medical utilization in constant dollars for the Hawaii Medicaid Project chronically ill group for the year before (white columns) and the year after (black columns) receiving targeted and focused treatment, other mental health treatment in the private practice community, or no treatment. Data are from Cummings (1997).

saved an average of $350 per year per patient, while the traditional setting raised medical costs by an average of $750 per year. In both the chronic and non-chronic groups, the no treatment situation was preferable to traditional psychotherapy. The latter result was so baffling that psychotherapists were interviewed about how they handled somatization. Surprising, instead of recognizing that their patient was somaticizing, the psychotherapists regarded the matter as an assertiveness issue and encouraged the patient to return to the physician, demanding more and more tests to "prove" that the symptoms were, indeed, reflecting a yet undiagnosed physical disease. Consequently, unnecessary costs continued to mount.

In testimony before the U.S. Senate in which Cummings presented the Hawaii Medicaid Project's preliminary findings, Senator Daniel K. Inouye of Hawaii, who conducted the hearing, observed, "The most powerful argument for mental health benefits is the evidence that they reduce inappropriate medical utilization" (*Congressional Record,* June 24, 1985, pp. S-8656 to S-8658). The lessons learned in the Hawaii Medicaid Project, where an entire innovative behavioral healthcare delivery system had to be created for the study, is that not only are organized settings imperative, but medical cost offset research cannot be parachuted into a traditional setting. The importance of focused, targeted interventions in an integrated system is being elicited in a growing body of subsequent research (Cummings et al., 1997; Kent & Gordon, 1997; Strosahl, 1997).

Why Is Somatization so Expensive?

It is not uncommon for a somaticizer, finally having exasperated the physician, who then makes a referral for psychotherapy, to abandon that physician and begin the investigation all over again with another doctor. Figure 9.4 illustrates the incidence of the 14 most common complaints confronting the primary care physician, and reveals that only 5% of these symptoms on average are based on physical, rather than psychological conditions. These most common complaints are chest pain, fatigue, dizziness, headache, edema, back pain, dyspnea, insomnia, abdominal pain, numbness, impotence, weight loss, cough, and constipation. Figure 9.5 addresses the first five of these and reveals that in 1,000 primary care patients, a surprising amount of money is required for evaluation of those manifesting stress, while a very small amount of money is adequate for the diagnosis of those with actual physical disease. For example, where $21,760 is spent to establish the somatization of chest pain, only $1,360 will diagnose the presence of an actual, existing organic cause (Kroenke & Mangelsdorf, 1989).

It is not so much that somaticizers are intractable, as it is the system that discourages their seeking appropriate psychotherapy. In an era of "physician glut," the fee-for-service primary care physicians are reluctant to refer high-utilizing patients for psychological treatment because this results in loss of income to themselves. In a capitated system, primary care physicians hesitate to refer to psychologists because the cost must come out of their risk pool, resulting in less profit. But even in an enlightened system where physicians recognize the need and refer appropriately, only 10% of these referrals ever follow through and actually

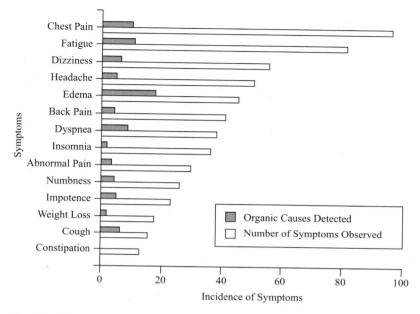

Figure 9.4 The incidence of 14 common symptoms (lighter shading) in 1,000 internal medicine outpatients, compared with those in which an organic disorder was detected (darker shading). Data are from Kroenke and Mangelsdorf (1989).

visit a psychotherapist. However, by having the psychologist on site in the primary care setting, the number of patients who accept the referral and enter treatment jumps to 80% (Slay & McLeod, 1997).

Supply Side Versus the Demand Side in Integrated Healthcare

Cost containment characteristically attempts to reduce costs by limiting the supply of unnecessary healthcare services. For example, in instances where short-term psychotherapy can be effective, long-term therapy is not reimbursed. Or where partial hospitalization is sufficient, full hospitalization is not authorized. The managed behavioral healthcare industry has now wrung all the fat out of the mental health/chemical dependency treatment system. There remains, however, a great deal of waste in the medical/surgical system, where costs continue to rise from (1) expensive technology and (2) inappropriate care. Addressing the demand side of the economic equation (i.e., reducing demand) through the use of population-based group programs may constitute true prevention.

Cummings and Cummings (1997) reported a comparison of supply side versus demand side economics in two outpatient behavioral care centers in the same system. Center A (experimental) implemented several psychoeducational programs and every patient who presented during two successive periods of 6 months, and who fell into any of five categories, was assigned to the corresponding psychoeducational program. These programs with their designated patients were as follows: (1) adult children of alcoholics; (2) agoraphobia and multiple phobias; (3) borderline personality; (4) independent living for chronic schizophrenia; (5) perfectionistic personality lifestyle. In Center B (control), every patient falling into any of the above five categories was routinely assigned to individual psychotherapy for two successive periods of 6 months each. All of the study patients for both centers were followed for a period of 2 years after their 6 months in treatment. Although there was not a randomized assignment of patients to control and experimental conditions because this would be tantamount to denying available services in Center A, the two groups from the two centers were comparable in all demographic characteristics (age, gender, socioeconomic level, education, ethnicity). Further, this arrangement permitted direct comparison between individual psychotherapy and population-based psychoeducational programs, which was not possible within the randomized assignment of patients in the Hawaii Medicaid Project.

As noted, there were two different periods of patient selection of 6 months' duration each in both centers. All patients had a 2-year follow-up after the initial 6 months. The total time of the experiment was 3 years, but only 2.5 years for each particular group. Because Center A was larger, there were 151 patients in the experimental group, while smaller Center B yielded 84 patients for the control group.

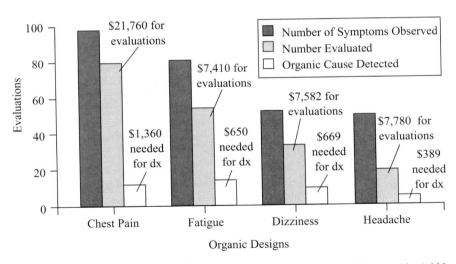

Figure 9.5 Evaluations and the cost per organic diagnosis for five symptoms in 1,000 internal medicine outpatients in 1988 dollars. Data are from Kroenke and Mangelsdorf (1989).

Table 9.1 A Comparison in the Use of Various Behavioral Health Services between an Experimental Group Assigned to a Psychoeducational Model, and the Control Group Assigned to the Traditional Model

	N		Group Sessions		Individual Sessions		Hospital Days		Emergency		Perscript		Return Visits	
	Expl	Cntrl	Expl	Cntrl	Expl	Cntrl	Expl	Cntrl	Expl	Cntrl	Expl	Cntrl	Expl	Cntrl
ACOA	38	12	570	46	76	132	1	11	6	8	16	24	53	38
Agoraphobia	23	8	460	0	46	122	14	21	9	37	26	28	38	63
Borderline	42	29	840	109	5	609	3	145	0	289	38	87	22	493
Indep. Living	22	18	422	315	21	72	26	183	4	51	41	68	251	488
Perfectionism	26	17	390	0	24	401	0	19	0	23	14	39	13	208
TOTALS	151	84	2682	480	172	1336	44	379	19	398	135	246	377	1290
MEANS			17.8	5.7	1.2	15.9	0.2	4.5	0.1	4.7	0.9	2.9	2.5	15.4

Legend:

ACOA: Adult Children of Alcoholics 15-Session Program
Agoraphobia and Multiple Phobias 20-Session Program
Borderline Personality Disorder 20-Session Program
Independent Living for Chronic Schizophrenics 25-Session Program
Perfectionism Leading to Disabling Episodes 15-Session Program

Note: Group therapy sessions for the control group were in traditional (i.e., non-psychoeducational) groups, while group sessions for the experimental group were all in psychoeducational programs.

Data are from Cummings and Cummings (1997).

The results are shown in Table 9.1, which reveals that for these five categories, the average number of psychoeducational sessions (experimental group) was only two more than the average number of individual sessions in the control group. Not even taking into account the cost differential (individual therapy ratio 1:1 between patients and therapists, psychoeducational 1:8 to 1:15), this resulted in a 90% reduction in demand for individual therapy, a 95% reduction in hospital days, a 97% reduction in emergency services (including emergency room visits and drop-in sessions), a 70% reduction in prescriptions for medication, and an 85% reduction in return visits.

For illustrative purposes, these findings can be translated into economic terms. Assuming an hour of individual psychotherapy costs $100, the cost of a psychoeducational group program of 1.5 hours would be $150 divided by the average patient group of 10, which equals $15 per patient. What is startling, this $15 per patient unit then goes on to save between 70% and 97% in hospitalization, individual psychotherapy, emergency room visits, medication prescriptions, and return visits.

Behavioral Healthcare Integration in Medicare

Healthcare for older adults is far more costly than that for the younger population. With the growing numbers of older Americans, and with per-patient costs steadily rising, the system is threatened with bankruptcy. The 1999 President's State of the Union Address devoted a significant amount of time to saving Medicare. Yet little attention has been paid to reducing costs through behavioral interventions since the general consensus in government has been that older adults are from a generation that does not avail itself of psychotherapy. The fact is that most psychotherapists like to address issues pertinent to a younger generation (dating, marriage, divorce, parenting, step-parenting, career, job loss, etc.) Research demonstrates that when programs relevant to older adults are made available (widowhood, retirement, loneliness, alienation, feelings of uselessness, chronic or debilitating illness in self or spouse, etc.), these patients will seek help in greater numbers than their younger counterparts (Hartman-Stein, 1997). This should not be surprising because the elderly are more at risk.

Appropriate behavioral interventions can not only save Medicare dollars, they can also spare older adults from a great deal of stress and pain. Two such programs will be briefly described as examples of the impact evidence-based programs can have in a population neglected by most psychologists.

The author and his colleagues (Cummings, 1997) found themselves having to create a new managed behavioral program when Humana was awarded responsibility for the healthcare of the first large population of Medicare recipients, 140,000 such older adults on the west coast of Florida, in 1987. American Biodyne became responsible for the behavioral care component, and HCFA, expecting the usual elderly penetration of only 0.5% for psychotherapy, was determined to set the capitation rate accordingly. American Biodyne challenged this, projecting a penetration rate of 5% to 7% to be accomplished by outreach and by the creation of relevant programs. The government agreed, but only after it was assured there would be a proportional return of the prospective funding if American Biodyne fell short of that level. Not surprising, the elderly flocked to American Biodyne at a rate exceeding 10%, threatening bankruptcy of the program. It was clear from the outset that effective programs had to be developed. This was accomplished, and among these were the bereavement program and the early Alzheimer's counseling program. The first of these was imperative inasmuch as a 5% mortality rate in this population yielded nearly 20 widows or widowers every day.

The Bereavement Program

The year before the death of a spouse, the surviving spouse characteristically has a lower healthcare utilization rate because of the concentration on the dying spouse's care. After the death, however, the surviving spouse demonstrates a skyrocketing healthcare utilization rate. Some of this reflects pent-up demand from the previous year, but the vast majority of this is the somaticized grief reaction. The bereavement study employed American Biodyne's familiar two-centers design (proximal as well as demographically comparable). An early outreach program was instituted in which the patient was identified and contracted within 2 weeks of widowhood. In Center A (experimental), a bereavement program was created that treated patients in special groups after those with depression, rather than bereavement, were screened out. Each group consisted of 5 to 8 mourners, depending on patient traffic. Fourteen 2-hour group sessions were spaced as follows: four semi-weekly sessions followed by six weekly sessions, and then by four concluding sessions held monthly. Center B (control) addressed the widowed patient without outreach, and with traditional referral and individual psychotherapy. All patients were followed for 2 years after the death of the spouse.

The results are clear-cut. The patients who participated in the bereavement program showed some increase the first year after the death of the spouse, reflecting the lack of personal medical attention during the previous caretaking year. The second year after the death of the spouse, healthcare returned to the rate of utilization expected of this age group. In contrast, the control group (traditional behavioral healthcare) demonstrated in the first year after the death of the spouse a healthcare rate twice that of the experimental group, and though it declined during the second year after the death, it remained 40% higher than that of the experimental group for that second year. After subtracting the cost of behavioral care, the bereavement program resulted in a saving of $1,400 per patient for the 2-year period, as shown in Figure 9.6. This amount, extrapolated to the general elderly population covered by this one health plan, translates to a potential saving of several million dollars. Even more important, however, this program can spare widowed older adults 2 years of avoidable suffering from physical symptoms and ill health.

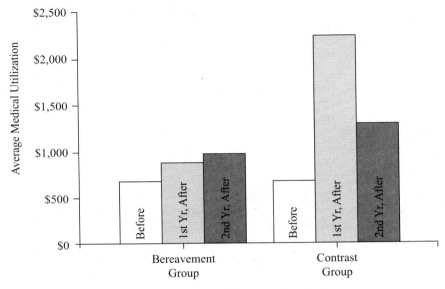

Figure 9.6 Average medical utilization for the year before and each of the 2 years after beginning the bereavement program, and for the same period for the contrast group who received individual psychotherapy rather than the bereavement program. Data are from Cummings (1997).

Early Alzheimer's Counseling

During this same period, a program focused on the caretakers of patients with early Alzheimer's dementia and on the patients themselves (Cummings, 1997). It has been noted for some time that the hardship imposed on the caretakers of Alzheimer's patients results in an increased rate of illness among the spouses or adult children caring for the person with dementia. The stress increases with both the length of the caretaking and the severity of the dementia, which is progressive and unpredictable, and is exacerbated by the patient's characteristic inability to show affection or gratitude.

The early Alzheimer's patient also experiences stress. Frequently disoriented when away from home, he or she soon experiences a characteristic "catastrophic emotional response" upon being disoriented in familiar surroundings. The response occurs before the dementia has damaged ego functioning; the patient is devastated by the experience, fears its recurrence, and is reluctant to leave home. There is a consequent narrowing of life space for both the patient and the non-afflicted spouse. The early Alzheimer's program patients were counseled to carry three telephone numbers of loved ones whom they were to call if they found themselves "lost," precluding the need for strangers to activate the emergency 911 systems with its consequent hospital involvement.

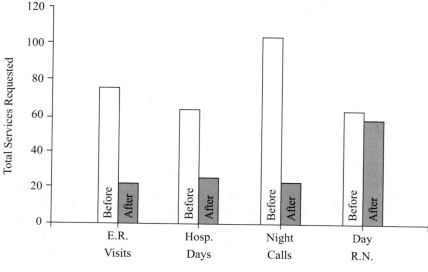

Figure 9.7 Reduction in outpatient (emergency room and drop-in clinic visits, night phone calls, and day advice nurse phone calls) and inpatient (hospital) services from the year before participating in the early Alzheimer's counseling program to the year following. Data are from Cummings (1997).

Ongoing counseling of caretakers on an as-needed basis, which included initial training in relaxation, guided imagery, and meditation, along with education regarding the course of the Alzheimer's syndrome, proved highly successful in reducing caretakers' incidence of illness and concomitant higher use of medical services. In addition, a hotline with immediate advice not only reduced the number of emergency calls to physicians when patients' behavior was baffling, but it also served as an emotional safety valve whenever caretakers' stress became unbearable. The costs of this behavioral program were ongoing over several years rather than the relatively brief 6.5-month duration of the bereavement project, but so were the consistently significant medical savings, which far more than offset these costs (see Figure 9.7).

Characteristics of Population-Based Group Programs

Most programs are verified expansions and modifications of the arthritis self-help course originally developed by Lorig and Fries (1990). In addition to an educational component tailored to the particular psychological or physical condition being treated, and the creation of a "buddy" support system, the protocols include the following objectives: (1) *Self-efficacy* (Bandura, 1977), which is a process of restoring self-confidence by performance of discontinued tasks that were once part of daily life. (2) Defeating *learned helplessness* (Seligman, 1975), which is the sense of being crippled by overwhelming feelings that dictate, "I no longer can do this." (3) Restoring a *sense of coherence* (Antonovsky, 1987) that there is still meaning in life, but in a different way than previously.

The Integrated Healthcare System of the Future

A number of large HMOs and regional group practices are making strides toward integrating behavioral healthcare in primary care, among them Kaiser Permanente (Kent & Gordon, 1997), Healthcare Partners (Slay & McLeod, 1997), Group Health Cooperative of Puget Sound, now Kaiser Group Health (Strosahl et al., 1997), Health Partners of Minnesota, and the Duke University Medical Center (Gunn et al., 1997). Most primary care physicians, faced with the daily array of as many as 80% of their patients reflecting psychological problems, welcome collaboration with behavioral care specialists (Lucas & Peek, 1997), but caution that integration must proceed slowly to overcome formidable barriers. Their view is that separate departments of psychiatry and medicine perpetuate the notion that the mind and the body are separate, but this long-standing tradition is entrenched and will not pass easily. In addition, behavioral health specialists, and psychologists in particular, are reluctant to leave their private solo practice offices so that they may be on location with the primary care setting. Finally, the carve-out companies that have captured 75% of the insured behavioral healthcare market are fiercely opposed to giving up their domain by "carving-in."

Fortunately, the integration of behavioral health with primary care can be accomplished in a continuum of steps, with a minimum of 18 months required to reach the level of behavioral care practitioners being on location, and 3 to 4 years before there is an obliteration of traditional departments in favor of population/disease-based teams. Figure 9.8 illustrates this continuum, beginning with a 1-800

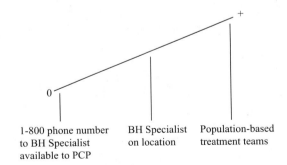

0

1-800 phone number   BH Specialist   Population-based
to BH Specialist   on location   treatment teams
available to PCP

Figure 9.8 Intensity (degree) of integration on a continuum from a 1-800 telephone number, through the midpoint in which behavioral health specialists are on location, to the eventual obliteration of departments in favor of population/disease-based treatment teams. Most programs (chemical dependency, depression, lifestyle, etc.) are before the midpoint.

number available to primary physicians for consultation with a psychologist 24 hours per day, proceeding to the midpoint in which psychologists are on location, and eventually reaching the level of departments being replaced by targeted teams. There is appreciable increase in collaboration when the behavioral specialist is on location, permitting the primary care physician to walk the patient the few feet down the hall where the three (physician, psychologist, and patient) address the patient's problem. In such an arrangement, even though the presenting complaint is regarded by the team as psychological in nature, the process is viewed by the patient as part of the totality of healthcare. It is precisely this lack of resistance by the patient that increases acceptance of psychotherapy from the national average of only 10% of referrals in the fragmented referral system, to 80% in the integrated model. The more the psychologist blends into the healthcare system, the less will be the patient's feeling of having been abandoned by the physician only to be stigmatized as a "mental case."

There are many examples of population-based teams (Cummings et al., 1997). In one setting, a teen-age clinic (ages 13 to 19 with ongoing parental consent), is composed of pediatricians, nurse practitioners, and psychologists/social workers. These practitioners do not report to the departments of pediatrics, nursing, or psychiatry, respectively, but rather to the teen-age clinic, which has its own administrative staff and budget. This accords freedom from having to beg for resources (money, staff) from such departments, and results in highly effective programs. In this instance, teenagers being seen without having to be accompanied by their parents were able to discuss freely issues of sex, drugs, and other matters typical of this age. The findings over a 4-year period revealed significantly lower rates of drug abuse, teenage pregnancy, and venereal diseases. Another example of such teams functioning independently of departments are back clinics, composed of primary care physicians, behavioral care specialists, and nurse practitioners who address one of the largest group of somaticizers, those with stress-related low back pain who would not be benefited by surgery. Still other examples are rheumatoid arthritis clinics (which include the difficult patients with fibromyalgia), childhood asthma programs, and diabetes clinics.

Eventually economic considerations, pressed by large employers and third-party payers, will insist on the integration of behavioral healthcare with primary care. All of the fat has been wrung out of mental healthcare, whereas enormous savings are yet to be realized in the medical/surgical system. Figure 9.9 dramatically illustrates that a 5%, 10%, or even 15% saving in the mental health/chemical dependency budget is scarcely a blip compared to such savings in medicine/surgery. Looking at the $1.2 trillion annual American health budget, a 10% saving through the appropriate treatment of the somaticizer would exceed the entire annual mental health/chemical dependency budget for that year. Research has demonstrated that in an integrated system, 5% to 10% medical cost offset is modest, indeed. Before the integration of behavioral healthcare with primary care occurs, however, the policy makers will have to put into place the required economic incentives. Current financial arrangements perpetuate the status quo.

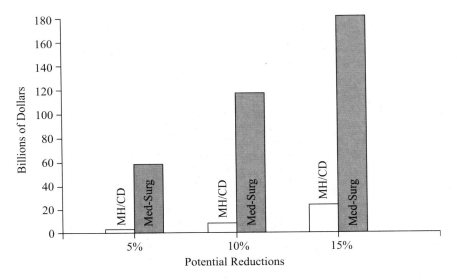

Figure 9.9 Reduction in billions of dollars potentially at the 5%, 10%, and 15% levels for the nation's mental health chemical dependency budget. Based on a total annual healthcare budget of $1.2 trillion in 1997. The estimates are from Cummings (1997).

The Behavioral Care Practitioner of the Future: A Golden Opportunity

Doctoral-level psychologists can no longer justify employment as psychotherapists as the trend among managed care companies and regional provider groups is to hire master's-level clinicians for that purpose. Any PhD who insists on competing as a therapist or counselor with MA psychologists will have to accept fees commensurate with that lower level, and, indeed, many doctoral psychologists are doing just that. The job market is grim for those insisting on traditional psychotherapy employment or private solo practice. At the same time, opportunities in health psychology are increasing. Several of the nation's largest health systems are firing traditional doctoral psychotherapists as they hire, instead, doctoral-level health psychologists who can not only be on location with primary care, but are trained to perform outcomes research, program planning, supervision of master's-level therapists/counselors, and other important activities. In some systems, health psychologists are participants along with physicians in practitioner/equity plans (Cummings et al., 1996).

The psychotherapy of the future is much different from that for which most psychologists have trained. Only 25% of the practitioner's clinical time will be in individual psychotherapy, which will be targeted and focused, and based on empirically derived amalgams of all the techniques (behavioral, cognitive behavioral, psychodynamic, strategic, systems). Another 25% will be in-group psychotherapy that is time-limited and closed. Open groups where patients wander in for a year or two and wander out again are outdated. In addition, 50% of the clinician's time will be in population/disease programs that will be both psycho educational and therapeutic. By adding the number of patients involved in such a configuration in a national healthcare system involving 14.5 million covered lives that employed such a ratio, less than 10% of patients are seen in individual psychotherapy (Cummings, 1996). The future doctoral practitioner in behavioral health will not only be (1) an innovative clinician, but also (2) a trained researcher, (3) a creative program planner, (4) a knowledgeable health psychologist, (5) a skilled manager, and (6) a compassionate, but astute businessperson (Cummings, 1996).

References

Antonovsky, A. (1987). *Unraveling the mystery of health: How people manage stress and stay well.* San Francisco, CA: Jossey-Bass.

Bandura, A. (1977). Self-efficacy: Toward a unifying theory of behavioral change. *Psychological Review, 84,* 191–215.

Cummings, N. A. (1993). Somatization: When physical symptoms have no medical cause. In D. Goleman & J. Gurin (Eds.), *Mind-body medicine* (pp. 221–232). Yonkers, NY: Consumer Reports.

Cummings, N. A. (1994). The successful application of medical offset in program planning and in clinical delivery. *Managed Care Quarterly, 2,* 1–6.

Cummings, N. A. (1996). The impact of managed care on employment and professional training: A primer for survival. In N. A. Cummings, M. S. Pallak, & J. L. Cummings (Eds.), *Surviving the demise of solo practice: Mental health practitioners prospering in the era of managed care* (pp. 11–26). Madison, CT: Psychosocial Press.

Cummings, N. A. (1997). Approaches in prevention in the behavioral health of older adults. In P. Hartman-Stein (Ed.), *Innovative behavioral healthcare for older adults: A guidebook for changing times* (pp. 1–23). San Francisco, CA: Jossey-Bass.

Cummings, N. A., & Cummings, J. L. (1997). The behavioral health practitioner of the future: The efficacy of psychoeducational programs. In N. A. Cummings, J. L. Cummings, & J. N. Johnson (Eds.), *Behavioral health in primary care: A guide for clinical integration* (pp. 325–346). Madison, CT: Psychosocial Press.

Cummings, N. A., Cummings, J. L., & Johnson, J. N. (Eds.). (1997). *Behavioral health in primary care: A guide for clinical integration.* Madison, CT: Psychosocial Press.

Cummings, N. A., & Follette, W. T. (1968). Psychiatric services and medical utilization in a prepaid health plan setting: Part 2. *Medical Care, 6,* 31–41.

Cummings, N. A., & Follette, W. T. (1976). Brief psychotherapy and medical utilization: An eight-year follow-up. In H. Dörken (Ed.), *The professional psychologist today* (pp. 126–142). San Francisco, CA: Jossey-Bass.

Cummings, N. A., Kahn, B. I., & Sparkman, B. (1962). *Psychotherapy and medical utilization: A pilot project.* Oakland, CA: Annual Reports of Kaiser Permanente Research Projects.

Cummings, N. A., Pallak, M. S., & Cummings, J. L. (Eds.). (1997). *Surviving the demise of solo practice: Mental health practitioners prospering in the era of managed care.* Madison, CT: Psychosocial Press.

Follette, W. T., & Cummings, N. A. (1967). Psychiatric services and medical utilization in a prepaid health plan setting. *Medical Care, 5,* 24–35.

Ford, C. V. (1983). *The somaticizing disorders: Illness as a way of life.* New York: Elsevier.

Ford, C. V. (1986). The somatizing disorders. *Psychosomatics, 27,* 327–337.

Gunn, W. B., Seaburn, D., Lorenz, A., Gawinski, B., & Mauksch, L. B. (1997). Collaboration in action: Key strategies for behavioral health providers. In N. A. Cummings, J. L. Cummings, & J. N. Johnson (Eds.), *Behavioral health in primary care: A guide for clinical integration* (pp. 285–304). Madison, CT: Psychosocial Press.

Hartman-Stein, P. (Ed.). (1997). *Innovative behavioral healthcare for older adults: A Guidebook for changing times.* San Francisco, CA: Jossey-Bass.

Jones, K. R., & Vischi, T. R. (1979). The impact of alcohol, drug abuse, and mental health treatment on medical care utilization: A review of the research literature. *Medical Care, 17*(suppl.), 43–131.

Jones, K. R., & Vischi, T. R. (1980). *The Bethesda consensus conference on medical offset: Alcohol, drug abuse, and mental health administration report.* Rockville, MD: Alcohol, Drug Abuse and Mental Health Administration.

Kent, J., & Gordon, M. (1997). Integration: A case for putting Humpty Dumpty together again. In N. A. Cummings, J. L. Cummings, & J. N. Johnson (Eds.), *Behavioral health in primary care: A guide for clinical integration* (pp. 103–120). Madison, CT: Psychosocial Press.

Kroenke, K., & Mangelsdorf, A. D. (1989). Common symptoms in ambulatory care: incidence, evaluation, therapy, and outcome. *American Journal of Medicine, 86,* 262–266.

Lorig, K., & Fries, J. (1990). *Arthritis helpbook* (3rd ed.). Reading, MA: Addison-Wesley.

Lucas, S. F., & Peek, C. J. (1997). A primary care physician's experience with integrated behavioral healthcare: What difference has it made? In N. A. Cummings, J. L. Cummings, & J. N. Johnson (Eds.), *Behavioral health in primary care: A guide for clinical integration* (pp. 371–397). Madison, CT: Psychosocial Press.

Pellitier, K. R. (1993). Between mind and body: Stress, emotions and health. In D. Goleman & J. Gurin (Eds.), *Mind/body medicine* (pp. 19–38). Yonkers, NY: Consumer Reports.

Ross, E. C. (1998, December 7). Plans present mixed bag of results for providers, subscribers. *Tallahassee Democrat,* pp. F1, 4.

Seligman, M. E. P. (1975). *Helplessness: On depression, development, and death.* San Francisco, CA: W. H. Freeman.

Slay, J. D., & McLeod, C. (1997). Evolving an integration model: The healthcare partners experience. In N. A. Cummings, J. L. Cummings, & J. N. Johnson (Eds.), *Behavioral health in primary care: A guide to clinical integration* (pp. 121–141). Madison, CT: Psychosocial Press.

Sobel, D. (1995). Rethinking medicine: Improving health outcomes with cost-effective psychosocial interventions. *Psychosomatic Medicine, 57,* 234–244.

Strosahl, K. (1997). Building primary care behavioral health systems that work: A compass and a horizon. In N. A. Cummings, J. L. Cummings, & J. N. Johnson (Eds.), *Behavioral health in primary care: A guide for clinical integration* (pp. 37–59). Madison, CT: Psychosocial. Press.

Strosahl, K., Baker, N. J., Braddick, M., Stuart, M. E., & Handley, M. R. (1997). Integration of behavioral health and primary care services: The Group Health Cooperative model. In N. A. Cummings, J. L. Cummings, & J. N. Johnson (Eds.), *Behavioral health in primary care: A guide for clinical integration* (pp. 61–65). Madison, CT: Psychosocial Press.

10 Behavioral Health in Primary Care
Dollars and Sense

Nicholas A. Cummings

Ever since the medical cost offset was discovered more than 35 years ago (Cummings et al., 1962) at the Kaiser Permanente health maintenance organization (HMO), the most important argument for the inclusion of behavioral healthcare in primary care has been that it saves medical and surgical costs, and reduces inappropriate physical utilization. Since that seminal research (Follette & Cummings, 1967; Cummings & Follette, 1968), researchers have conducted scores of studies, many of which elicited the medical cost offset effect, while others did not. In order to be meaningful, the savings in medical utilization must exceed the costs of providing the behavioral healthcare interventions. Some studies have shown a negative effect, painfully demonstrating that traditional mental healthcare services cannot be parachuted into a traditional medical delivery system without incurring disappointing results.

A recently reported study (Fraser, 1996) reveals just how disastrous the results can be. A managed care organization (MCO) obtained an important delivery contract on the basis of promising medical cost savings. The negotiations were market driven in conjunction with misguided clinicians who bypassed the experts in medical cost offset. Neither knowing how to conduct medical cost offset research nor having the ability to deliver the necessary and appropriate interventions, no medical-surgical savings were realized and the client canceled the contract. In contrast, one Blue Cross/Blue Shield organization revealed that, in a year when most health plans were raising their premiums, they did not have to do so because of the medical cost offset realized.

This article will focus on how and when behavioral health interventions produce the medical cost offset effect and when they do not. In order to do so, it will review three generations of medical cost offset research, and conclude with the most recent findings as to what circumstances enhance the effect, and what circumstances depress the potential effect.

The Discovery of Somatization

In the 1950s, the physicians at the Kaiser Permanente Health Plan, the prototype of the modern HMO, found to their surprise that 60% of physician visits were by patients who had no physical disease (Cummings & VandenBos, 1981). These patients were "diagnosed" in their medical charts as *hypochondriacs* in keeping with the parlance of the time. This unfortunate term was subsequently changed to that of *somatizer*, reflecting their *somatization*, a newly coined word in the medical nomenclature. It must be emphasized that this term has no relationship to the diagnosis of Somatiform Disorder in the current DSM-IV (American Psychiatric Association, 1994). Rather, it is defined as follows: Somatization is the translation of emotional problems into physical symptoms, or the exacerbation of a disease by emotional factors or stress.

Somatization inevitably results in the overutilization of healthcare, overloading the system. Originally it was erroneously believed that it was the function of the HMO in that when all barriers to access to healthcare are removed, patients will somaticize. Currently it is a generally accepted figure that between 60% and 70% of all physician visits are by somaticizers, and when one adds the visits resulting from faulty or unhealthy lifestyles, the figure approaches 90% (Mechanic, 1966, 1991). The reason it was first discovered in an HMO setting is because capitated physicians were not compelled to declare a diagnosis where there was none, while fee-for-service physicians had to enter a diagnosis on the insurance form, even if preliminary, in order to be reimbursed. Consequently, the factor of somatization was obscured and even inadvertently hidden.

Medical Cost Offset

The history of medical cost offset can be roughly divided into three generations, each with its own set of discoveries and constellation of problems. It parallels the evolution of healthcare delivery, and as the system moved steadily and swiftly from fee-for-service to managed care, so did the challenges for medical cost offset investigations. It has been extensively described (Cummings, 1991, 1993, 1996a) and will only be summarized here.

The First Generation: 1960–1980

Medical cost offset research was catapulted into the scientific literature following the discovery at Kaiser Permanente that 60% of physician visits were by somatizers and the seminal research by Cummings and his colleagues (Cummings et al., 1962; Follette & Cummings, 1967; Cummings & Follette, 1968, 1976) that medical utilization typically is reduced by 62% over 5 years following the application of behavioral interventions, and that the reduction in costs substantially exceeds the costs of providing the behavioral healthcare services. Furthermore, without any additional behavioral healthcare services, the utilization of medicine and surgery, both outpatient and inpatient, steadily declined to an ultimate level and stayed down, as compared to a group of high utilizers who did not receive any behavioral healthcare services. The typical Cummings and Follette effect is shown in Figure 10.1.

During these decades, the National Institute of Mental Health (NIMH) sponsored a number of investigations, and the Alcohol, Drug Abuse and Mental Health

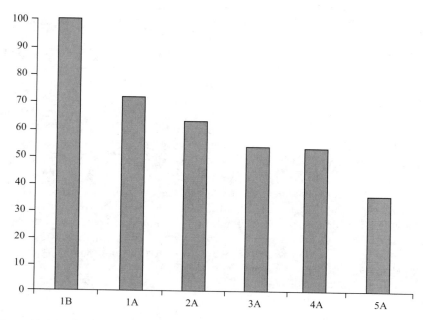

Figure 10.1 Average medical utilization for the year before (1B) and the 5 years after (1A, 2A, 3A, 4A, and 5A) behavioral intervention (from Follette & Cummings, 1967).

Administration (ADAMHA) summarized 28 medical cost offset studies (Jones & Vischi, 1979), all but one of which showed the effect. The end of the decade was marked by the Bethesda Consensus Conference in 1980, which concluded not only that medical cost offset was real, but that the array of studies varied from savings that were highly significant to those that were not sufficient to cover even the cost of providing the behavioral healthcare services. It further noted the methodological difficulties inherent in the retrospective design of these studies, with the recommendation that future research be prospective with a control group even if this meant that those in the control group would be denied services. In spite of the difficulties reflected in this first generation of studies, the Bethesda Consensus Conference concluded that the healthcare system is burdened by patients with no real physical disease whose symptoms are caused by stress. Without psychotherapy, it was believed these persons would suffer needlessly.

The report of the Bethesda Consensus Conference (Jones & Vischi, 1980) was never widely disseminated because it appeared only a few weeks before the end of the Carter administration and the scientists who convened it left government service when the next administration took office. That report noted that medical cost offset is more likely to occur in organized settings, and it recommended that future research determine what factors increase medical-surgical cost savings and what factors mitigate such savings. To overcome the limitations of past studies, it recommended that a way be found to conduct controlled experiments and to address the problem of how medical cost offset research could aid in program planning and in clinical delivery (Jones & Vischi, 1980).

In regard to the integration of behavioral healthcare into primary care, the era ended with two very significant events in the Kaiser Permanente Health Plan where the medical cost offset effect was first discovered. The first of these was the design and implementation of the nation's first comprehensive prepaid psychotherapy benefit. Prior to this monumental event, the conventional wisdom in healthcare was that psychotherapy could not feasibly be covered as an insurance benefit because it had the potential to bankrupt the system. The conclusion at Kaiser Permanente was that, because of the overloading of the medical-surgical system by the somatizer, no comprehensive healthcare delivery system could operate without psychotherapeutic interventions. Within these conclusions was the finding that the treatment of choice for 85% of the somatizers was brief focused psychotherapy. The 15% of patients who needed and received longer-term psychotherapy tended to substitute psychotherapy visits for physician visits, and therefore did not demonstrate any overall cost savings except in the reduction of medical-surgical hospitalization.

Advocates for the inclusion of psychotherapy, and especially of long-term psychotherapy in health insurance, overlooked the fact that medical cost offset was the result of interventions of brief therapy of the type later known as "HMO therapy." This led to the first series of studies that embarrassingly did not result in enough medical cost savings to offset the unnecessary expenditures of long-term therapy. Although this generation of research revealed a minority of patients need longer-term psychotherapy, this should be determined by the patients' condition, not therapist bias or ineptitude. The lesson learned is that if 85% of patients can benefit from brief therapy (average 6–7 sessions), then the longer-term treatment of those who really need it can be successfully financed.

The second event in regard to the integration of behavioral healthcare into primary care was a series of demonstration projects, early and noble experiments, indeed, in which this integration was actually accomplished. These will be described in the next article.

The Second Generation: 1980–1990

This second generation of studies numbers about 80, and along with merely replicating previous findings, the majority of researchers turned to addressing the concerns and issues discussed at the Bethesda Consensus Conference. But as momentum was building, suddenly all activity stopped as managed behavioral care "carve-outs" sought to tether out-of-control psychiatric and chemical dependency treatment costs by removing behavioral healthcare from the medical-surgical delivery system. In addition, mental healthcare costs were so high that their provision would more than swallow up any medical cost offset effect. Integration all but came to an abrupt halt.

As unfortunate as this turn of events seems in retrospect, the carve-outs actually saved the mental healthcare benefit from extinction. Congress's enactment of diagnosis-related groups (DRGs) had dramatically tethered medical-surgical costs, but inadvertently encouraged the hospital industry's survival tactic of turning thousands of empty hospital beds into psychiatric (especially adolescent psychiatric) and chemical dependency treatment services. Faced with the fact that this was now driving the double-digit inflation in healthcare, third-party payers began to drop the mental health/chemical dependency (MH/CD) benefit from their coverage. By curtailing the accelerating inflation rate of MH/CD, the managed behavioral care industry prevented the extinction of the benefit, an accomplishment for which sufficient credit has not been accorded the carve-outs. Nonetheless, carving out behavioral healthcare is the very antithesis of integration. When Cummings (1986) defined the parameters of the carve-outs, he pointed out that their necessity was solely economic and for about a 10-year period, a fact overlooked and resisted by the carve-out industry, which now fears its own extinction inasmuch as it has outlived its usefulness. As important as the carve-outs were in their time, we are now confronted with the task of carving back in.

This second generation of medical cost offset research enunciated very clearly the methodological difficulties involved, and charted a course for the future. The first and foremost difficulty was that most healthcare settings did not possess the information systems needed to conduct such research. The carve-out arrangement only exacerbated the problem; if the informatics was deficient within a health plan, that between it and its carve-out was virtually nonexistent. Embarrassed by this, actuaries found it easier to ignore the medical cost offset phenomenon than to acknowledge their data-processing shortcomings. The current emphasis (third generation) on outcomes research and accompanying drives toward sophisticated medical informatics has heralded a brighter future for researchers.

A second major difficulty in conducting medical offset research stems from practice disparity among psychotherapists. Psychotherapists display a seemingly infinite number of competing and warring approaches to treatment, and most research employs a "lumping" of practitioners who may be canceling each other out. The emergence of organized settings is more likely to result in more homogeneity among psychotherapists. For example, in HMOs in which practitioners are trained and monitored in effective short-term psychotherapy, significant medical cost offset is usually elicited (Cummings & Follette, 1968, 1976; Goldberg et al., 1970, 1979), while in a fee-for-service setting in which practitioners characteristically practice longer-term therapy, a dosage effect seems to prevail (Schlesinger et al., 1983). In the latter study, the greatest savings occurred with hospitalization, inasmuch as the higher costs of longer-term therapy subtracted from the potential savings in ambulatory healthcare. Thus, there needs to be greater specificity in selecting providers and treatment.

Most somatizers are not referred for psychotherapy because the non-psychiatric physicians who see them recognize less than one fourth of those with emotional distress or chemical dependency (Glazer, 1993; Glazer & Bell, 1993). The problem is greater in fee-for-service settings where incentives for referral are absent. In a study by the RAND Corporation (1987), physicians who were capitated were more likely to refer patients for psychotherapy than were fee-for-service physicians, and the likelihood of referrals markedly decreased in geographical areas where there was a surplus of physicians, resulting in the "patient scarcity" phenomenon. Some studies have sought to train non-psychiatric physicians to recognize the somatizer and to appropriately refer him or her for psychotherapy. Even screening with computer printouts to primary care physicians has been utilized with mixed results (Cummings, 1995). However, to maximize referral to a psychotherapist, in addition to increasing physician cooperation, an outreach program directed at the somatizer may be necessary.

Medical offset studies need to be prospective and controlled, in contrast to most previous studies, which relied on retrospective data and multiple regression analysis. Such studies are subject to selection bias and do not answer the question of whether so-called positive results are a statistical regression to the mean (Fiedler & Wight, 1989). Further, they would have to include a randomly selected group of somatizers who do not receive psychotherapy. The denial of services is not generally contractually permitted by the third-party payer and constitutes an ethical dilemma for the practitioner. One way of addressing the problem is by a phase-in of a new psychotherapy benefit. A random phase-in could include the required control group, at least until the implementation of psychotherapy benefits. It remained for the next (third) generation of medical cost offset research to adequately address this problem. While the concentration of effort to control MH/CD costs all but curtailed medical cost offset research, a large number of second-generation studies helped to clarify the role of stress and unhealthy lifestyles in relation to medical utilization and to identify and promote issues of wellness. This body of literature is extensive, and somatization as a lifestyle has been reviewed by Ford (1983) and Pelletier (1993). The relationship between stress and somatization, which was not well understood when Kaiser Permanente dealt with this problem in the 1950s, will continue to occupy a significant sector of the healthcare field. Medical overutilization can be affected by programs designed to promote healthy lifestyles (Ford, 1983, 1986).

The Third Generation: 1990 to the Present

The unprecedented growth of managed behavioral health plans over the past decade has provided large organized settings that have shown a revitalized interest in medical cost offset research. These companies are under considerable pressure to empirically demonstrate claims of quality, efficiency, and effectiveness. Outcomes research is experiencing a surge of activity, with contract research organizations springing up to meet the demand. Today, most of the unnecessary costs in delivering behavioral healthcare have been eliminated, and managed care organizations are turning to answer whether, how, and when such services can have an effect on unnecessary medical and surgical costs.

The forerunner and prototype of this new medical cost offset research is the Hawaii Medicaid Project (Cummings et al., 1993; Pallak et al., 1994), conducted over a period of 7 years with the entire Medicaid population of the Island of Oahu (Honolulu) and in a managed behavioral care setting specifically organized for that purpose under the auspices of the federal Health Care Financing Administration (HCFA). The study was designed to meet the several scientific criticisms delineated in the second generation of medical cost offset research.

The Hawaii Medicaid Project was (1) prospective in design with (2) all Medicaid eligibles (N = 36,000) randomly assigned to experimental and control groups, keeping families intact. It was in a specially created (3) organized setting that accorded (4) standardization of psychotherapists by 6 months of prior training and perpetual monitoring and case management in a staff (salaried) model. All practitioners were half-time, and 15% of their time was spent in quality assurance and adherence to the (5) empirically derived treatment protocols in which they were trained. (6) Access was enhanced by a series of satellite centers in high-density Medicaid areas, as well as a main center placed at the Ala Moana Shopping Mall where all Oahu public transportation converges. House calls were routine for those who could not come to any center. (7) An aggressive outreach program was coupled with (8) programs designed to encourage physician, social work, agency, and community participation. Every month, the top 15% of users of health services as defined by frequency, who accounted for 80% of Medicaid costs, were outreached by mail, telephone, and, for patients who responded to neither of these, by house call from a registered nurse dressed in full regalia and carrying a black bag. In contrast to the psychotherapists who very seldom were invited into the house, the registered nurses were never refused entrance.

Interesting, this controlled prospective study confirmed years of retrospectively derived results. The cost of creating the behavioral healthcare system was recovered by medical-surgical savings within 18 months, and the significant reduction in medical utilization continued thereafter with no additional behavioral healthcare required to maintain the cost savings. These were estimated to be $8 million per year in constant dollars, with the greatest savings attributed to the group with a chronic medical diagnosis. This group consisted of high utilizers who suffered from diabetes, hypertension, chronic airway and respiratory diseases, ischemic heart disease, and rheumatoid arthritis, and who account for 40% of all Medicaid costs in Hawaii.

In contrast, the control group, which was seen in the fee-for-service private sector for psychotherapy, revealed a 17% increase in medical-surgical utilization, which was not statistically different from the 27% increase in control group patients who received no MH/CD services whatsoever. These results are found in Figures 10.2 and 10.3.

Hawaii was chosen as the site for this study because of its liberal Medicaid benefit of up to 52 sessions per year and renewable every year with any psychiatrist or psychologist in the community of the patient's own choosing. This permitted a direct comparison of the effectiveness and efficiency of empirically derived

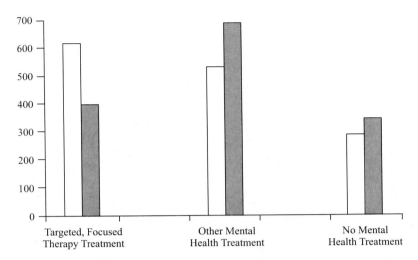

Figure 10.2 Non-chronic group. Average medical utilization in constant dollars for the Hawaii Medicaid Project non-chronic group for the year before (lightly shaded columns) for those receiving targeted and focused treatment, other mental health treatment in the private practice community, and no mental health treatment (from Cummings et al., 1993).

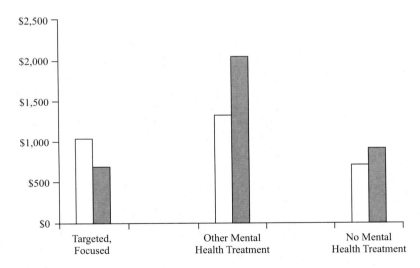

Figure 10.3 Chronically ill group. Average medical utilization in constant dollars for the Hawaii Medicaid Project chronically ill group for the year before (lightly shaded columns) and the year after (darkly shaded columns) for those receiving targeted and focused treatment in the private practice community, and no mental health treatment (from Cummings et al., 1993).

protocols delivered in a standardized setting versus traditional psychotherapy delivered in a laissez-faire private sector. The superiority of focused interventions designed and targeted to specific conditions, often in group psychoeducational format, was demonstrated in this and other settings (Goleman & Gurin, 1993) and may indicate that such protocols may be the psychotherapeutic wave of the future. These programs will be described in detail in a subsequent article in this volume.

Finally, the third generation of medical cost offset research indicates the importance of this methodology in program planning (Cummings, 1994). Results are in hard data, such as measurable reductions in units of medicine and surgery delivered, as compared to soft variables known as patient satisfaction, reported happiness, well-being or adjustment, and other rather difficult-to-quantify responses. Perhaps even more important, and as reluctant as healthcare practitioners may be to admit it, the results impinge on that almighty "bottom line" which, in this era of diminishing resources, is the ultimate determiner.

Now that managed care covers 70% of America's insured, some believe it is no longer possible to demonstrate medical cost offset as there is very little fat left. Nothing could be farther from the truth. Although managed care has reduced the acceleration of the inflationary spiral, it has not reversed it. There is still considerable waste and duplication in the system, and medical-surgical savings through behavioral health interventions have yet to more than scratch the surface. Two examples will be described. The first is a demonstration of how medical cost offset research must adapt to managed care realities, and the second demonstrates how dramatic savings can be realized in an efficient and effective managed care setting by a simple, heretofore untried behavioral health intervention.

The Reverse Medical Offset Threat

When the medical cost offset phenomenon was first demonstrated, a frequent criticism from traditional psychotherapists was that psychological or other physical symptoms would replace the physical symptoms in remission (symptom substitution). However, an 8-year follow-up study showed otherwise: not only had the somatizing abated, but patients had actually resolved the underlying stress that had resulted in their original symptomatology (Cummings & Follette, 1976). This finding seemed to put an end to the criticism called *transfer of equivalence* by more traditional psychotherapists. Less clear was the relationship between medical and psychiatric hospitalization.

Several studies have shown that hospitalized medical patients with psychiatric comorbidity have longer hospital stays and that psychotherapeutic consultation in the hospital can reduce the length of stay (Levenson et al., 1986; Hengeveld et al., 1988; Fulop et al., 1989). However, what is the fate of a patient who presents for psychiatric hospitalization and is denied admission? Does that patient subsequently have a greater incidence of medical hospitalization? Such a finding would clearly be a *reverse* medical cost offset effect.

To investigate this question, Pallak and Cummings (1992) followed for 1 year every patient who presented for psychiatric hospitalization within a 6-month period in a managed care program and who was either admitted to a psychiatric hospital or was diverted to outpatient psychotherapy. They were interested in whether patients who presented for psychiatric hospitalization and were denied admission were more likely to be admitted for medical and surgical hospitalization for an ostensibly non-psychiatric diagnosis. Patients who accepted outpatient psychotherapy either in lieu of psychiatric hospitalization or subsequent to discharge from a psychiatric unit, whether they were diverted or hospitalized psychiatrically, were not likely to be admitted to a medical or surgical unit. Both psychiatrically diverted *and* hospitalized patients who did not accept outpatient psychotherapy were more likely to be medically or surgically hospitalized during the subsequent year. The critical variable determining hospitalization was whether patients received outpatient psychotherapy.

The Managed Medicare Bereavement Program

It has long been recognized that in the first year or two following the death of a spouse, the surviving widow or widower demonstrates a significant and often startling increase in medical utilization. Cummings (1991) studied a group of 140,000 older adults who were receiving their Medicare benefits through a large managed care company. These retirees living in Florida were yielding about 20 widows and widowers every day, most of whom reduced medical utilization the year before the spouse died, ostensibly because they were too busy caring for the ill and dying spouse to attend to their own healthcare needs, only to strikingly increase medical utilization the year following the death of the spouse.

An aggressive but sensitive and compassionate outreach program contacted the survivor shortly after the death of the spouse and screened each one for signs of depression (reflecting unresolved issues with the deceased that would hamper bereavement) and those who were essentially in mourning with often severe sadness, but not pathological depression. The former were referred to psychotherapy for depression, while the latter were referred to a group program for bereavement. Because this older generation is characteristically respectful of the doctor and compliant with medical advice, acceptance of referrals was high.

The bereavement program consisted of 5 to 8 mourners in each group depending on patient traffic. There were 14 sessions of 2 hours duration each, spaced as follows: 4 semi-weekly sessions, followed by 6 weekly sessions, and concluding with 4 monthly sessions for a total treatment period of 6.5 months. The program was psychoeducational in nature, imparting information about the process of mourning, encouraging the patients to experience it as painful healing, and providing relaxation techniques and guided imagery to help them over the most stressful periods. A "buddy system" paired patients for mutual support and accessibility as needed. Patients were encouraged to discontinue antidepressant medication or use it sparingly as this may reduce the sadness but interferes with the natural healing process and prolongs it. The thrust of the program was to enhance self-efficacy, reduce learned helplessness, and restore a sense of coherence, all of which are described in greater detail in a subsequent article.

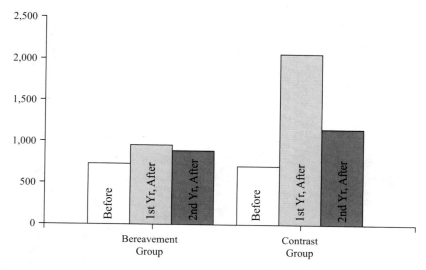

Figure 10.4 Average medical utilization for the year before and each of the 2 years after beginning the program, and for the same period for the contrast group who did not receive bereavement counseling. Amounts are in 1988–1992 dollars (from Cummings, 2004).

The medical utilization of 323 patients in this experimental group was compared with that of 278 widowed older adults in a nearby center of the same managed care company where the bereavement program had not been implemented. All patients were followed for 2 years except for a small number who did not live the entire 2 years following participation in the bereavement program. As is seen in Figure 10.4, following the death of the spouse, the medical utilization of the bereavement program group rises somewhat higher than is expected of this age group, but then declines the second year after. The group not receiving the bereavement program demonstrated a sharp increase in medical utilization the first year after, with the increase being twice that of the bereavement program group. And although average medical utilization was considerably reduced in the second year after, it remains 40% higher than that of the bereavement program participants. The savings in medical utilization of the experimental group over the control group was $1,400 per patient for the 2 years. Extrapolated to the older adult population in this 140,000 Medicare cohort alone, this amount translates potentially to several million dollars. But even more important, it spared these widowed older adults 2 years of avoidable suffering from physical symptoms and psychologically induced ill health.

Where's the Beef?

Considering the overwhelming evidence, this author has maintained that traditional services cannot be parachuted into a traditional setting with the expectation

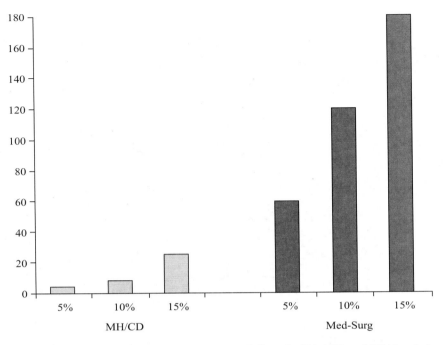

Figure 10.5 Reduction in billions of dollars potentially at the 5%, 10%, and 15% levels for the nation's mental health/chemical dependency budget (first three columns) and these percentages for the nation's medical/surgical budget.

of finding medical cost offset. A recent project known as the Fort Bragg Study has demonstrated that *improved* traditional behavioral healthcare services cannot be injected into an *improved* traditional setting to obtain medical cost offset (Bickman, 1996). After spending $80 million to greatly increase access and to provide longer-term psychotherapy to more people, costs significantly increased, leading the researchers to conclude that more is not necessarily better. Some of the least costly nontraditional behavioral healthcare services are the most efficacious in ameliorating patient pain, anxiety, and depression, in enhancing disease management, and in promoting prevention.

The cost containment that can be realized in MH/CD pales by comparison with the cost containment that lies potentially in medicine and surgery. Dollar amounts tend to obscure the importance of the comparison inasmuch as practitioners, like the general public, have become inured to large monetary sums being bandied about. Figure 10.5 is startling in that it dramatically shows the difference for 5%, 10%, and 15% cost savings in MH/CD (the first three columns) versus the same percentages in total healthcare (last three columns). All are in billions of dollars, and the 5%, 10%, and 15% reduction figures are modest estimates when most medical cost offset research demonstrates 15% to 60% savings. This figure graphically reveals that a 10% savings in medicine and surgery far exceeds the entire MH/CD budget of the United States!

The healthcare costs that might be saved through behavioral interventions, especially in a cutting-edge integrated program, have not begun to realize their potential.

Summary

More than 35 years of medical cost offset research, spanning 3 generations of activity, reveal that the cost offset is greater (1) in organized settings where (2) behavioral healthcare and primary care are somehow integrated, and where (3) the behavioral health interventions and the delivery system are cutting edge rather than traditional. Furthermore, it is enhanced by (4) standardized treatment procedures involving nontraditional modalities with (5) psychotherapists who have been standardized through training and subsequent monitoring. (6) The latest in informatics is critical, and the referrals of somatizers (7) are increased by capitation and suppressed by fee-for-service financial arrangements. (8) Controlled prospective studies are needed, but where they have been conducted they tend to confirm findings from years of less scientific retrospective research.

For years the medical cost offset has been blurred by methodological, delivery, and informatics problems, but a set of clear conditions is emerging under which significant savings can be demonstrated. For years advocates of psychotherapy, particularly of long-term psychotherapy in health insurance, have confused the issue by misusing the medical cost offset literature as "proof" that traditional psychotherapeutic services should be included in every health plan. To the contrary, the evidence now points to innovation in both behavioral health interventions and primary care delivery systems as the crucial factor.

References

American Psychiatric Association (1994). Diagnostic and statistical manual, 4th ed. (DSM-IV). Washington, DC: American Psychiatric Press.
Bickman, L. (1996). A continuum of care: More is not always better. American Psychologist, 51, 689–701.
Cummings, N. A. (1986). The dismantling of our health system: Strategies for survival of psychological practice. American Psychologist, 41, 426–431.
Cummings, N. A. (1991). Arguments for the financial efficacy of psychological services in health care settings. In J. J. Sweet, R. G. Rozensky, & S. M. Tovian (Eds.), *Handbook of Clinical Psychology in Medical Settings* (pp. 223–232). New York: Plenum.
Cummings, N. A. (1993). Somatization: When physical symptoms have no medical cause. In D. Goleman & J. Gurin (Eds.), *Mind-body medicine* (pp. 221–232). Yonkers, NY: Consumer Reports.
Cummings, N. A. (1994). The successful application of medical offset in program planning and in clinical delivery. Managed Care Quarterly, 2, 1–6.

Cummings, N. A. (1995). Assessing the computer's impact: Professional concerns. Computers in Human Behavior, 1, 293–300.

Cummings, N. A. (1996a). Does managed mental heal care offset costs related to medical treatments? In A. Lazarus (Ed.), *Controversies in managed mental health care* (pp. 213–227). Washington, DC: American Psychiatric Press.

Cummings, N. A. (1997). Approaches in Prevention in the Behavioral Health of Older Adults. In P. Hartman-Stein (Ed.), Innovative behavioral healthcare for older adults: A guidebook for changing times (pp. 1–23). San Francisco, CA: Jossey-Bass.

Cummings, N. A. (2004). Approaches in prevention in the behavioral health of older adults. In P. Hartman-Stein (Ed.), *Innovative behavioral health of older adults: A guide-book for changing times* (pp.1–23). San Francisco, CA: Jossey-Bass.

Cummings, N. A. (1997). Pioneering Integrated Systems: Lessons Learned, Forgotten, and Relearned. In N. A. Cummings, J. L. Cummings, & J. N. Johnson (Eds.), Behavioral health in primary care: A guide for clinical integration (pp. 23–35). Madison, CT: Psychosocial Press.

Cummings, N. A., Dörken, H., Pallak, M. S., & Henke, C. J. (1993). The impact of psychological intervention on health care costs and utilization: The Hawaii Medicaid Project. In N. A. Cummings & M. S. Pallak (Eds.), Medicaid, managed behavioral health and implications for public policy, Vol. 2: Healthcare and utilization cost series (pp. 3–23). South San Francisco, CA: Foundation for Behavioral Health.

Cummings, N. A., & Follette, W. T. (1968). Psychiatric services and medical utilization in a prepaid health plan setting: Part 2. *Medical Care, 6,* 31–41.

Cummings, N. A., & Follette, W. T. (1976). Brief psychotherapy and medical utilization: An eight-year follow-up. In H. Dörken (Ed.), The professional psychologist today. (pp. 126–142). San Francisco, CA: Jossey-Bass.

Cummings, N. A., Sparkman, B., & Kahn, B. R. (1962). Psychotherapy and Medical Utilization. Unpublished pilot project (pp. 33-43). Kaiser Permanente Hospital and Medical Center, San Francisco, CA.

Cummings, N. A., & VandenBos, G. R. (1981). The twenty-year Kaiser-Permanente experience with psychotherapy and medical utilization: Implications for national health policy and national health insurance. Heath Policy Quarterly, 1, 159–175.

Fiedler, J. L., & Wright, R. B. (1989). The medical offset and effect and public policy. New York: Praeger.

Follette, W., T., & Cummings, N. A. (1967). Psychiatric services and medical utilization in a prepaid health plan setting. Medical Care, 5, 25–35.

Ford, C. V. (1983). The somaticizing disorders: Illness as a way of life. New York: Elsevier.

Ford, C. V. (1986). The somaticizing disorders. Psychosomatics, 27, 327–337.

Fraser, J. S. (1996). All that glitters is not always gold: Medical offset effects and managed behavioral health care. Professional Psychology: Research and Practice, 27, 335–344.

Glazer, W. (1993, June–July). Approaching hidden psychiatric illness in PPOs: The "medical offset" effect. AAPPO Journal, 15–21.

Glazer, W., & Bell, N. (1993). Mental health benefits: A purchaser's guide. Brookfield, WI: International Foundation of Employee Benefits Plans Press.

Goldberg, I. D., Krantz, G., & Locke, B. Z. (1970). Effect of a short-term outpatient psychiatric benefit on the utilization of medical services in a prepaid group practice medical program. Medical Care 8, 419–428.

Goleman, D., & Gurin, J. (1993). Mind-body medicine. New York: Consumer Reports Books.

Hengeveld, M. W., Ancion, F. A. J. M., & Rooihans, H. H. G. (1988). Psychiatric consultations with depressed medical inpatients: A randomized controlled cost-effectiveness study. International Journal of Psychiatric Medicine, 18, 33–43.

Jones, K. R., & Vischi, T. R. (1979). The Impact of Alcohol, Drug Abuse, and Mental Health Treatment on Mental Health Utilization: A Review of the Research Literature. Medical Care, 17(12, suppl.), 43–131.

Jones, K. R., & Vischi, T. R. (1980). The Bethesda Consensus Conference on Medical Offset. Alcohol, drug abuse, and mental health administration. Rockville, MD: Alcohol, Drug Abuse, and Mental Health Administration.

Mechanic, D. (1966). Response factors in illness: The study of illness behavior. Social Psychiatry, 1, 52–73.

Pallak, M. S., & Cummings, N. A. (1992). Inpatient and outpatient psychiatric treatment: The effect of matching patients to appropriate level of treatment in psychiatric and medical-surgical hospital days. Applied and Preventive Psychology: Current Scientific Perspectives, 1, 83–87.

Pallak, M. S., Cummings, N. A., Dörken, H., & Henke, C. J. (1994). Medical costs, Medicaid, and managed mental health treatment: The Hawaii Study. Managed Care Quarterly, 2, 64–70.

Pelletier, K. R. (1993). Between mind and body: Stress, emotions and health. In D. Goleman & J. Gurin (Eds.), Mind/Body Medicine (pp. 19–38). Yonkers, NY: Consumer Reports.

Schlesinger, H. J., Mumford, E., Glass, G. V., Patrick, C., & Sharfstein, S. (1983). Mental health treatment and medical care utilization in a fee-for-service system: Outpatient mental health treatment following the onset of a chronic disease. American Journal of Public Health, 73, 422–429.

11 Medical Costs, Medicaid, and Managed Mental Health Treatment

The Hawaii Study

*Michael S. Pallak, Nicholas A. Cummings,
Herbert Dörken, and Curtis J. Henk*

Following mental health treatment, patients often show reductions in medical costs and utilization—often large enough to offset the costs of mental health treatment.[1–5] Access to mental healthcare services may reduce medical costs and utilization for at least two reasons. On one hand, patients under emotional distress may present with physical and somatic problems and thereby seek medical services for relief. In this view, substantial proportions of medical utilization may be misdirected in that the underlying emotional distress remains unaddressed. Symptomology continues to evolve and medical costs continue an upward trend, despite the physician's best efforts, because the emotional problem remains untreated.

Consistent with this view, Cummings and Follette reported that 60% of visits to physicians did not result in a confirmable medical or biological diagnosis.[2] Thus mental health treatment may forestall increasing medical costs by providing treatment appropriate to the underlying emotional distress that drives medical utilization. As a result, change in medical costs relative to initiation of mental health treatment represents a powerful empirical measure of clinical outcome.[6,7]

On the other hand, emotional distress may exacerbate existing medical conditions, complicate treatment, and thereby result in increased medical costs and utilization. Similarly, medical conditions per se may involve or trigger emotional components that complicate treatment if unaddressed and may make patients more vulnerable to other sources of emotional distress.

If so, the implications extend well beyond the typical 2% to 4% penetration rates[8] for mental healthcare services or the 5% of medical patients with somaticization disorder.[9] For example, Schlesinger et al. found that outpatient mental health treatment reduced medical costs after 3 years for patients with chronic medical diagnoses of airway-respiratory problems, ischemic heart disease, diabetes, and

This project was supported by Health Care Financing Administration (HCFA) Contract No. 11-C-98344/9 to the State of Hawaii for which the Foundation for Behavioral Health was the subcontractor. Although the final report has been accepted by the state and by HCFA, this paper does not necessarily reflect the opinions of either. Drs. Cummings and Dörken were, respectively, principal investigator and co-principal investigator for the contract.

hypertension.[10] Empirically, about 40% of the national population may have one or more of these diagnoses.[8,10]

From a policy perspective, effective programs to encourage mental health treatment could be implemented by outreaching to subgroups with high medical utilization rates. In short, the literature suggests a policy of increased access to outpatient mental health services rather than a policy of restricted access through various barriers such as deductibles and copay requirements now incorporated in most healthcare reform initiatives.

In general, managed care has received increased attention as a mechanism for restraining medical costs in public programs such as Medicaid.[11,12] At present, however, the literature regarding the relationship between mental health treatment and medical costs has been generated from employed populations,[4,5] and little is known about the relationship between mental health treatment and medical costs in Medicaid populations. For example, Fiedler and Wight in a retrospective review of Medicaid claims data from Georgia and Michigan found little relationship.[13]

In contrast, the present prospective study examined the relationship between managed mental health treatment, traditional fee-for-service mental healthcare available under Medicaid, and medical costs within the Medicaid population on Oahu, Hawaii. In addition, Medicaid enrollees with or without chronic medical diagnoses of ischemic heart disease, hypertension, diabetes, or respiratory problems were tracked in relation to mental healthcare services and medical services utilization. This article also extends previous analyses[14–16] by examining medical services utilization in terms of hospital days, physician office visits, emergency department visits, and controlled drug prescriptions, as well as medical costs.

Method

About two thirds of Medicaid enrollees on Oahu were randomly assigned to eligibility for managed mental health services (the experimental condition) in addition to mental health treatment services typically available in the fee-for-service format, and the remaining were not (the control condition). Managed mental health treatment was provided in a brief therapy format described elsewhere[8,17,18] as targeted, focused mental health treatment (TFMHT), while patients who needed and could benefit from longer-term therapy received longer-term treatment.

In addition, due to the time-limited service period (3.5 years), an outreach effort to those in the experimental condition and to high medical utilizers was incorporated.[8] The prospective design enabled comparisons among patients who used only managed mental health services (TFMHT), patients who used only traditional mental health services otherwise available under Medicaid (OMHT), patients who used both managed and traditional mental health services (BOTH) at some point, and patients who never used any form of mental health treatment (NoMHT).

These results were from Medicaid enrollees with 30 months of continuous eligibility. Medical costs and utilization were compared from the year preceding the 6-month period in which MHT was initiated and from the year following. For the NoMHT group, the middle 6-month period of the five periods was designated as the "MHT" period for comparison of change with the MHT groups. A total of 611 Medicaid enrollees in the 30-month eligibility cohort received managed mental health services. The results below were replicated also with patients who had 18, 42, or 54 months of continuous eligibility,[8] although the *ns* were smaller in the latter two cohorts.

Results

Medical Cost Trends for Medicaid Enrollees with or Without Chronic Medical Diagnoses

Medical cost trends are summarized in Table 11.1. All costs are in constant dollars and exclude costs of mental health treatment.

Initial Pretreatment Medical Costs

As one might expect, patients with chronic medical diagnoses had higher medical costs than patients without these diagnoses. For example, for the baseline group of enrollees who never used mental health treatment (NoMHT), medical costs for patients with chronic medical diagnoses were about 251% of those for patients without these medical diagnoses ($1,338 vs. $553, $p < 0.0001$).

Consistent with the literature, patients who used traditional other mental health treatment (as in the OMHT groups) also had higher initial medical costs than patients who never used mental health treatment ($1,187 vs. $533, $p < 0.05$; $1,745 vs. $1,338, $p < 0.12$, respectively), although the latter was attenuated.

Table 11.1 Medical Costs and Change in Medical Costs 12 Months Pre- and Post-MHT for Patients with Chronic Medical Diagnoses (CMD) or without (NONCMD)*

	N	Cost pre-MHT	Cost post-MHT	Change in cost	Percent change
CMD patients					
NoMHT[†]	4,307	1,338	1,694	+356	+27.0%
OMHT[‡]	169	1,745	2,045	+300	+17.0%
TFMHT[§]	227	2,654	2,126	−528	−20.0%
BOTH[/]	209	3,150	3,110	−40	−1.0%
Non-CMD patients					
NoMHT	6,837	533	511	−21	−4.0%
OMHT	199	1,187	907	−280	−24.0%
TFMHT	136	864	633	−231	−27.0%
BOTH	91	1,662	938	−724	−44.0%

Source: Adapted from Cummings, N. A., et al. *The Impact of Psychological Services on Medical Utilization.* HCFA Contract No. 11-C-98344/9. Baltimore, MD: Health Care Financing Administration, 1992.

* All cost entries represent means in 1983 constant dollars.

† NoMHT = enrollees who never used mental health services.

‡ OMHT = enrollees who used other traditional mental health services available under Medicaid.

§ TFMHT = enrollees who used only managed mental health services, i.e., targeted, focused, mental health treatment.

/ BOTH = enrollees who used both traditional and managed mental health services at some point.

Finally, patients who used managed mental health services (as in TFMHT, BOTH) had higher initial medical costs than NoMHT or OMHT enrollees (p < 0.0001), consistent with the outreach effort.

Change in Medical Costs

Table 11.1 summarizes change in medical costs as well as percentage change. For enrollees who never used mental health treatment (the NoMHT baseline), patients with chronic medical diagnoses increased medical costs by 27%—reliably different from the 4% decline in costs obtained for patients without these diagnoses (+$356 vs. –$21, p < 0.0001). From one perspective, enrollees with chronic medical diagnoses had higher medical costs initially and accounted for all of the medical cost increase (in constant dollars) obtained in Medicaid in this study.

Medical Cost Change for Enrollees with Chronic Medical Diagnoses

Traditional mental health treatment (OMHT) had little effect on medical costs for enrollees with chronic medical diagnoses. For example, medical costs for this group increased by 17% and did not differ reliably from the 27% increase from enrollees in the baseline group who never used mental health treatment.

In contrast, medical costs declined in the managed care groups (TFMHT, BOTH) relative to the baseline group of enrollees who never used mental health treatment (p < 0.0001) and relative to enrollees who used traditional mental health treatment (p < 0.001). Relative to baseline, these represented 47% and 28% declines in medical costs for the managed mental health treatment groups, respectively.

> *Traditional mental health treatment had little effect on medical costs for enrollees with chronic medical diagnoses.*

Medical Cost Change for Enrollees without Chronic Medical Diagnoses

Medical costs for patients who used traditional mental health treatment declined by about 24%, although not reliably different from the 4% decline in the NoMHT baseline (t < 1.00).

In contrast, medical costs in the managed mental health groups (TFMHT, BOTH) declined by 27% and 44%, respectively, and were reliably different from the baseline provided by patients who never used mental health treatment as in NoMHT (p < 0.05).

When pooled together, the three mental health treatment groups declined in medical costs relative to the baseline provided by enrollees who ever used treatment. However, those who used traditional mental health treatment had about three times as many outpatient mental health visits as did the managed treatment group.[8,14]

The medical cost trends were clearly different between enrollees with or without the four chronic medical diagnoses. Enrollees with these diagnoses had sharp continuing increases in medical costs in contrast to enrollees without these diagnoses who declined in cost.

Traditional mental health services (as in the OMHT group) had little impact on the rising cost trend for enrollees with these diagnoses—and costs increased at about the same rate as NoMHT patients.

In contrast, those enrollees who received managed mental health treatment (as in the TFMHT and BOTH groups) declined relative to the NoMHT baseline and relative to patients who used traditional mental health services.

Trends in Medical Services Utilization

Medical services utilization was examined in order to have a fuller picture, especially regarding inpatient and outpatient utilization trends. These results are summarized in Tables 11.2 to 11.6 and generally followed the trends obtained for medical costs, as one would expect.

In general, for each category of utilization, enrollees who used mental health services had higher levels of medical services utilization. Similarly, those enrollees with chronic medical diagnoses had utilization levels about twice as high as for enrollees without these diagnoses. Detailed analyses of differences in initial utilization levels are not presented here.

Medicaid Enrollees with Chronic Medical Diagnoses

Medicaid enrollees who used managed mental health services (as in the TFMHT and BOTH groups) declined in hospital days (Table 11.2) and emergency department visits (Table 11.3) relative to patients who never used mental health services

Table 11.2 Number of Hospital Days and Change in Hospital Days 12 Months Pre- and Post-MHT for CMD and NONCMD Patients

	N	Days pre-MHT	Days post-MHT	Change in days	Percent change in days
CMD patients					
NoMHT	4,307	0.84	0.92	+0.08	+9.8%
OMHT	169	1.79	1.59	−0.20	−11.0%
TFMHT	227	2.92	1.87	−1.05	−36.0%
BOTH'	209	4.37	4.04	−0.33	−7.5%
Non-CMD patients					
NoMHT	6,837	0.36	0.28	−0.08	−23.0%
OMHT	199	1.46	0.76	−0.70	−48.0%
TFMHT	136	1.02	0.39	−0.63	−61.0%
BOTH	91	1.68	0.52	−1.16	−69.0%

Source: Adapted from Cummings, N. A., et al. *The Impact of Psychological Services on Medical Utilization.* HCFA Contract No. 11-C-98344/9. Baltimore, MD: Health Care Financing Administration, 1992.

(p < 0.01) and relative to enrollees who used traditional mental health services (p < 0.01).

Enrollees who used traditional mental health services increased in physician office visits (Table 11.4) and in the number of controlled drug prescriptions (Table 11.5) relative to enrollees who never used mental health services (p < 0.001) and relative to enrollees who used managed mental health services. In contrast, managed mental health patients declined in physician office visits (p < 0.001) and in controlled drug prescriptions either absolutely or relative to enrollees who never used mental health services and relative to enrollees who used traditional mental health services (p < 0.02).

Table 11.3 Number of Emergency Department Visits and Change in Number 12 Months Pre- and Post-MHT for CMD and NONCMD Patients

	N	Pre-MHT	Post-MHT	Change	Percent change
CMD patients					
NoMHT	4,307	0.31	0.31	0.00	0.0%
OMHT	169	0.55	0.62	+0.07	+13.0%
TFMHT	227	0.89	0.67	−0.22	−24.0%
BOTH	209	1.25	1.10	−0.15	−13.0%
Non-CMD patients					
NoMHT	6,837	0.17	0.18	+0.01	+7.0%
OMHT	199	0.32	0.36	+0.04	+14.0%
TFMHT	136	0.20	0.25	+0.05	+25.0%
BOTH	91	0.72	0.45	−0.27	−38.0%

Source: Adapted from Cummings, N. A., et al. *The Impact of Psychological Services on Medical Utilization.* HCFA Contract No. 11-C-98344/9. Baltimore, MD: Health Care Financing Administration, 1992.

Table 11.4 Number of Physician Office Visits and Change in Number 12 Months Pre- and Post-MHT for CMD and NONCMD Patients

	N	Pre-MHT	Post-MHT	Change	Percent change
CMD patients					
NoMHT	4,307	7.58	6.92	−0.66	−8.6%
OMHT	169	8.89	11.34	+255	+27.0%
TFMHT	227	13.49	12.59	−0.90	−6.7%
BOTH	209	17.90	16.77	−1.13	−6.3%
Non-CMD patients					
NoMHT	6,837	4.22	3.84	−0.38	−9.0%
OMHT	199	5.29	5.68	+0.39	+7.4%
TFMHT	136	5.96	5.64	−0.32	−5.4%
BOTH	91	7.62	7.17	−0.45	−5.9%

Source: Adapted from Cummings, N. A. et al. *The Impact of Psychological Services on Medical Utilization.* HCFA Contract No. 11-C-98344/9. Baltimore, MD: Health Care Financing Administration, 1992.

Table 11.5 Number of Controlled Drug Prescriptions and Change in Number 12 Months Pre- and Post-MHT for CMD and NONCMD Patients

	N	Pre-MHT	Post-MHT	Change	Percent change
CMD patients					
NoMHT	4,307	2.03	2.25	+0.22	+11.0%
OMHT	169	2.93	4.79	+1.86	+64.0%
TFMHT	227	5.18	4.95	−0.23	−4.5%
BOTH	209	11.01	11.86	+0.85	+7.7%
Non-CMD patients					
NoMHT	6,837	0.66	0.76	+0.10	+15.3%
OMHT	199	1.91	3.14	+1.23	+65.0%
TFMHT	136	1.63	1.41	−0.22	−13.5%
BOTH	91	4.75	5.33	+0.57	+12.0%

Source: Adapted from Cummings, N. A., et al. *The Impact of Psychological Services on Medical Utilization.* HCFA Contract No. 11-C-98344/9. Baltimore, MD: Health Care Financing Administration, 1992.

Table 11.6 Number of Diagnostic (Lab and X-Ray) Procedures and Change in Number 12 Months Pre- and Post-MHT for CMD and NONCMD Patients

	N	Pre-MHT	Post-MHT	Change	Percent change
CMD patients					
NoMHT	4,307	3.71	4.22	+0.51	+13.7%
OMHT	169	6.16	8.14	+1.98	+32.1%
TFMHT	227	9.02	8.81	−0.21	−2.3%
BOTH	209	10.38	11.86	+0.90	+8.7%
Non-CMD patients					
NoMHT	6,837	1.96	2.24	+0.28	+14.3%
OMHT	199	3.27	3.50	+0.23	+7.0%
TFMHT	136	3.89	4.14	−0.25	−6.4%
BOTH	91	4.30	4.96	+0.66	+15.3%

Source: Adapted from Cummings, N. A., et al. *The Impact of Psychological Services on Medical Utilization.* HCFA Contract No. 11-C-98344/9. Baltimore, MD: Health Care Financing Administration, 1992.

Finally, managed mental health patients also declined in the number of diagnostic procedures (Table 11.6) relative to enrollees who did not use mental services or used other traditional mental health services ($p < 0.05$).

Medicaid Enrollees without Chronic Medical Diagnoses

From Table 11.2, enrollees who used traditional mental health services declined in the number of hospital days relative to enrollees who did not use mental health services ($p < 0.08$). The managed mental health groups declined by 61% and 65%, respectively, reliably different from the baseline provided by those who never used mental health services ($p < 0.02$).

From Table 11.3, there were no differences for change in emergency room visits among the groups of enrollees who did not use mental health services, used other mental health services, or used managed services. However, those who used both types of mental health services declined by 38% in the number of emergency department visits—reliably different from the baseline ($p < 0.001$).

For physician office visits (Table 11.4), enrollees who used traditional mental health services increased relative to the baseline provided by enrollees who never used mental health treatment ($p < 0.08$), while the managed mental health groups did not increase relative to the baseline. Enrollees who used traditional mental health services had sharp increases in the number of controlled drug prescriptions (Table 11.5) relative to enrollees who never used mental health services and relative to those who used managed mental health services ($p < 0.01$). There were no reliable differences among groups for change in diagnostic procedures (Table 11.6).

Discussion

These results have several implications for healthcare policy, as well as for public programs such as Medicaid, in terms of the potential role for mental health services. On one hand, it seems clear that managed mental health treatment was associated with declines in medical costs. In addition, analyses presented elsewhere[8,14,15] indicated that the costs of managed treatment were recovered in 5 to 6 months in terms of reduced medical costs. For the BOTH subgroup, with its higher medical utilization rate, treatment costs were recovered in about 21 months. Clearly, managed mental health treatment holds potential as a clinically effective and cost-effective tool by which to address healthcare costs.

On the other hand, these results provided a clearer picture of the effect of more traditional mental health treatment (OMHT) on medical costs in Medicaid. Previous analyses, aggregated over patients with and without the four chronic medical diagnoses, indicated little effect on medical costs for traditional treatment and hence little cost-effectiveness.[14] The present results were disaggregated by whether enrollees had one or more of the four chronic medical diagnoses, and indicated, at least for patients without these chronic medical diagnoses, that costs of traditional treatment would have been recovered in about 2 years. OMHT patients used 12.2 MHT visits at a cost of $48 per visit for a total cost of $586. OMHT generated medical cost reduction of $280 per year and would have resulted in cost recovery in 2.1 years (about 25 months).

Managed MHT has substantial potential for medical cost reduction for patients with one of the chronic medical diagnoses tracked in this study. We noted earlier that these patients accounted for the overall increase in annual medical costs and represented about 40% of the Medicaid population. Thus, providing managed mental health treatment directed toward these patients and their emotional distress resulted in stable declines in both inpatient and outpatient medical services and costs.

• • •

Medicaid enrollees with one of the chronic diagnoses were consistently higher utilizers of medical services in the absence of managed mental health treatment. It seems clear that programs to identify and provide early managed interventions would have value in ameliorating emotional distress that drives medical utilization. Patients with these chronic diagnoses had medical problems that continued and these patients remained higher utilizers. However, it seems evident that the emotional distress involved can be cost-effectively addressed with reliable reductions in medical services costs and utilization.

References Notes

1 Follette, W. T., & Cummings, N. A. (1967). Psychiatric services and medical utilization in a prepaid health plan setting. *Medical Care, 5*, 25–35.
2 Cummings, N. A., & Follette, W. T. (1968). Psychiatric services and medical utilization in a prepaid health plan setting: Part II. *Medical Care, 6*, 31–41.
3 Jones, K., & Vischi, T. (1979). The impact of alcohol, drug abuse, and mental health treatment on medical care utilization: A review of the research literature. *Medical Care, 17*(12, Suppl.), 43–141.
4 Mumford, E., Schlesinger H. J., Glass, G. V., Patrick, C., & Cuerdon, T. (1984). A new look at evidence about reduced cost of medical utilization following mental health treatment. *American Journal of Psychiatry, 141,* 1145–1158.
5 Holder, H. D., & Blose, J. O. (1987). Mental health treatment and the reduction of healthcare costs: a four-year study of U.S. federal employees enrollment with the Aetna Life Insurance Company. In R. M. Scheffler & L. F. Rossiter (Eds.), *Advances in health economics and health services research* (Vol. 8) (pp. 102–116). Greenwich, CT: JAI Press.
6 Pallak, M. S. (1989). *Managed mental health and medical cost-offset in a Medicaid population.* Address given at the Behavioral Healthcare Tomorrow Conference, Crystal City, VA.
7 Pallak, M. S., & Cummings, N. A. (1994). Outcomes research in managed mental healthcare: Issues, strategies, and trends. In S. A. Shueman, S. L. Mayhugh, & B. S. Gould (Eds.), *Managed behavioral healthcare: A search for precision* (pp. 205–221). Springfield, IL: Charles C. Thomas.
8 Pallak, M. S., Cummings, N. A., Dörken, H., & Henke, C. J. (1992). *The impact of psychological services on medical utilization* (HCFA Contract No. 11-C-98344/9 report). Baltimore, MD: Health Care Financing Administration. 59, 27–40.
9 Smith, R. G. (1991). *Somaticization disorder in the medical setting.* Washington, DC: American Psychiatric Press.
10 Schlesinger, H. S., Mumford, E., Glass, G., Patrick, C., & Sharfstein, S. (1983). Mental health treatment and medical care utilization in a fee-for-service system: Outpatient mental health treatment following the onset of a chronic disease. *American Journal of Public Health, 73*), 422–429.
11 Freund, D. A., & Neuschler, E. (1986). Overview of Medicaid capitation and case-management initiatives. *Health Care Financing Review, Annual Supplement,* 21–30.
12 Wilensky, G. R., & Rossiter, L. F. (1991). Coordinated care and public programs. *Health Affairs, 10*(4), 62–67.
13 Fiedler, J. L., & Wight, R. B. (1989). *The medical offset effect and public health policy.* New York: Praeger.

14 Pallak, M. S., Cummings, N. A., Dörken, H., & Henke, C. J. (1993, Fall). Managed mental healthcare, Medicaid and medical cost-offset: The impact of psychological services in the Hawaii Medicaid Project. In N. A. Cummings & M. S. Pallak (Eds.), *Medicaid, managed behavioral health and implications for public policy* (pp. 27–40). South San Francisco, CA: Foundation for Behavioral Health.

15 Pallak, M. S., & Cummings, N. A. (1994). Managed mental healthcare, Medicaid and medical cost-offset: In S. Feldman & W. Goldman (Eds.), *New directions in mental health services: Managed mental healthcare* (pp. 76–97). Springfield, IL: Charles C. Thomas.

16 Pallak, M. S., Sibulkin, A. E., & Kiesler, C. A. (1993). Managed mental healthcare, Medicaid and medical cost-offset. *Behavioral Healthcare Tomorrow, 2,* 76–97.

17 Oss, M. (1991). Arguments for the financial efficacy of psychological services in healthcare settings. In J. J. Sweet, Ronald H. Rozensky, & Steven M. Tovian (Eds.), *Handbook of clinical psychology in medical settings* (pp. 66–72). New York: Plenum.

18 Cummings, N. A. (1991). Brief, intermittent therapy throughout the life cycle. In C. Austad & W. H. Berman (Eds.), *Psychotherapy in HMOs: The practice of mental health in managed care* (pp. 35–45). Washington, DC: American Psychological Association.

12 Universal Healthcare

Readings for Mental Health Professionals

Nicholas A. Cummings

> If all economists were laid end to end, they still wouldn't read a conclusion.
> George Bernard Shaw

As we are reminded of George Bernard Shaw's statement from more than a century ago, this can be said doubly for healthcare economists. And if healthcare has bedeviled economists for decades, mental healthcare is so baffling that economists try to avoid it entirely. Seldom is mental healthcare mentioned in texts addressing healthcare in general, and even the Institute of Medicine (IOM) (2001) in its landmark report, *Crossing the Quality Chasm: A New Health System for the 21st Century,* totally sidestepped the subject The absence of mental healthcare would suggest either that mental healthcare is not important, or that the IOM had left a gaping hole in its otherwise comprehensive study of our health system. This article will address a number of policies and events that have either promoted or inhibited the effective delivery of mental healthcare services, will also discuss the difficulty of interpreting and applying mental healthcare data, and finally will touch on the political and economic debate that surrounds the financing of healthcare, particularly mental healthcare.

The author's style in this article is somewhat reminiscent of the story of two rams standing on the edge of a cliff and looking down at a flock of ewes grazing in the valley below. The younger ram suggested they run down and get a couple. The older and much wiser ram interjected that they should walk down and get them all. This author claims no particular wisdom, but rather would walk us through the too many issues confronting the mental healthcare delivery system in which he has been an activist participant for well over half a century. Since in mental healthcare delivery there are no straight lines from here to there, I apologize in advance for meandering, and also for proffering no easy solutions. Henry L. Menken is reputed to have said, and this author agrees, "For every complex issue there is a simple solution that is wrong" (Kennedy, 2004).

The Importance of Presidential Mental Health Commissions

As of this writing, President Bush's New Freedom Commission on Mental Health has rendered its final report (Hogan, 2003), stating that mental and emotional conditions are more prevalent than previously believed, and stressing the importance of access and even national screening to facilitate early detection and treatment. Many Americans believe that presidential mental health commissions are routine, like the ubiquitous energy commissions appointed by every president since Franklin D. Roosevelt. There have been only three presidential mental health commissions in our nation's history, and all in the past half century, and although it is too early to tell the outcome of President Bush's Commission, the first two resulted in great gains in the delivery of mental healthcare services. The first such by President Kennedy (1961–1963) was not officially a commission, but a task force he brought together to design what later became our community mental health centers. Because of my early work in prepaid healthcare at Kaiser Permanente, I was invited and privileged to participate. As President Kennedy was assassinated before he could see his innovative ideas come to fruition, the Community Mental Health Centers Act was eventually signed by his successor, President Johnson. This gave a tremendous boost to behavioral care, spreading these services across the land as it put psychologists and social workers in rural areas in significant numbers for the first time.

The second presidential mental health commission, and the first one bearing that title, was appointed by President Carter (1977–1980). Without giving herself the title of chair, the First Lady enthusiastically led this commission, participated in its meetings, and energized its members. She insisted that all facets of mental healthcare had to be addressed, and divided the members into a series of panels. Again I was privileged to serve, this time on the panel grappling with the costs and financing of mental healthcare. Mrs. Carter took particular interest in our group, stating that unless the problems of costs and financing were resolved, not much else would happen. We rendered our commission report just 2 months before President Carter lost his reelection bid, abruptly ending the influence of this commission. But our work did result in the Mental Health Act of 1980, which mandated a minimum of 20 psychotherapy sessions in health maintenance organizations, and made psychotherapy and counseling integral parts of all health insurance.

The fact that there have been only three presidential commissions does not necessarily suggest that mental health is a low priority in our nation, although at times it would seem so. Healthcare is considered a top priority in Washington, but other than the ill-fated Rodham Clinton Health Care Task Force (1993–1994), there has never been a presidential healthcare commission. This is because healthcare is mired in politics, and addressing it is regarded as political suicide. The demise of Mrs. Clinton's efforts has only underscored that belief, and presidents have restricted their efforts to high-sounding campaign speeches and state of the union addresses, all falling far short of implementation. Nonetheless, significant healthcare legislation has emerged, such as the Hill Burton Hospital Construction Act of the late 1950s, Medicare and Medicaid in 1965, the HMO enabling act of 1975, and recently President Bush's bipartisan drug benefit for seniors.

Several Stupid Stories: Lessons to Be Learned

The railroad industry was America's 19th-century success story, only to become a 20th-century failure. Within an amazingly short time, its steel rails had spanned the nation, and seemingly shrunk the continent as it made travel and shipment of goods rapid and affordable for the first time. By the middle of the 20th century, however, the once prosperous railroads began a precipitous decline into bankruptcy and had to be rescued by the federal government. Along had come air travel, air cargo, and trucking, all affordable and far more rapid than the cumbersome railroads. The railroads had made an irreversible mistake; believing they were in the "railroad business" rather than in the "transportation business," they missed the opportunity to own and operate the transportation systems that superseded them. Scrambling to survive, they finally began looking at technologies available to them, and later in the 20th century they developed container cargo and piggyback shipping (loading and unloading large containers directly on ships or trucks, respectively), but it was too late. They lost their primacy forever. But through these technologies the railroads have learned how to survive. Fifty years ago, 2 million Americans worked for the railroads. Thanks to new freight technology, the railroads now ship twice as much cargo and with only 150,000 employees.

Another 19th-century miracle was the telegraph that had made instant communication to all parts of the nation possible for the first time. Rivaling the railroad companies for stupidity, the telegraph companies decided they were in the telegraph business, when in reality they were in the communication business. Seeing that the telegraph wires already spanning the continent could be easily modified to accommodate the telephone, Alexander Graham Bell attempted to sell his invention to the telegraph companies. The response was an emphatic rejection, in essence saying it was in the telegraph business, and saw no future in the telephone. Where once it could have owned the telephone, Western Union is now an archaic little company through which one can wire money to a distant recipient.

Our stupid stories continue into the 20th century. The giant IBM did not comprehend that it was in the information business, not the mainframe business. This decision resulted in the myopic declaration that Americans would never want an electronic machine in their homes. Along came Steve Jobs and Michael Dell, the personal computer was soon an affordable reality, and the information age was in full swing as the PC became almost as common in every home as a television set. Down plunged IBM's stock. Similarly, Xerox pioneered efficient dry copiers and was inordinately successful for decades as it essentially had the copier market to itself—not realizing it, too, was in the information business and not just the copier business. Other companies like Ricoh, Sharp, and Kyocera transformed the simple copier into a computer, a scanner, a fax, and a host of other functions that reflected they knew they were in the information business. Xerox adapted too late and is now lagging in the industry.

Sadly, we in mental healthcare are replicating this lack of foresight and understanding by insisting that we are in the mental health business, when in reality, we are a part of the healthcare industry. Primary care physicians (PCPs) know that the mind and the body are not separate entities, and they are providing 80% of the mental health services right in the primary care setting, including psychological advice, counseling, and the dispensing of antidepressants and other psychotropic medications (Cummings et al., 2001). Sadly compounding this stupidity, psychologists and social workers see themselves narrowly as in the psychotherapy and counseling business, while psychiatrists regard themselves as in the mental health medication and hospitalization business.

Parity Legislation: Separate and Unequal

One of the nation's most successful legislative efforts has been the drive for parity. Mandating equal expenditures with physical healthcare for mental healthcare, parity laws have been enacted in 34 states and the federal government, a remarkable achievement were it not for the fact that less money is being spent on mental healthcare today than before the parity laws (Carnahan, 2002). The managed care companies and the health insurance industry, fearing runaway costs for mental healthcare, put in place more draconian requirements to qualify for mental healthcare than for physical care. Yet the political battle to renew the federal parity law and to enact such laws in the remaining 16 states that do not have them continues with vigor. In the end it merely makes mental healthcare advocates appear successful and to justify contributions from rank-and-file practitioners frightened by their dwindling practices.

Unfortunately, the drive for parity merely perpetuates the separation of mental health from physical health. Separate but equal did not work in education before the civil rights movement inasmuch as white schools were more "equal" than black schools. The idea that mental healthcare is entitled to one half of the nation's $1.4 trillion budget, especially when the physical healthcare system is providing 80% of the mental healthcare, rounds out our list of stupid stories. It will be only after mental health is an integral part of healthcare and is funded as part of healthcare that it will be appropriately funded.

Access and Stigma May Largely Be Self-Created Artifacts

As long as we maintain two separate silos, one labeled healthcare and the other mental healthcare, we are inadvertently restricting access. As stated, 80% of mental healthcare is dispensed by PCPs, while only 10% of those referred to the separate mental health system ever cross the chasm of stigma, resistance, and access by actually seeing a behavioral health specialist. PCPs are in the trenches with the patient, and behavioral care providers (BCPs) should be there in the primary care setting with them. Research in systems where BCPs are co-located with PCPs reveals that 85% to 90% of patients identified as needing psychological services will accept that help because the PCP can merely walk the patient the short distance down the hall to the office of the immediately available BCP (Strosahl, 2001). Called the "hallway handoff" in settings where primary care and behavioral healthcare services are integrated, the patient is receiving mental health services where she or he expects to receive them: in the healthcare system, not a separate system in another location called "mental health," that has all sorts of resistances and stigmas attached to it.

The experience at Walter Reed Army Medical Center, one of our nation's healthcare showcases where presidents have received care, is illuminating. According to one report (James, 2004), the earlier problems until recently replicated those investigated and later corrected at Tripler Army Medical Center. In 1997, the following deficiencies were extant at Tripler: (1) psychiatry and psychology were away from the mainstream of the hospital, resulting (2) in a 50% to 60% no show rate attributed (3) to a stigma associated with going to the mental health part of the building. (4) Consultations were frequently lost or misplaced and (5) mental health staff members were not showing up for their assigned duty to see walk-in emergencies. (6) Psychiatrists were simply inefficient and ineffective managers, and (7) it took anywhere from 3 to 8 weeks for a patient to be seen for medication evaluation. A plan was implemented that placed the mental health outpatient clinic in the middle of the family practice department (i.e., primary care setting), and the seven deficiencies were largely overcome. In 2003, the same plan became an initiative at the Walter Reed Army Medical Center where most, if not all of the seven deficiencies found at Tripler, were manifest (James, 2004). The lesson to be learned, as one researcher put it, is that even across the street is too far away.

Since the problems of access and stigma seem to essentially evaporate in the integrated behavioral health/primary care setting, the following finding should not be surprising. In American Psychological Association (APA)–conducted focused groups, stigma was seen as a distant second in a list of impediments to seeking psychotherapy. Rather, the participants identified "it doesn't work" as by far the number one reason they would not undergo psychotherapy (Saunders, 2003). These embarrassing results were not widely disseminated; rather the APA later authorized a more structured, limited item poll, leaving out the choice that psychotherapy may not be effective as a reason for not seeking it. Responding to the available choices in this national poll, cost and lack of insurance coverage were the main barriers, while stigma continued to be less important in seeking treatment (Association for the Advancement of Psychology, 2004). Confirming the APA findings, the National Association of Addiction Treatment Providers (NAATP) found that 41.2% of those not seeking addiction treatment in 2003 stated they were not ready to give up their using, 32.2% pointed to cost or insurance barrier, while only 17.2% feared a stigma (NAATP, 2004).

As long as separate systems of healthcare and mental healthcare exist, stigma will continue to be a ready excuse for low utilization of mental healthcare services. In a recent review (Corrigan, 2004), stigma is well conceptualized and its effects on the individual are convincingly presented. Less convincing is the argument presented that stigma is the primary reason persons needing services do not seek them, or persons receiving services fail to adhere to the psychiatric regimen. Even President Bush's New Freedom Commission advocates anti-stigma programs as a way of improving the mental health system (Hogan, 2003). Whether, as some findings suggest, stigma is less significant than practitioners believe, or whether this stigma disappears when a patient feels a part of the *health* as opposed to the mental health system, making behavioral care an integral part of primary care would be an effective way of addressing these barriers.

Encouraging is that many authorities within the APA, which usually lags behind in delivery innovation, see the future role of the psychologist heavily in primary care and working closely with primary care physicians (Kerstine, 2004). Important, the 2005 APA president has made the integration of psychology in primary care a major thrust of his administration (Levant, 2004).

The Evolution of Technology and Personnel in Mental Healthcare

Mental healthcare seems painfully static at times, yet a historical perspective reveals a series of relatively frequent and often massive changes so that various periods within the past century are hardly recognizable today. In retrospect, some of these changes even constitute upheavals that resulted in the disaffection of large cadres of practitioners and their ideologies. A chronology of the more significant waves is summarized in Table 12.1, with dates given representing modal approximations of events that developed not discretely, but over a number of years.

Table 12.1 Practitioners and Their Technologies. The significant waves in mental health beginning with the 19th century through the early 21st century, with approximate dates, personnel, and technologies that characterized each successive period.

	Personnel:	*Technology:*
1850–1920	Psychiatrists	Descriptive psychiatry
1920–1980	Psychoanalysts (MD and lay)	Psychoanalytic methodologies
1948–1950	Post–WW II training stipends	V. A. and the new NIMH
1950	Psychologists	Migration to private practice
1965	All personnel	Community MH Centers Act
1975	Psychiatrists	Remedicalization begins
1960	Psychologists/social workers	Family therapy movement begins
1965	Psychiatry	Medicare enacted; psychiatrist only
1970	All personnel	Insurance coverage gains momentum
1975	Social workers	Migration to private practice
1978	Psychologists	Licensed in all 50 states
1979	Psychiatric nurse practitioners	Rapid emergence with Rx authority
1980	All personnel	Mental Health Act of 1981 (Carter)
1980	Psychologists/social workers	Brief therapy movement begins
1980	Psychologists	Cognitive revolution begins
1985	All practitioners	Managed behavioral healthcare begins
1990	Psychoanalytic therapists	Psychoanalysis begins rapid decline
1990	Psychologists/social workers	Family therapy loses prominence
1990	M.A.-level counselors	Migration to private practice
1995	Psychologists/social workers	Cognitive revolution is complete
1995	Psychologists	Included in Medicare
2000	All practitioners	Managed behavioral care 175 M lives
2000	Psychiatrists	Biomedical revolution is complete
2000	Psychoanalytic therapists	Psychoanalysis loses prominence
2003	All personnel	Bush MH Commission report complete
2003	All personnel	Momentum for primary/behavioral care
2004	Psychologists	Prescription authority in NM and LA

Descriptive Psychiatry

In the 19th century and immediately thereafter, psychiatry was essentially descriptive, addressing mostly the severely mentally ill for whom mandated institutionalization and physical restraint were the primary treatments. It also saw discoveries, such as hypnosis, and it was absorbed by a number of oddities with which it tantalized its few adherents, such as multiple personalities, astasia abasia, sleepwalking, and automatic writing, to name only a few. Psychology was in its earliest phase, establishing primitive laboratories and conducting basic experiments on illusions, psychological aspects of the five senses, and the beginnings of learning theory. While the American Psychiatric Association (APA) was founded in 1850, the American Psychological Association did not come into being until 1892. Through its first president, G. Stanley Hall, psychology began a scientific look at education, while an initial interest in philosophy and religion was defined by its third president, William James, also known as the father of American psychology. Soon this interest in education and spirituality were superseded by the German psychophysicists, and the laboratory that sought to emulate the physical sciences characterized the majority of psychology for decades. Psychotherapy as we know it today simply did not exist.

Freudian Preeminence

Psychotherapy as we know it today is an outgrowth of the Freudian tradition, which after establishing a foothold in Europe, began to spread to the United States following the increased travel and communication that characterized the post–World War I era. This interest spiked incredibly following World War II, and the degree to which Americans espoused psychoanalysis was reflected in movies, literature, music, and the news media, as well as by a seemingly insatiable demand for services. Psychoanalytic institutes proliferated, but Freudian therapy was not limited to those who traversed the long, arduous years of psychoanalytic training because the preponderance of psychiatrists, psychologists, and social workers was conducting psychoanalytically oriented psychotherapy without such training. There were offshoots, with leaders such as Carl Jung, Alfred Adler, Melanie Klein, and a number of others, and, as time went on, with the Neo-Freudians (e.g., Harry Stack Sullivan, Frieda Fromm Reichman) psychoanalysis became more interpersonal and ego oriented. Nonetheless, all of these offshoots were rooted in the principle of unconscious determinism, with the personality shaped by experiences in infancy and early childhood.

Psychoanalytic thought dominated treatment for most of a half century, and its rapid ascendancy was rivaled only by the swiftness of its demise. Criticized for its lack of a scientific foundation, and plagued by the interminable nature of psychoanalytic therapies, the death knell came when managed behavioral care organizations stopped paying for psychoanalytic treatment. Psychoanalytic institutes shrank and even disappeared, and even the famed psychoanalytically oriented Menninger Clinic closed its doors in the late 1990s. By the dawning of the 21st century, psychoanalysis was not only in decline, but also in disrepute.

The Cognitive Revolution

The beginning of the 21st century marks the era of the cognitive revolution, with cognitive behavioral interventions supplanting psychoanalysis. Behaviorism, which rejects the Freudian concept of unconscious determinism, has always been congenial to the academic setting, so it has been around for at least 75 years. The original radical behaviorism, which even rejects cognition, dominated the early clinical psychology training programs, but it produced mostly academicians, with an almost indiscernible number of clinicians practicing outside university and government settings. The rising tide of cognitive behaviorism had overwhelmed radical behaviorism by the mid-1980s and is producing most of the currently minted psychological practitioners. It received unexpected impetus in the new thrust for scientifically validated therapies inasmuch as it is much more amenable to quantification than were the older interpersonal and psychoanalytic therapies, and it has the advantage of being university based where most of the psychology training is taking place. In its zeal to overthrow interpersonal therapies, however, it threw out the baby with the bathwater, resulting in a sterile and often inflexible treatment approach that neglects individual differences in its one-size-fits-all templates. For example, cognitive behavioral interventions for depression will receive a differing response depending on whether the depressed patient is an alcoholic, a borderline personality, bereaving, or simply a neurotic. Additionally, cognitive behavior therapy (CBT) has been less able to address the many negative behaviors and therapeutic resistance of Axis II patients.

A Possible Rapprochement May Be Emerging

Thomas Kuhn (1996) has documented that scientists seldom if ever embrace new theories, and retire still believing in what was current in their heyday. Mental health practitioners more than replicate this pattern, perpetuating psycho-religions, often fiercely. Psychotherapy progresses as the high priests of the psycho-religions die or retire. Presently, however, there may be occurring a surprising melding of CBT and interpersonal psychotherapies. It all began as innovators in behaviorism began dressing up interpersonal interventions in behavioral and cognitive nomenclature and injecting them into CBT and even into radical behaviorism. Such thrusts as Acceptance and Commitment Therapy are slipping through the back door effective interventions that have been extant in psychoanalysis for decades, and were taken to new effectiveness by gestalt, Ericksonian, systems, solution-focused, and other brief therapies, and they are being heralded as brilliant innovations by the historically challenged behaviorists.

Beginning in the early 2000s, this rapprochement has become more open, with articles boldly championing the utility of combining analytic and behavioral therapies (Callaghan et al., 2004). And if wonders will never cease, the usually behaviorist-derided "chairwork" (i.e., the gestalt intervention of having the patient talk to an empty chair) has suddenly been discovered to be a form of cognitive restructuring (Kellogg, 2004). If as may be happening, two psycho-religions actually merge and evolve to a greater effectiveness, it will be the first time in the history of psychotherapy.

The Biomedical Revolution

Overlapping the cognitive revolution, and ascending to equal if not even greater importance, is the biomedical revolution, which substitutes medication for counseling. In the 1970s, the psychiatric profession began what it called its "remedicalization," a gradual process of abandoning psychotherapy in favor of medication. In the ensuing years, psychiatric residencies deemphasized and even discontinued psychotherapy training, while psychology became the preeminent psychotherapy profession, with social workers doing most of the actual therapy.

Several factors gave impetus to the biomedical revolution, principal among them being the discovery of more effective antidepressants and other psychotropic medications. HMOs and other managed behavioral care organizations saw these newer medical treatments to be cheaper and more manageable than behavioral interventions. The pharmacology industry began direct advertising to consumers, and patients, having seen the promotions on television, began requesting and even demanding medications. Soon depression became the common cold of psychiatry, with patients demanding antidepressants for normal mood fluctuations just as decades ago patients began demanding antibiotics for the common cold. The medical profession and the psychiatric profession in particular encouraged this by redefining most, if not all behavioral difficulties to be of genetic or biological origin. Primary care physicians, having been unsuccessful in getting patients to accept psychological referrals, took advantage of the new medications and began prescribing them in lieu of arguing with reluctant patients who might otherwise benefit from psychotherapy (Cummings, 2005b). A startling example in the decline of referrals for psychotherapy is demonstrated in the current paucity of post-psychiatric hospitalization referrals. In 1990, almost 95% of discharged patients were referred for outpatient psychotherapy, but by 2000, the figure had declined to only 10% (Carnahan, 2002).

The National Institutes of Mental Health (NIMH) are rapidly moving toward biomedicine, with increasingly more funds allocated for biomedical than behavioral research. The largest mental health pressure group, the National Association for the Mentally Ill (NAMI), representing mostly relieved family members of mentally ill patients who are better managed on the new medications, strongly support the expansion of biomedicine in mental health.

EBTs and the End of Name-Dropping

The beginning of the 21st century is characterized by the movement toward evidence-based treatments (EBTs), creating a schism between academic/science-based psychologists and those in full-time practice who insist clinical experience is as important as research evidence. The lines are being drawn, and although the battle will continue for some time, the psychological "name-dropping" that has been used as authority has rapidly faded. It was typical during the entire 20th century to quote a psychotherapist of stature (e.g., Freud, Jung, Erickson, Perls) as evidence, rather than to cite research. That practice is losing credibility rapidly, and with it is fading authoritative leadership, defined as psychotherapy movements centered about individuals, or what this author has termed "psycho-religions."

Economic Factors

Although the transitions described earlier occurred over time, they eventuated in upheavals that saw the disappearance of descriptive psychiatry, then the fading of psychoanalysis as it gave way to the cognitive revolution, and finally the displacement of much cognitive therapy by the biomedical revolution. All of these resulted in severe economic hardship to the technologies that were successively disaffected, especially since each revolution looks back disdainfully on its immediate predecessor. At the present time there are two major competing technologies, cognitive behaviorism and biomedicine (i.e., dispensing psychotropic medications), each so critical of the other that they appear to be ideologies, or even "psycho-religions." A minority of cooler heads is paying attention to the research that points to one or the other as more effective with certain conditions, while still other conditions are best treated by a combination of behavioral counseling and medication (Antonuccio et al., 1999).

It is the position of this article that the patient is best served by the coexistence of cognitive behavioral interventions and psychotropic drugs. Two things need to happen. First, cognitive therapy must continue its modification to incorporate useful technologies (e.g., the defense mechanisms, techniques for overcoming resistance, basic pathology) that were thrown out in haste in the cognitive revolution. In turn, biomedicine must recognize its limitations that it now attempts to overcome by adding more and more medications (called a med cocktail) when previous medications do not work. It must also cease its scorn of "talk therapy" and accept that many conditions are not medical, but behavioral. Both have to recognize that the mind and the body are not separate, and behavioral/primary care is the wave of the future.

While the battle continues, third-party payers are discovering that the new psychotropic medications are expensive and in perpetuity, while counseling can often achieve therapeutic goals with less total expenditure and in a fraction of the time. When psychotropic medications do not work, psychiatrists are prone to keep adding more medications, calling this a therapeutic cocktail for which chemical restraint, not therapy, is more often the end result. Interesting, in spite of a growing backlash, psychologists accelerated their effort to attain prescription authority, and by 2004 had succeeded in two states, New Mexico and Louisiana. This early success will undoubtedly gain momentum, and it remains to be seen whether future psychologists will retain their identity as behavioral therapists, or succumb to the expediency of the prescription pad.

The Brief Psychotherapy Movement and the Role of Third-Party Reimbursement

Superimposed upon all the foregoing treatment waves, and beginning post World War II, has been the brief psychotherapy movement that economic realities forced upon an uncongenial mental health establishment. A firestorm erupted when Alexander and French (1946) published their blueprint for brief psycho-analytically oriented psychotherapy, even though their definition of brief was in excess of 150 sessions. Extensive research at Kaiser Permanente, the nation's first HMO, revealed that most patients received maximum benefit from brief psychotherapy, and less than 20% of patients required long-term psychotherapy (Follette & Cummings, 1967; Cummings & Follette, 1968; Cummings & Van-denBos, 1981). Following the Mental Health Act of 1980, when coverage for psychotherapy became an integral part of health insurance, most third-party pay-ers began imposing session limits, with 52 sessions (one year at once a week) being the most frequent benefit As research demonstrated that with brief therapy most patients improved sufficiently within 18 sessions, and that without session limits a phenomenon known as "therapeutic drift" emerged (Lambert, 1992), 20 sessions became the modal benefit. In therapeutic drift, patients who were not improving kept coming, while therapists allowed them to do so in the hope that something would happen, all in an atmosphere where a third party was paying the bill.

By the late 1980s, brief psychotherapy had become the main form of outpatient psychotherapy (Budman & Gurman, 1988), so when managed behavioral care imposed even more stringent session limits, most psychotherapists were practic-ing more or less a form of brief psychotherapy. It was psychoanalysts and other long-term psychotherapists who suddenly had the economic rug pulled out from under them, and had to rely on a dwindling number of affluent patients willing to pay out of pocket for unrestricted services. Although there was much research demonstrating the efficacy of short-term therapy, the practice of brief therapy fol-lowed its long-term predecessor into regarding clinical experience as paramount, resulting in a host of brief therapy psycho-religions. Family therapy (i.e., systems theory) erupted at the Ackerman Institute (New York) and the Mental Research Institute (Palo Alto), became part of the brief therapy movement, and swept across the country from each coast, only to eclipse by the 1990s. Parallel to it were the other movements such as those of Milton Erickson and the gestalt therapy of Frederick (Fritz) Perls whose techniques have permeated brief therapy even though their psycho-religions have lost preeminence.

The Futile Economics of Parity

The drive for parity, defined as equal healthcare benefits for mental and physi-cal illness, has been one of the most successful legislative campaigns in his-tory of healthcare advocacy. By 2003, parity laws had been enacted in 34 states and the federal government, a dazzling political achievement rendered inert by economic factors. There is less money being spent on mental healthcare after these parity laws than before their enactment. The third-party payers, fearing a spiking of mental healthcare costs, put in place more draconian hurdles to qualify for receiving behavioral care than physical care. Furthermore, prescribing psychotropic medication can be construed as mental healthcare when no behavioral interventions have been rendered. The end result is that these legislative campaigns give lobbyists a deceptive success to justify the financial contributions made by their constituents, while these same constituents, not realizing the end result is a negative, can believe progress is being made to bolster their sagging practices.

From an economic standpoint, it is folly to believe that any statute could force the allocation of half of the $1.4 trillion annual healthcare budget from physical to mental health, especially since 80% of mental healthcare is being delivered by non-psychiatric physicians and mostly in the primary care setting.

Who Is a Mental Health Practitioner? Everyone

The seemingly insatiable demand for psychotherapy that followed the post–World War II era was squeezed by the relatively small number of psychiatrists in practice at the time. Most were elderly with European accents, and they practiced long-term psychoanalysis that itself limited the availability of practitioners. Confronted by this reality, and believing that there would never be enough psychiatrists, the federal government undertook the large-scale funding of training not only for psychiatrists, but also psychologists and social workers, and later even paraprofessionals. Psychologists and social workers had proven their effectiveness in the military, and the NIMH and the Veterans Administration (VA) hoped their newly minted non-medical psychotherapists would staff the underserved public institutions. It is a little remembered fact that the federal government befuddled for all time the definition of a psychotherapist, embracing and funding all disciplines and non-disciplines, as well as paraprofessionals who in time inevitably demanded recognition as professionals.

Chafing under the psychiatric domination of the public institutions, the newly trained psychologists were the first to enter the domain of independent practice. There was no licensure or public recognition of psychology, but the young psychologists solved these problems by affiliating with established psychiatrists who, unable to keep up with the demand for their services, were happy to have their help. In addition, they provided the valuable service of administering batteries of psychological tests, at that time deemed imperative before undertaking psychotherapy. Organized psychiatry formally opposed state licensure of psychologists, but because of widespread public acceptance of psychologists, all 50 states had statutory recognition (licensure or certification) by 1979.

Social workers were next to mount their campaign for statutory recognition, but as of 2004 they have yet to attain this in all 50 states. Concurrently, master's-level counselors, marriage and family therapists (MFTs), addiction counselors, and others have attained success in more or fewer states, with psychiatric nurse practitioners having joined psychiatry and psychology as a ubiquitous mental health profession. As might have been predicted, psychologists sought to prevent licensing of social workers and all the others who came after them, as social work, too, has with those that came after them. To complicate matters more, in states that have not enacted master's-level counselor licensure, one can practice as a "counselor" as long as the titles that have statutory recognition (i.e., psychiatrist, psychologist, and social worker) are not used. The public has sought to address this confusion by adopting the all-encompassing term "therapist." So now, who is a therapist? Almost everyone is, or 650,000 individuals who have some kind of state statutory recognition, and by adding the unlicensed or uncertified, the total number might easily exceed 1 million, perhaps three or more times the number needed.

A perusal of rosters of practitioners licensed to do psychotherapy or counseling reveals that the ranks of social workers, marriage-family therapists, counselors, psychiatric nurse practitioners, and other master's-level licensees far outweigh the number of doctoral-level psychologists licensed to practice, and who are essentially offering their services as psychotherapists. Similarly, the networks of managed behavioral care companies list a plethora of master's-level psychotherapists. This overwhelming number of non-doctoral psychotherapists firmly establishes the reimbursement scale for psychotherapy on a pre-doctoral level. If doctoral psychologists are to compete, they must offer services their master's-level counterparts cannot perform, and they must reflect doctoral-level skills not attained by counselors and social workers.

As long as these turf wars continue among a glut of practitioners, and with no culture to separate the wheat from the chaff, mental healthcare will be hampered by an oversupply of competing disciplines, psycho-religions, and an unprecedented variability in competence, along with near quackery and actual quackery. Doubtless the NIMH and VA did not anticipate this state of affairs when this author entered the independent practice of psychotherapy in 1948 under government auspices.

Chicken Little, Our Healthcare Sky Is Falling

Listening to the constant stream of reports in the media, one would conclude that the American health system is rapidly becoming unraveled. We are told that we spend more money than anyone else in the world, and have less to show for it than other developed countries. In spite of this barrage, Americans tend to believe they have the best health system in the world, and survey after survey reveals that we like the healthcare we receive (Barlett & Steele, 2004a, 2004b). The press would have healthcare reform a top priority, but as late as only 4 weeks before the 2004 presidential elections, only 4% of those polled thought such reform was a top priority (ABC News/*Washington Post*, 2004). When foreign potentates, or ordinary people with seemingly impossible medical conditions, seek care, they come to the United States. How can we be the best and the worst health system at the same time?

Polarization of the Experts

Increasingly the health dialogue is becoming polarized between those who favor universal healthcare and those who would continue the current free-market system, and each side tends to interpret events and statistics in keeping with its predetermined position. Under the premise that people will not eat squid but will relish calamari, the code words for government medicine are "universal healthcare" and "one payer system," while those who would continue the present system refer to it as "freedom of choice" or the "free market." The first proponents see the current system as wasteful, inefficient, and plagued with fraud and duplication, while resulting in more than 45 million Americans being left without health coverage. Their opponents see universal healthcare as synonymous with high taxes, rationing, big government, and bureaucratic interference with free choice of physician and treatment. The latter belief is bolstered not only by the experiences of nationalized healthcare throughout the world, but also by a provision in the ill-fated Rodham Clinton plan, the last serious universal healthcare proposal. This would have punished any physician operating outside the government system with a $10,000 fine and 6 months in prison, with corresponding sanctions against patients utilizing them, thus eliminating free choice of physician.

Only three things can be said with certainty: (1) healthcare information is processed and then interpreted according to ideology, not veracity; (2) the debate is contentious and the voices strident; and (3) anyone charting a middle ground, or seeing both truth and error in each point of view, will be damned by both sides. Such may be the fate of this article.

Mental Health Weighs In

Most psychiatrists and psychologists favor universal healthcare and are often eager to join in sounding the alarm that Americans are underserved, while most physicians oppose it There is a growing barrage of articles purporting to show that Americans are increasingly under stress and nothing is being done about it, thus supporting universal healthcare. A recent example was the front-page lengthy story headlined and syndicated to hundreds of newspapers just before Labor Day, pointing to an alleged stress explosion in the workplace, with scores of mental health practitioners chiming in and lending credence (Schwartz, 2004). This article had three themes: (1) employees today are driven to work longer hours, (2) so that stress levels are soaring, (3) resulting in higher levels of job-related sickness and accidents. Seligman (2004) challenged the report, replete with quotes from experts, showing that this new crisis is based on nothing more than junk statistics. According to the Bureau of Labor Statistics (see Figure 12.1), workdays lost because of anxiety, stress, or neurotic disorders have significantly and steadily declined since they peaked in 1993.

More important, psychiatry and psychology are seeking to increase their revenue base by enlarging the pool of potential patients through expanding existing diagnoses to include more and more persons, and creating syndromes and

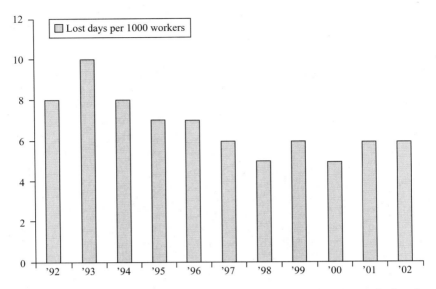

Figure 12.1 Private-sector workdays lost because of anxiety, stress, and neurotic disorders.

disorders by grouping any collection of symptoms, so that treatment for these newly discovered conditions will be insurance reimbursable (Wright & Cummings, 2005). Perhaps the most startling example was seen when the American Psychiatric Association redefined attention deficit/hyperactivity disorder (ADD/ADHD) several years ago, and by doing so it quadrupled the number of potential patients who would qualify under that diagnosis (Cummings & Wiggins, 2001). Hopefully saner voices will prevail. In a rare and remarkably candid article, a past president of the APA who is also the current president of the APA's Division of Independent Practice, acknowledges psychology's dereliction in contributing to the costly system that was a "major catastrophe in the making" had not managed care come along. He calls for protecting the incomes of psychotherapists before they have to go out of business, but only by first supporting "efforts to protect and advance the public interest in a fair and equitable health care system" (Fox, 2004, p. 158).

Healthcare Research Is Difficult to Interpret

Medical and behavioral research performed under ideal conditions such as randomized clinical trials is indispensable, but it seldom translates as intended out of the laboratory and into the delivery system. Consider that it is only after the FDA has approved a drug for use that all of the limitations, including death and disfigurement, are discovered. The purity of the laboratory requires subjects (patients) with only the condition being examined, whereas in the real world there are few if any patients who do not have co-morbidities that require poly-pharmacy for which most possible interactions have never been investigated. Interpreting healthcare statistics is even more elusive, and more often results in inaccuracy.

The complexities of healthcare delivery are so vast that they lend themselves to inaccurate conclusions. There are seemingly myriads of examples, and only two will be presented here as illustrative of well-meaning, but erroneous conclusions. For 2 decades, it was widely believed that the higher rate of breast cancer deaths among African American women was due to their seeking medical care much later in the development of such cancers than do white women. In 2004, it was discovered that African American women are more prone to carry a gene that prevents the production of the enzyme that blocks growth of breast cancer cells. Similarly, for more than a decade, it was believed that the relatively small number of heart catheterizations among African American men was due to the lack of adequate care accorded minorities. In 2004, it was discovered that the relevant death rate between white and African American male heart patients was the same, and that the higher rate of catheters accorded white males was due to defensive medicine, not adequate or necessary care.

In mental healthcare, logicians and philosophers remain skeptical of the level of confidence that can be placed on experimental results obtained when measuring the efficacy of one treatment modality over another (Lakatos & Musgrave, 1974). As Mechl (1978, p. 822) stated, "Putting it crudely, if you have enough cases and your measures are not totally unreliable, the null hypothesis will always be falsified, regardless of the truth of the substantive theory." Dumont and Fitzpatrick add, "It is commonplace . . . that we normally research those problems that are most amenable to neat and easy solutions. . . . Thus, we attack the easiest problems first." Meehl goes on to further quote a remark by Dumont and Fitzpatrick (F. Dumont & M. Fitzpatrick, 2007, vol. 16, page 17, Fault Lines in the Great EST Debate. Journal of Contemporary Psychotherapy, vol. 16, page 10.), ". . . for every study that identifies a statistically significant benefit of treatment, there may be an equal number of studies that report a statistically significant benefit that is useless."

The Negation of Supply and Demand by Mental Healthcare

This and several succeeding sections will additionally address economic issues, and the faint of heart may wish to skip them. However, in so doing, they will overlook the hot-button issues in healthcare and mental healthcare today. The first of these involves a look at the reasons the economic laws of supply and demand do not operate, or only partially apply within healthcare.

The Provider Controls Both Supply and Demand

By determining both the treatment and its frequency, the provider determines both supply and demand. Physicians, being in control of the process, merely render more treatment, particularly more costly procedures, to a declining number of available patients. In psychotherapy, a reduction in the number of referrals can be subverted by increasing the length of treatment (longer-term psychotherapy) as well as its frequency (twice or three times a week instead of once a week). In other words, a dozen patients seen twice a week almost interminably are equivalent to scores of brief therapy referrals and will constitute a nearly full-time private practice. Called "unconscious fiscal convenience" (Cummings, 2005a, 2005b), this allows a skilled psychotherapist to inadvertently foster dependency and discourage and even prevent many patients from terminating. This will result in a perpetual caseload that needs only a few occasional referrals.

These mental health practices are called *demand creation* (Feldstein, 1996) by economists, and have been essentially eliminated by the time-limited psychotherapy required by third-party payers. But other forms of demand creation are flourishing, such as inventing a syndrome for which the psychotherapist already has a treatment. Psychotherapy has a number of established treatments for depression, and by a new syndrome, seasonal affective disorder (SAD), the state of feeling "blue" in the gloom of winter, these established techniques could be applied to an entire new population. Stretching our credulity even further, NIMH identified "reverse SAD" that ostensibly afflicts persons during daylight savings time (Spencer, 2003). Psychology already had the treatment, but the new disorders were created, thus expanding the number of persons who could be regarded as patients and for whom insurance coverage could be provided. Systematically the definition of depression has been expanded to encompass the slight mood swings involved in daily living. Similarly, bereavement counseling techniques were transposed to the new "grief and crisis counseling" that is rushed to the scene of every disaster, despite evidence it is ineffective and even deleterious (McNally, 2003). Interventions developed by military psychologists for treating combat post-traumatic stress disorder (PTSD) were transported to civilian stress reactions, most of which do not begin to approach the trauma of combat. Cummings (2005a) delineated the process by which this demand is created, while Lilienfeld et al. (2003) and Lilienfeld et al. (2005) have addressed the proliferation of dubious diagnoses and their treatments that have been spawned in the era of the psychotherapist glut.

How the Patient Inadvertently Distorts Demand

Before 1942 and the advent of the third-party payer system, the doctor–patient relationship was simple and one that had endured for more than 2,000 years dating back to Hippocrates: the physician was pledged to treat the patient, first doing no harm, and the patient was obligated to follow the doctor's regimen and to pay the fee. If the doctor was not helpful, extravagant, or insisted on unnecessary services, the patient merely found another physician. Once the employer or the government began paying for healthcare, 60 years of studies demonstrate, patients overly utilize care because it is free (Gingrich, 2003; Sowell, 2003; Friedman, 2004). For example, a patient with a minor knee injury might demand an MRI, refusing to wait the 2 weeks' time in which minor injuries improve. If the patient were paying out of pocket for this costly procedure, the doctor's advice to wait would be readily heeded. In psychotherapy, it is usually manifested in a different way called "therapeutic drift" (Cummings, 2005a). Both patient and psychotherapist may continue treatment despite no improvement because a third party is footing the bill. Even with no progress, the patient can narcissistically enjoy having the semi-weekly full attention of a renowned therapist for a full hour, all for free! This is called *artificial demand,* created by variables being in the wrong juxtaposition rather than by need (Feldstein, 1996). Various ways are being suggested to return decision making and responsibility back to the doctors and their patients as will be discussed later.

A different type of artificial demand known as *misperceived demand* (Feldstein, 1996) is the medical/surgical overutilization that occurs because of somatization, defined as translating psychological stress into physical symptoms. It is well-established that 60% to 70% of all patient visits to primary care are by patients who have no physical disease, or have a physical disease exacerbated by psychological factors (see, for example, Cumming et al., 2002, for an extensive review and healthcare delivery solutions). Somatization is reduced by as much as 65% in healthcare settings in which behavioral healthcare is part of primary care.

Managed Care

In the 1980s, healthcare became the last major sector of our economy to industrialize, having lagged far behind the industrializations of manufacturing (1900s), energy (1930s), transportation (1950s), and retailing (1970s). The first manifestation of this industrialized healthcare was managed care, the corporate ownership of healthcare financing and delivery made possible by the elimination of laws limiting the corporate practice of medicine and by the application of antitrust laws to the health system, all of which took place in the 1970s. Within a decade, managed care became the dominate force in healthcare delivery, and managed behavioral healthcare emerged as separate companies that managed that sector, known as "carve-outs." By the mid-1990s, 175 million Americans received their mental healthcare through managed behavioral healthcare organizations (MBHOs). These carve-outs began as utilization review and other monitoring device entities, but soon copied American Biodyne, which was the first national comprehensive managed behavioral healthcare company.

By the beginning of the 21st century, the MBHOs had lost much of their punch, thanks to a backlash that initiated a host of laws and regulations limiting their management of behavioral care. By early in 2000, the MBHOs had become essentially monitoring, network management, and payment centers, and in the transition a number of bankruptcies and near bankruptcies occurred. The largest MBHO, Magellan Behavioral Health, restructured and emerged from Chapter 11 financially sound. The industrialization of healthcare, as well as mental healthcare, continues, but with a much different morphology, and it will continue to evolve in the future. Once a sector industrializes, there is no returning to the cottage industry that preceded it.

Managed care, including managed behavioral care, did not manage care, but managed costs. Companies like American Biodyne that resulted in cost-efficiency through managing effective mental healthcare were impossible to replicate in a corporate, rather than health-driven environment. Not that doctors were doing a better job of managing costs, but only in a few instances (e.g., American Biodyne) was there a melding of best practices with Edwards Deming efficiencies. Managed care imploded from a self-created backlash. It (1) had forgotten that patients vote as well as complain to their members of Congress, and it (2) falsely believed employers were their ultimate customers, not the patients.

In the discussions of the implosion of managed behavioral healthcare as implemented in the 1980s, neglected is the fact that managed care as originally conceived was never implemented. Managed care was conceptualized by the Jackson Hole Group beginning in the 1970s. It was so named because all their meetings were held in that town in Wyoming where the Federal Reserve Board also meets, and it was comprised of some of the nation's most prestigious health economists (e.g., Paul Elwood, Alain Enthoven). Summarized, it called for every employer to provide a choice of basic coverage at employers' expense, and a series of upscale plans, each at employees' choice and costs, ranging from bronze to platinum. Employees would always have a choice of managed care and indemnity plans, priced accordingly. Full information on every choice was accorded employees, who could switch plans once a year. Integral to the Jackson Hole concept was that no employee would be forced to accept managed care over indemnity insurance. Very few employers ever implemented such a choice, which would have significantly lowered patient complaints, and might have spared the backlash. In one setting, Stanford University, where faculty and other employees have a choice between managed care and indemnity insurance, 76% choose the HMO (Enthoven, 2003).

Consumerism

Information that would enable a patient to choose the health plan with the best value for the premium dollar is integral to the consumer movement in America, and the CEO of the APA sees this as the next step in healthcare (Bradshaw, 2004a, 2004b). It is intended that the most efficient and effective health plans would also have the lowest premiums. Ideally the consumer has influenced health plans to become more effective and efficient, thus lowering the premium. The idea of an informed purchaser connecting with a low-cost health plan certainly sounds appropriate, but unfortunately consumerism would end health insurance as we know it. The fastest way for a health plan to lower costs is to eliminate potential enrollees who are sick or likely to become sick. It is fundamental in our present system that the 80% of insured who use little healthcare pay for the 20% who use most of the services, thus resulting in an equal premium for the sick and the healthy. Given full information there is little doubt that buyers would gravitate to health plans that cherry-pick healthy enrollees and thus have lowered pay-out and a very low premiums. This leaves the 20% of Americans needing extensive services facing an astronomical premium, with enrollment in what could be termed "sick plans" rather than health plans, essentially ending third-party payment.

The Cost of Healthcare and the 45 Million Uninsured

A perusal of the past 15 years indicates that the cost of healthcare and the cost of automobiles have risen about the same proportionally. However, in 2004, healthcare costs are rising at a faster rate than automobile prices, whereas for the first half of the 15-year period the opposite was true. The reason is that for a number of years managed care dramatically lowered the healthcare inflation spiral, but in the past 5 years the number of laws and regulations encumbering managed care have resulted in its inability to continue controlling costs. So for a number of years automobile inflation was exceeding healthcare inflation, but now the opposite is true. There are currently more government regulations that lead to healthcare cost increases than are now hampering the auto industry. The startling difference, however, is that whereas almost every American has at least one automobile, 45 million do not have health insurance. Everyone buys a car, even if it is a clunker, but it is expected that health insurance will be provided. How many Americans forego buying a car and begin riding the bus so they can pay for health insurance?

The 45 million uninsured have become a political football, but who are they? They are not the poor who are covered under Medicaid. The figure does include uncounted college students, especially graduate students, who are too old to be covered by their parents' health plans, but for whom mom and dad are providing a healthcare safety net. It probably includes many undocumented (i.e., illegal) immigrants. But the majority is young entrepreneurs who have started their own small business, and cannot afford healthcare for themselves or their employees. These small businesses are providing 60% of the new jobs in America, and the solution is legislation that will encourage them to band together and buy healthcare at a "bulk price" as do large corporations. Such legislation is proposed, but politics that would rather perpetuate the issue than solve it are hampering the outcome; thus, the figure keeps growing annually from its original 40 million 4 years ago to estimates in 2004 that put it at a yet to be defined, and perhaps overblown 45 million.

One other variable is overlooked. Many of these small businesses are mom-and-pop operations, such as one or two married couples, several single women, or other such arrangements, that have other than the owners only one or two employees, but often none at all. These entrepreneurs are usually in their early 30s and have less than a 5% risk of a catastrophic medical condition. As are most entrepreneurs, they are not risk aversive, and would rather take that risk in favor of using the money that would go to health insurance to grow their fledgling businesses.

Medical Savings Accounts

The overwhelming evidence that third-party payment systems destroy the doctor–patient relationship, resulting in the patient abdicating responsibility for both healthcare costs and his or her own health (Gingrich, 2003; Sowell, 2003), has prompted Nobel Laureate Milton Friedman (2004) to strongly favor tax-free medical savings accounts. The non-spent portions of the medical savings accounts

158 Nicholas A. Cummings

can be carried over into succeeding years and accountholders still enjoy the tax benefits accorded these accounts. Eventually a healthy individual could cash in some of the accrual. It rewards good health, it encourages a healthy lifestyle, and since one's own money is being spent, the patient is prudent in the use of care and demanding in its quality. It restores the doctor–patient relationship extant for the more than 2,000 years that preceded health insurance. In mental health, it would end therapeutic drift, unnecessarily prolonged psychotherapy, the proliferation of dubious diagnoses, and the unskilled practitioner.

This all seems viable, but in time the medical savings account system would encounter some of the same difficulties eventually facing consumerism. Medical savings accounts are not suitable for the chronically ill or persons with preexisting conditions, although they can be a boon to small businesses. In time the healthy would gravitate to the medical savings account system, leaving the sick to face ever-increasing premiums in what has become an expensive "sick plan" (Brock, 2004).

One must ask, however, if those who maintain a healthy lifestyle must be punished by having to pay for those who continue to smoke, overeat, and maintain a sedentary lifestyle? Or should they be rewarded? This issue will be addressed later.

Tort Reform

Frivolous lawsuits directly cost the health system $28 billion annually, but the indirect cost of defensive medicine is estimated to be another $60 to $100 billion. This exceeds the amount of money necessary to provide coverage to the 45 million uninsured. The health systems of other nations do not have to bear this burden, and many have totally eliminated frivolous lawsuits by simply outlawing contingency arrangements by which the plaintiff pays nothing, but the lawyers collect 50% of the judgment plus all their costs. A number of states have capped noneconomic (i.e., pain and suffering) payments, and in 2004, a number of such bills are pending, especially in states where doctors are rapidly exiting because of astronomical malpractice insurance costs. Patients are suffering because of a shortage of physicians in their states, and in Nevada, a pregnant woman must travel to California for prenatal care. In Las Vegas, both trauma centers closed in response to the bleak litigious environment in which trial lawyers advertise on large billboards, and critical patients must be transported to the Los Angeles area. Similar plights confront patients in a number of other states suffering from runaway litigation awards. Vaccines are often in short supply, with the 2004 shortage of the flu vaccine only the latest example, with child vaccines perpetually in short supply, because American manufacturers avoid the litigious environment confronting the manufacture of vaccines. California experienced a mass exodus of physicians decades ago, solved the problem by a combination of tort and insurance reform, and is now considered a mecca for physicians and their patients.

It would seem that tort reform is an obvious solution, were it not that the subject has become mired in partisan politics. Trial lawyers spend millions of dollars defending their lucrative practices, and they have become one of the largest contributors to the Democratic Party, unfortunately making the matter a partisan Democrat versus Republican issue.

Medical Errors

Medical errors have become an enormous problem that can be virtually eliminated by (1) electronic recordkeeping and (2) transparency of data. The first is resisted by a medical culture that likes cellular phones but dislikes electronic recordkeeping, and a health system that concentrates on the costs of instituting such a system without looking at the magnitude of future cost savings.

No corporation would be successful today without the transparency of data that enable it to elicit and correct production errors immediately. This principle so integral to business is absent in the healthcare industry because transparency means lawsuits. Who would admit a medical error, even though this is the first step to eliminating an error system, when such an admission will surely result in a deluge of lawsuits? Tort reform that will eliminate frivolous lawsuits while compensating victims of medical error, and also encouraging data transparency so as to substantially reduce future errors and its victims, is a challenge that must be faced with a bipartisan effort that is long overdue.

Universal Healthcare

From the foregoing, one might prematurely conclude that universal healthcare would eliminate many of the problems of our market-driven system. Polls seem to show that the majority of Americans favor universal healthcare, but these polls are not conclusive in that the questions are usually framed so as to render the positive response, making any respondent not so disposed appear lacking in compassion. Where universal healthcare has been instituted, which is every industrialized nation except the United States, it works well in the beginning but then costs accelerate exponentially, unacceptably increasing the tax burden, so that controls and rationing must be instituted. The Province of Ontario (Canada) in 2004 had to end its system of free healthcare for all by instituting premiums along with the other controls and rationing that have been put in place over prior years (Mackie, 2004). Several years ago Ontario announced in the beginning of December that the healthcare budget had been exhausted, and no healthcare would be paid for until after the new budget came into effect the first of the year.

Again, taking the highly touted Canadian system of universal care as an example, it is now plagued with "a number of shortcoming, including the growing shortage of doctors and nurses, the lengthening of waits for cancer care and surgery, and the mounting cost of drugs for an aging population" (Krauss, 2004, p. 11). Additionally, the cost to the taxpayer has grown 40% since its enactment in 1975, while furthering the silent rationing of care that manifests itself in long waits. The system would be even more stressed were it not that so many

Canadians, despairing waiting, cross into the United States and pay out of pocket for immediate care.

Included in this volume is an updated reprint of a universal care financing proposal that evolved from a study initiated by the National Academies of Practice in 1994 (see Dörken chapter 11 in this volume). It is intended to build in the kinds of safeguards and controls that would prevent draconian measures in the future that would be necessary to curb ever-accelerating costs. The study was conducted in response to the absence of financing considerations in the thousands of pages of the Rodham Clinton Healthcare Task Force report that was unable to grapple at all with cost and financing.

A Viable Healthcare Model: A Beginning

It is time we returned decision making in healthcare to the doctors and their patients, but under an accountable system where both are held responsible for their side of the doctor–patient equation. It would preserve the employer-sponsored coverage as well as the existing coverage for the poor, veterans, and the elderly (e.g., Medicare, Medicaid, Veterans Administration, TriCare), but it restores the responsibility of the patient to use the system wisely, while the doctor provides effective quality care without excessive treatment. It presupposes the elimination of frivolous lawsuits that will encourage data transparency, thus reducing and eliminating medical errors. It is a return to small, manageable, integrated group practices in which doctor and patient know and respect each other, and patients' psychological needs are addressed along with their physical health. It is a responsible system, serving the patient while also respecting the doctor.

Employer and Payer Responsibility

An enrollee is guaranteed a prepaid basic health plan that is adequate, and is provided the information to make a choice among several plans offered. These are basic bronze plans, and totally at employer expense. Additionally, each potential enrollee is provided information on plans rated silver, gold, and platinum with successively higher premiums to the insured above the basic bronze plan offered by the employer or agency. Such upgraded plans are voluntary, but always at an added increment to the basic plan payable by the subscriber. Information on available health plans is kept current and the enrollee may make a change at a prescribed date annually.

Preventive services that include intensive health education, integration of behavioral health into primary care, training the patient to manage chronic disease and stress, and essentially create incentives for the patient assuming responsibility for his or her health are integral, covered services. Whereas prevention accounts for less than 5% of today's healthcare budget, it would be substantially increased. As an example of today's unworkable system, the physician is reimbursed for treating the consequences of diabetes (amputations, blindness, etc.), but is not reimbursed for services that would prevent these unfortunate and costly consequences.

Patient Responsibility

The patient has the responsibility of keeping appointments and following the medical and psychological regimen prescribed, and the doctor has the option of refusing to treat an intractable patient. This would rarely occur, but would have a sentinel effect on patient responsibility. A copayment is required for every visit, as much as $5 for most plans, but a modest $1 for the indigent and elderly. As modest as this copayment is, research has shown it decreases unnecessary utilization without curtailing the seeking of needed services (Cumming et al., 2002).

The patient is taught responsibility for maintaining a healthy lifestyle, which includes nutrition, activity, and attitude (Gingrich, 2003). These include eating healthy foods, avoiding overeating, not smoking, moderate use of alcohol, and no recreational drugs. Activity not only includes regular exercise, but having a healthy social involvement, spirituality, and other endeavors that lead to contentment. Attitude means reduction of anger, elimination of stress, and maintaining a positive psychology. The person with a chronic illness is taught best how to manage that illness. Gingrich (2003) calls this health before healthcare (i.e., prevention is preferable to treatment). Incentives toward healthy lifestyles are provided throughout the health system, and if all else fails, he believes there are ways to mandate them.

Government Responsibility

The federal government could do much to make health insurance available (Forbes, 2004). For example, (1) by allowing individuals to deduct health insurance premiums just as corporations do, this would not only offset the cost of the premiums, it would create an incentive to purchase such insurance. (2) Enact legislation that has been pending in Congress that would permit consumers to buy health insurance policies offered anywhere in the United States. Currently one can only purchase policies approved by each state for sale in that state. This would establish a national standard and get around the excessive state regulations that enormously increase premiums. (3) New federal legislation allows employers to offer their employees tax-free health savings accounts (HSAs) (Forbes, 2004). In these HSAs, money for medical purposes can be deposited by either employer or employee free of tax, it can continue to grow tax free, and it can be spent for medical purposes tax free. If withdrawn for any other purpose, it is subject to taxation. Also, these HSAs can choose to have high deductibles, making health insurance policies infinitely cheaper, and reconnecting in a financially responsible manner the patient responsibility for one's own healthcare. HSAs have portability inasmuch as they are owned by the worker, not the employer, so the policy accompanies the employee no matter how frequently he or she changes jobs. If all of these incentives were in place, the 45 million uninsured would nearly disappear within a short time.

Morphology of Physician Practice

Primary care group basic practices will be divided into patient cohorts of 20,000 to 30,000 enrollees assigned to each group practice. Each primary care provider (PCP) shall be expected to carry a reasonable patient load, with a smaller patient load expected in upscale practices providing such so-called healthcare frills as same-day-appointments, longer appointment time with each patient, house calls as may be appropriate, and other niceties not unessential and absent in basic care. By limiting the patient cohort for each group, the advantages of small group practice are maintained. For each eight PCPs, there is one behavioral care provider (BCP) with a minimum of two per setting so that one BCP is always available for the hallway handoff.

Where such small, cohesive group practices exist, electronic data keeping has been attained rapidly and with relatively moderate cost. Medical errors are significantly reduced and the paperwork that currently is drowning most doctors becomes more manageable.

The third-party payer contracts with each group practice on a fee-for-service basis, and monitors each group practice and compares effective and efficient group practices with those less so. It enables the latter to learn from the more successful groups, but also takes into account those groups whose cohort may have a higher percentage of seriously ill patients. Groups are liable for medical errors, but tort reform has capped noneconomic judgments and eliminated frivolous lawsuits. The third-party payer may cancel or not renew a contract with a substandard group, but it is important that the financial structure is such that it will attract skilled physicians and thus upgrade each group.

It is intended that as much as 80% of behavioral care is performed within the primary care setting, thus greatly reducing the need for referrals to specialty care that is caring for the chronically mentally ill. The PCPs are encouraged to upgrade their skills to include the first tier of other specialties (e.g., minor surgery, routine dermatology, and even uncomplicated prenatal care), in keeping with the trend to expand the range of primary care. This would significantly reduce the cost by eliminating unnecessary specialty referrals.

The third-party payer reimburses the physicians for preventive services, something that is lacking in today's system. The present system is shortchanging those physicians conscientious enough to provide health education, patient training in management of chronic disease, and other preventive services that would eventually reduce healthcare costs significantly.

Finally, the health plan makes available business advice as well as courses in business, since the absence of business acumen has caused many a medical group practice to fail.

Summary and Conclusions

This article has attempted to walk the reader through the dense forest of healthcare complexities in a succinct, straightforward, and nonpartisan manner. With space limitations undoubtedly some topics have received too brief attention, and there are other topics that may not have been included. The author has also provided a beginning model for returning the health system to the doctors and patients, but with accountability for the doctor and responsible use for the patient. Mind/body dualism would end with behavioral care being an integral part of primary care. In struggling to steer a middle course, the effort will inevitably receive criticism from both sides, as healthcare has become highly politicized and ideological.

While grappling with the unexpected volumes of primary care patients manifesting emotional and psychological distress as first discovered in the newly nationalized post–World War II British system, the prescient Michael Balint (1957) predicted that to meet this exigency physicians would have to become more like psychologists, and psychologists would have to become more like physicians.

References

ABC News/Washington Post Poll (2004, October 4). Washington, DC.

Alexander, F., & French, T. M. (1946). *Psychoanalytic therapy: Principles and applications.* New York: Ronald Press.

Antonuccio, D. O., Danton, W. G., & DeNelsky, G. Y. (1999). Raising questions about antidepressants. *Psychotherapy and Psychosomatic Medicine, 68*(1), 3–14.

Association for the Advancement of Psychology. (2004, Summer). APA poll: Most Americans have sought mental health treatment but cost, insurance still barriers. *AAP Advance,* 12.

Balint, M. (1957). *The doctor, his patient, and the illness.* New York: International Universities Press.

Barlett, D. L., & Steele, J. B. (2004a). *Critical condition: How healthcare in America became big business—and bad medicine.* New York: Doubleday.

Barlett, D. L., & Steele, J. B. (2004b, October 11). Healthcare can be cured: Here's how. *Time,* 50–51.

Bradshaw, A. (2004a, January–February). What will follow managed care? "Consumerism" will guide change in healthcare, APA's CEO says. *National Psychologist, 13*(1), 1, 3.

Bradshaw, A. (2004b, January–February). What will follow managed care? National health is coming, predicts pioneer in managed care. *National Psychologist, 13*(1), 1, 3–4.

Brock, F. (2004, September 21). Weighing the risks in a health savings account. *New York Times,* pp. 17, 20.

Budman, S. H., & Gurman, A. S. (1988). *Theory and practice of brief therapy.* New York: Guilford Press.

Callaghan, G. M., Gregg, J. A., Marx, B., Kohlenberg, B. S., & Gifford, E. (2004). Fact: The utility of an integration of functional analytic psychotherapy and acceptance and commitment therapy to alleviate human suffering. *Psychotherapy: Theory, Research, Practice, Training, 41*(3), 195–207.

Carnahan, I. (2002, January 21). Asylum for the insane. *Forbes,* 33–34.

Corrigan, P. (2004). How stigma interferes with mental healthcare. *American Psychologist, 59*(7), 614–625.

Cummings, N. A. (2005a). Expanding a shrinking economic base: The right way, the wrong way, and the mental health way. In R. H. Wright & N. A. Cummings (Eds.), *Destructive trends in mental health: The well-intentioned road to harm.* New York: Brunner-Routledge (Taylor and Francis), 70–102.

Cummings, N. A. (2005b). Treatment and assessment take place in an economic context. In S. O. Lilienfeld & W. O'Donohue (Eds.), *The great ideas of clinical science: The 18 concepts every mental health researcher and practitioner should know.* New York: Brunner-Routledge (Taylor and Francis Group), 120–137.

Cummings, N. A., & Follette, W. T. (1968). Psychiatric services and medical utilization in a prepaid health plan setting: Part II. *Medical Care, 6,* 31–41.

Cumming, N. A., O'Donohue, W. T., & Ferguson, K. E. (2002). *The impact of medical cost offset on practice and research: Making it work for you.* Foundation for Behavioral Health: Healthcare Utilization and Cost Series, Volume 5. Reno, NV: Context Press.

Cummings, N. A., O'Donohue, W., Hayes, S. C., & Follette, V. (Eds.). (2001). *Integrated behavioral healthcare: Positioning mental health practice with medical/surgical practice.* San Diego, CA: Academic Press.

Cummings, N. A., & VandenBos, G. R. (1981). The twenty years Kaiser Permanente experience with psychotherapy and medical utilization: Implications for national mental health policy and national health insurance. *Health Policy Quarterly, 1*(2), 159–175.

Cummings, N. A., & Wiggins, J. G. (2001). A collaborative primary care/behavioral health model for use of psychotropic medication with children and adolescents: Report of a national retrospective study. *Issues in Interdisciplinary Care, 3*(2), 121–128.

Dumont, F., & Fitzpatrick, M. (2007). Fault lines in the great EST debate. *Journal of Contemporary Psychotherapy, 16,* 7–27.

Enthoven, A. (2003, May). Remarks to the World Health Care Congress. Washington, DC.

Feldstein, P. J. (1996). *Healthcare economics* (5th ed.). Albany, NY: Delmar.

Follette, W. T., & Cummings, N. A. (1967). Psychiatric services and medical utilization in a prepaid health plan setting. *Medical Care, 5,* 25–35.

Forbes, S. (2004, September 20). Insuring healthcare coverage. *Forbes, 33.*

Fox, R. E. (2004). It's about money: Protecting and enhancing our incomes. *Independent Practitioner, 24*(4), 158–159.

Friedman, M. (2004, January 27). Keynote address to the World Health Care Congress, Washington, DC.

Gingrich, N. (2003). *Saving lives and saving money.* Washington, DC: Alexis de Tocqueville Institution.

Hogan, M. F. (2003). New freedom commission report: The president's new freedom commission—Recommendations to transform mental healthcare in America. *Psychiatric Services, 54,* 1467–1474.

Institute of Medicine (2001). *Crossing the quality chasm: A new health system for the 21st century.* Washington, DC: National Academy of Sciences.

James, L. (2004, September 21). Personal communication.

Kellogg, S. (2004). Dialogical encounters: Contemporary perspectives on "chairwork" in psychotherapy. *Psychotherapy: Theory, Research, Practice, Training, 41*(3), 310–320.

Kennedy, E. (2004, October 9). *Comments made on the U.S. Senate floor regarding healthcare.* Washington, DC: C-Span Cable Network.

Kerstine, K. (2004). Healthcare change is coming: What do we do? *Monitor on Psychology, 35*(9), 56–57.

Krauss, C. (2004, September 23). Canadian healthcare deal adds $14 billion to ailing fund. From the *New York Times Syndicate. San Francisco Chronicle,* p. A11.

Kuhn, T. (1996). *The structures of scientific revolutions.* Chicago, IL: University of Chicago Press.

Lakatos, I., & Musgrave, A. (Eds.). (1974). *Criticism and the growth of knowledge.* Cambridge: Cambridge University Press.

Lambert, M. J. (1992). Psychotherapy outcome research: Implications for integrative and eclectic therapists. In J. C. Norcross & M. R. Goldfried (Eds.), *Handbook of psychotherapy integration* (pp. 94–129). New York: Basic Books.

Levant, R. F. (2004). 21st century psychology: Toward a biosocial model. *Independent Practitioner, 24*(3), 128–139.

Lilienfeld, S. O., Lohr, J. M., Lynn, S. J., & Fowler, K. (2005). Pseudoscience, nonscience, and nonsense in contemporary clinical psychology. In R. H. Wright & N. A. Cummings (Eds.), *Destructive trends in mental health: The well-intentioned path to harm* (pp. 187–218). New York: Brunner-Routledge (Taylor and Francis).

Lilienfeld, S. O., Lynn, S. J., & Lohr, J. M. (Eds.). (2003). *Science and pseudoscience in clinical psychology.* New York: Guilford.

Mackie, R. (2004, June 10). Ontario budget will re-introduce health-care premiums. *Canada*, pp. 1, 9.

McNally, R. J. (2003, September 12). As extensively quoted in S. Begley, Is trauma debriefing worse than letting victims heal naturally? *Wall Street Journal*, p. B1–2.

Mechl, P. E. (1978). Theoretical risks and tabular asterisks: Sir Karl, Sir Ronald, and the slow progress of soft psychology. *Journal of Consulting and Clinical Psychology, 46*, 806–834.

National Association of Addiction Treatment Providers. (2004, September). 20.3 million needed addiction treatment and did not get it in 2003. *NAATP Visions, 10*, 10–14.

Saunders, T. R. (2003). Personal communication.

Schwartz, J. (2004, September 3). Always on the job, employees pay with health: The stress explosion. *New York Times Syndicate*, pp. 1, 13–14.

Seligman, D. (2004, October 18). New crisis—junk statistics. *Forbes*, 118–119.

Sowell, T. (2003). *Applied economics.* New York: Basic Books.

Spencer, J. (2003, May 22). When blue skies bring on the blues: Research shows why some despair on sunny days and relish gloom of winter. *Wall Street Journal*, p. D1–2.

Strosahl, K. (2001). The integration of primary care and behavioral health: Type II changes in the era of managed care. In N. A. Cummings, W. O'Donohue, S. C. Hayes, & V. Follette (Eds.), *Integrated behavioral healthcare: Positioning mental health practice with medical/surgical practice* (pp. 45–70). San Diego, CA: Academic Press.

Wright, R. H., & Cummings, N. A. (Eds.). (2005). *Destructive trends in mental health: The well-intentioned path to harm.* New York: Brunner-Routledge (Taylor and Francis).

13 We Are Not a Healthcare Business

Our Inadvertent Vow of Poverty

Nicholas A. Cummings, Janet L. Cummings, and William O'Donohue

By 1980, psychology had become the premier psychotherapy profession in America. Our last state had enacted psychology licensure (Missouri in 1979), and psychiatry had decided to "remedicalize," abandoning psychotherapy to psychologists as it became an essentially prescribing and hospitalizing profession. Social work was still struggling to obtain statutory recognition, and master's-level counselors and marital/family therapists were just beginning the arduous path toward establishing their respective professions. Popular polls asking women to list their most desirable husband year after year revealed psychologists to be the number one choice. The media were unceasingly favorable toward us, and story after story heralded that psychology was about to solve many of society's problems. We were riding high. Then 15 years later, or circa 1995, psychology began a precipitous decline that continues. What happened? What did we do wrong? We suggest that an analysis of these questions will reveal that a revolution needs to take place: clinical psychology needs to move to take its rightful place as a healthcare business with all the strategic, training, attitudinal, and practice changes this implies.

A Brief Retrospective

After decades of struggle to establish its new profession, psychology was understandably enjoying having come of age. But while it was basking in its arrival as the nation's premier psychotherapy profession, healthcare was beginning to industrialize, ushering in changes unthinkable a few years earlier. The enactment by Congress in 1985 of diagnosis-related groups (DRGs) in medicine and surgery was the first effective salvo in this industrialization. The second was by the Supreme Court, which established that healthcare was subject to the antitrust laws, and the restrictions on the corporate practice of medicine were thrown out. The inability of the government to establish DRGs for mental healthcare led to the complacency that mental healthcare was impervious to industrialization. Not so, said the senior author of this paper, who heeded the harbingers as he began to warn the profession of the sea changes just ahead (Cummings, 1985; Cummings & Fernandez, 1985; Cummings, 1986).

The term "managed care," and more specifically, "managed behavioral care," had not yet been coined, so Cummings (1986) referred to what was about to occur as the giant corporations sweeping over our profession like a swarm of locusts. Unless psychology owned the industrialization of behavioral care, it would own us. He announced (Cummings, 1986) that he was establishing American Biodyne as a model to be emulated. He would cap its enrollment at 500,000 covered lives, and he invited psychologists to come and spend as much time as necessary to enable them to go out and form 50 such companies. In this way, psychology, not the locusts, would own the new wave of industrialization.

The American Psychological Association (APA) was immediately not only skeptical, but oppositional. Particularly vocal were Bryant Welch, the first head of the newly created APA Practice Directorate, and Rogers Wright, the executive director of the Association for the Advancement of Psychology (AAP). Where would Nick Cummings ever obtain half a million enrollees for such an unworkable scheme? Laughably, he was accused of having added grandiosity to his paranoia. Even after managed care, as it came to be called, was entrenched, the APA's official position was that it was a passing fad (Wright, 1992; Cantor, 1993). For 3 years, Cummings kept his promise, but when no one came to learn other than corporations, he took his foot off the brake and enrollment skyrocketed to 20 million in the succeeding 5 years. Several copycat companies were formed, but none other than American Biodyne was psychology-driven, even to the point where medical directors reported to psychologist clinical directors. Now in his 70s, and tiring of working 90-hour weeks while being constantly attacked by his own profession as well as that of psychiatry, Cummings took American Biodyne public and left the company in 1994. Two years later, a survey of practicing psychologists revealed they were frustrated by managed care, but they had fallen prey to assurances by the APA and planned to "hang tough" until managed care collapsed (Saeman, 1996). Psychology had missed the opportunity to own managed behavioral care.

Why No One Came

That a large 100,000-member organization like the APA, which is well staffed and funded and sponsors a plethora of ostensibly well-informed study committees and task forces, could make such a far-reaching and egregious (to its members) error is curious. That is, it is curious until one delves into the belief system of psychologists. There are two pervasive beliefs, or near universal biases, both of which are highly counterproductive to the success of the delivery of psychological services: (1) the practice of psychology is not part of healthcare, and further (2) it is not a business.

Psychology Practice Is Not Healthcare

In the 60 years the senior author has been a psychotherapist, as well as all of our collective experiences as psychotherapists, the worst accusation that could be leveled at a colleague, or in critiquing a therapeutic approach, was for someone to exclaim disdainfully, "That's the medical model!" Recoiling, the accused would backpedal to reestablish acceptable credentials that reflected the psychosocial, behavioral, or humanistic models, declaring loudly that psychology is not healthcare. Psychology has failed, however, to establish an economic base to sustain itself, so it paradoxically insists that psychotherapy be reimbursed by the health system. In so doing, it plays the dubious double-game that mental health is separate and different from the general healthcare industry, a stance that isolates us even more.

As will be seen later, this dichotomy has led not only to our underfunding, but to a stepchild status in the health system. A plethora of examples shows how such a narrowing of identity has harmed other successful industries. The railroads were the most successful industry of the 19th century, but their insistence they were in the railroad industry and not the transportation industry resulted in their being usurped by trucking and air cargo, both endeavors railroads could have once owned. The telegraph industry, the miracle of the same century, failed to define itself beyond the telegraph to the rightful focus as the communications industry. As a result, it rejected the then newly invented telephone and subsequently withered. It is fascinating that at that time telegraph lines had already crisscrossed the continent, and it would have taken only a minor adjustment to adapt them to the telephone. Other examples are numerous, for many companies failed to identify with the broader, impending focus. In more recent history, IBM failed to see it was in the communication industry rather than in mainframe manufacture, concluding the American people would never accept the scaled down "cyber-machine" in their homes, thus letting Steve Jobs of Apple and Michael Dell introduce and dominate the early desktop computer industry. Similarly Xerox, which dominated the copier industry for years, remained myopic, allowing a number of upstarts to redefine the copier as a communication device by adding faxes, scanners, telephones, and even computers. The railroads eventually recovered by adding container cargo and piggyback, IBM and Xerox adapted and recovered by emulating their new competition, but none of these industries could regain their preeminence. On the other hand, Western Union and Postal Telegraph have never recovered, and they remain outmoded "messengers" through which one can wire money to a distant recipient. The telephone, however, has become cellular, has joined with the Internet, and is enormous.

Facing the same medical dominance that has incensed psychology, the professions that established themselves after medicine have redefined what used to be called "medical care" into "healthcare," and have carved a successful place in the system of healthcare. One does not hear the outmoded term "medical model" as the ostensible enemy among dentists, nurses, optometrists, osteopaths, pharmacists, and podiatrists, all of whom enjoy autonomy, growth, and continuing success in *healthcare*. Only among psychologists (and to a lesser extent among social workers and other so-called mental health practitioners) is healthcare equated solely with medicine (Dranove, 2000).

We Are Not a Business

With the industrialization of healthcare, business courses have become a routine part of the curriculum in medical, dental, nursing, and all other healthcare schools, but not in psychology. Additionally, the healthcare national organizations sponsor and strongly promote continuing education business courses for their members already in practice, but not in psychology. As a consequence, all health professions are expanding into new practice horizons and delivery systems, but psychology remains mired in its traditional 50-minute hour in its private offices, shrinking in income as Medicare, Medicaid, and managed care continue to ratchet down their already ridiculously low reimbursement fees. Your plumber and auto mechanic charge more per hour.

It is true that Medicaid and Medicare are also reducing fees in medicine and the other healthcare professions, but these have expanded their services, and it is the frequency of these services (termed procedures), not the time the practitioners spend, that increases their incomes. But psychotherapy has mired itself in one main service, the 50-minute hour, which managed care has limited in both frequency and number of sessions. As much as 90% of psychotherapy is dispensed in the 50-minute hour model, remanding the psychotherapist to an ever-decreasing practice income. We have voluntarily boxed ourselves in.

Psychology has demonstrated a pervasive anti-business bias that reflects a belief that psychology is a compassionate profession, and a person cannot succeed in business and remain compassionate. By default, the practice of psychology has become almost an eleemosynary endeavor that perpetuates itself by attracting students who share our anti-business bias, thus remanding the practice of psychology to remain a compassionate and underpaid profession. One recent graduate confided that she could not make her student loan payments as her overhead exceeded her practice income and she was going farther into the hole. When it was suggested she needed some business and marketing courses, she haughtily replied she did not become a psychologist to make money. When asked if she became a psychologist to lose money, she became speechless and sullen.

The "poster child" of all professional organizations for helping its members out of the hole is the American Dental Association (ADA). Twenty years ago, dentistry was a dying profession. Fluoridation of the water supply had so reduced caries (tooth cavities), the mainstay of dentistry, that most dentists were retiring early and students were not entering the field. The ADA sprang into action, instituted business and marketing courses in dental schools, and embarked on a national reeducation campaign for its members. As a result, dentistry has expanded into new services that are lucrative because the public wants them and is willing to pay for them, and the profession is revitalized to the extent that many dentists are enjoying incomes higher than those of primary care physicians. In contrast, our APA has been impotent, unable to lead psychology practice out of its doldrums.

Our Rightful Place as a Healthcare Profession

The list of paradoxes currently plaguing psychology and used to justify the contention that we are not a healthcare profession is long and perplexing. Only a few of the more blatant ones are enumerated here (from Cummings & O'Donohue, 2008).

- We are not a healthcare profession, but we should be reimbursed by health insurance for our (non-healthcare) services.
- We treat "clients," not "patients" (this switch occurred in the 1970s), but we should be paid by healthcare systems, both governmental and private, set up to take care of patients.
- Physicians, nurses, dentists, podiatrists, optometrists, osteopaths, naturo-paths, chiropractors, pharmacists, and veterinarians have patients, while law-yers and psychologists have clients.
- We deliver "mental *health* services," but we are not a healthcare profession.
- Medicine is guilty of mind-body dualism, but we will not integrate into pri-mary care so we can finally declare that Rene Descartes is dead.
- We do have an oxymoronic group of colleagues who call themselves health psy-chologists who help physicians with diseases and really do not do psychotherapy.
- Real psychotherapy involves self-actualization, with such things as marital counseling, mindfulness, and rebirthing far more fun than such mundane interventions as helping diabetics comply with their medical regimens or helping somatizers resolve the causes of their high medical utilization.

These paradoxes have produced nonsensical beliefs by psychologists willing to go to the extreme to prove we are not a health profession and that we do not treat disease.

- Schizophrenia is not a brain condition, but the result of poor life choices (William Glasser), schizophrenogenic parents, especially mothers (Gregory Bateson, Leo Kanner), or the result of widespread poverty and oppression (George Albee).
- Alcoholism is not a disease. Tissue or neurological changes are absent, genetic or other predispositions do not exist, and a chronic inebriate can be rendered a social drinker by cognitive therapy (Linda Sobell).
- No medication is helpful in mental and emotional conditions since there is no disease pathology involved (George Albee, Fred Baughman, William Glasser).

It is no wonder, then, that very few psychotherapists treat schizophrenia, severe addictions, or chronic mental conditions. Rather, they continue overwhelmingly to treat what Paul Ellwood 40 years ago called the "worried well" of the health system. This is why the requirement of medical necessity by insurers strikes ter-ror in the hearts of psychotherapists, who insist that the health system pay for treatment that does not address illness in patients who are not sick. The preferred justification for psychotherapy is some variant of self-actualization, a term that masquerades under many names, but which for 60 years has not been satisfacto-rily defined.

An Awakening

Since the beginning of the 21st century there has been a renewed interest in the integration of behavioral care into primary care, with behavioral care providers (BCPs) co-located and working side by side with primary care physicians (PCPs). Surprising, such a system was first proposed half a century ago by Balint (1957), whose prescient insights were largely ignored. He saw physicians becoming more like psychologists, and psychologists more like physicians. Following the pioneering publication by the authors (Cummings et al., 1997), several textbooks have now been written describing the training, practice, and research of what is termed "integrated behavioral/primary care" (Cummings et al., 2001; O'Donohue et al., 2005; O'Donohue et al., 2006; Robinson & Reiter, 2007). Such co-location, surprisingly, was proffered more than half a century ago by Balint (1957). During this period, extensive health systems (e.g., U.S. Air Force, Kaiser Permanente Health System, the Cherokee Health System, and a number of VA hospitals, military treatment facilities, and TriCare programs) now have behavioral care providers, mostly psychologists, co-located in the primary care setting. However, only a few clinical psychology doctoral programs (e.g., Forest Institute of Professional Psychology, University of Nevada, Reno, Argosy, Hawaii, and the School of Professional Psychology at Wright State University) have instituted graduate programs to train BCPs. Consequently, facilities that have instituted such integrated services have had to rely on in-service training.

In an innovative attempt to move beyond the controversy, Barlow (2004) proposed that evidence-based interventions that are applicable to healthcare be termed "psychological treatments," while all else would retain the appellation "psychotherapy" and its practice would continue in the usual manner. Only the first would be eligible for reimbursement by the healthcare system, however, while the latter would have to be paid out of pocket or the practitioners would have to find an alternative means of payment. As might be expected, this only increased the level of contentiousness. While psychology dallies, the emerging industry has forged its own vocabulary, substituting for Barlow's psychological treatments such terms as "behavioral care" and "behavioral interventions." This reflects that although currently most BCPs are psychologists, they can also be drawn from specifically trained psychiatric nurse practitioners, social workers, counselors, and other therapists.

Where Are Our Patients?

Our patients are in the healthcare system, as psychological problems are first presented to a physician to whom all care is usually entrusted. It is estimated that PCPs are treating up to 80% of their patients who present psychological problems, making the primary care setting the de facto mental health system of the United States.

Decades ago it was discovered that 60% of visits to primary care were by patients who either had no physical illness but were somaticizing stress and emotional issues, or their physical illness was exacerbated by psychological problems (Follette & Cummings, 1967). Additionally, it was found that brief psychotherapy would reduce substantially the overutilization of medical care that was burdening the system (Cummings & Follette, 1968). Within a decade, these findings were replicated in a score of other studies (Jones & Vischi, 1979), and PCPs began routinely referring these somatizers to psychotherapy. All this has now changed, as PCPs have learned to prescribe the newer psychotropic medications and referrals to psychotherapy have drastically fallen. These front-line physicians found considerable resistance existed toward such a referral, and all too often the patient responded with anger and resentment. Of those who on the surface accepted the referral, less than 10% ever entered into psychotherapy. On the other hand, medication was readily accepted even though in many instances it resulted in no demonstrable change in the patient's somatizing behavior (Cummings, 2006). A stark example of the decline in referrals for psychotherapy is found in the freefall of referrals following psychiatric hospitalization. In 1990, nearly 95% of patients released from psychiatric hospitals were referred for outpatient psychotherapy. By 2000, the number had precipitously fallen to 10%, as discharged patients were given medication instead (Carnahan, 2002). While psychology remains aloof from the healthcare system, often practicing in private offices far from medical settings, primary care physicians who used to refer patients for counseling are now prescribing and managing with the new psychotropic medications instead of arguing with reluctant patients who might otherwise benefit from psychotherapy.

There is a profound need to reevaluate our non-healthcare stance, perhaps even to revise our graduate training, and to reeducate psychologists as well as the general public that behavioral care is an integral and indispensable part of treatment. The alternative is continued decline as we are rendered nearly obsolete by the biomedical revolution.

Overcoming Our Economic Illiteracy

Among practicing psychologists is widespread misunderstanding of the economic forces that impinge on practice, suppress current incomes, and that will shape the future of healthcare delivery, either positively or negatively. Many practitioners suffer from an anti-business bias that blinds them to pertinent information that would be helpful to both them and their patients (O'Donohue et al., 2002). They complain they are seeing more patients for less money, and the managed care companies pay less an hour for psychotherapy than plumbers are paid for their work. Taking into account the wide educational disparity between doctoral psychologists and plumbers, they despair that society is treating them unfairly. It is not a matter of fairness, for economic principles explain why plumbers are relatively well paid, whereas psychologists are underpaid. These principles remain a mystery to most psychologists. To put it sadly and bluntly, most psychologists are economic illiterates (Cummings, 2006). In the lament, "All I want is an income commensurate with the years it took to obtain my doctorate," the complainer is oblivious to the fact that labor, along with goods and services, is subject to the laws of supply and demand. A simple illustration is appropriate.

The Case of the Mortar-Carrying Bricklayer and the Plight of Psychology

A former patient who had recently moved into the community from another state was not able to get a job in his skillset as a bricklayer, and in desperation accepted a minimum-wage laborer's job carrying the mortar up the scaffolding to the bricklayers. He complained that even though he was working as a hod-carrier, he should be paid according to a bricklayer's scale because he was a journeyman bricklayer. One day, in a fit of pique, he fell off the scaffolding, and now recovering from two broken bones, insisted he should be paid by the bricklayer's workers' compensation scale, not that of a laborer. As I listened, he reminded me of so many of our colleagues who are doing the same work as master's-level psychotherapists but want to be paid according to a higher doctoral pay scale. However, economic principles, not fairness, determine remuneration (from Cummings, 2007). Consider the following:

- A perusal of state rosters of licensed psychotherapists or counselors reveals that master's-level practitioners (social workers, psychiatric nurse practitioners, marriage and family therapists, counselors) far outnumber the psychologists licensed to practice.
- Similarly, the managed care networks are populated largely by master's-level providers, establishing the scale on the lower level, not at the doctoral level.
- The precipitously declining numbers of referrals for psychotherapy creates a glut of practitioners that further suppresses compensation.
- The absence of entrepreneurial and business training now found in all healthcare professions other than our own has prevented our profession from innovating new practice opportunities like those found flourishing in expanded dentistry, nursing that now dominates emergent care, and physicians who have refined the marketing and delivery of cosmetic and concierge medicine and surgery.
- Finally, our failure to establish ourselves as an integral and necessary part of healthcare has contributed to our being replaced by the biomedical revolution.

The Failure of Parity

The enactment of parity (i.e., rendering third-party reimbursement for behavioral healthcare to be equivalent to reimbursement for physical healthcare) in 44 states as well as in the federal government constitutes perhaps the most successful legislative effort in the history of mental healthcare. The sad fact remains that expenditures in mental healthcare are less now than they were before parity, as the percentage of the national healthcare budget that goes to mental healthcare has shrunk from 7% to less than 5% (Carnahan, 2002). The managed care companies, as well as the government, simply instituted more draconian hurdles for mental healthcare than for physical healthcare. The well-intentioned "every-willing-provider" laws that mandate acceptance into managed care networks of every qualified applicant had their own negative effect. They created a larger practitioner pool vying for the diminishing number of referrals.

Had we been more economically savvy, we would have anticipated that legislation is almost invariably trumped by economics. The often attempted rent control legislation is one painful example. Intended to aid the struggling renter, it only increased the shortages of available housing as landlords abandoned properties in rent-controlled districts and the building of new affordable housing sharply diminished (Sowell, 2003).

Characteristics of a Business

- In spite of psychologists' contention that psychotherapy practice is not a business, but rather a "helping profession," it demonstrates all the attributes of a business.
- The practitioner offers a marketable service that the consumer wants.
- Seeking and receiving the service places the patient in the role of customer.
- The provider is licensed to dispense that service and is taxed on the income.
- The service is provided at the practitioner's office, which constitutes his or her business location, and the customer (patient) willingly comes to this office.
- In providing the service the practitioner must generate a revenue stream that will offset overhead (the cost of doing business). Generating a sufficient patient load is called marketing, even though the techniques differ from the marketing of most commodities.
- Income above and beyond overhead, taxes, and other expenses constitutes the margin of profit.
- Unless the psychologist is determined to engage in an eleemosynary endeavor, the inability to attract customers (clients), to collect payment for services, or to meet expenses constitutes a business failure, even though professional parlance would prefer to call it an unsuccessful practice.

In summary, the sooner a practitioner accepts that practice is business and sets about learning business principles and methods, the more likely is that psychologist to succeed. Psychotherapy acumen is a must, but it has to be augmented with a firm knowledge of business methods. We have seen too many excellent psychotherapists struggling without knowing why their practices are not generating sufficient income to sustain a livelihood.

Both American Biodyne and the integrated behavioral/primary care models of practice are unabashedly in the healthcare business, and the results are startling when compared with traditional psychological care. In contrast to traditional referrals in which only 10% enter psychotherapy, when the PCP has only to walk the patient down the hall to the BCP, 85–90% of patients in this so-called hallway handoff enter behavioral treatment. This is a nine-fold increase in referrals

(O'Donohue et al., 2006). Additionally, the method leverages the physicians' time, releasing the PCP to attend to more profitable procedures for which she or he is trained.

The American Biodyne Model is based on over 20 years of evidence-based research and field demonstrations, and although freed from the 50-min hour, it actually expands psychotherapeutic services, even to addressing issues that are usually excluded by managed care because they do not qualify as medical necessity (Cummings and Cummings 2000). As a successful healthcare business model, it remains unparalleled and is still being used in a number of flourishing venues. It was originally based on capitation (the financial structure in which the providers are paid an agreed upon monthly flat fee per member per month, or pmpm), freeing the practitioners to provide any needed services rather than the ones usually covered by third-party fee-for-service reimbursement. Unfortunately, most psychologists who have tried capitation failed miserably because the payment method is geared to innovation, not the delivery of the relatively inefficient traditional therapy they were providing.

Entrepreneurship

Practice is becoming more difficult as the result of ever-increasing competition, professional "overcrowding," and lowered demand, and therefore innovation is required for practice to survive. The process of business innovation is called entrepreneurship and is different from entrepreneurial. The latter essentially means the management, marketing, and other important ongoing aspects of an established business. On the other hand, an entrepreneur is one who creates, organizes, manages, and assumes the *risk* of an *innovative* business enterprise. Note that the key words are *risk* and *innovative*, and are the very attributes that are so absent in professional psychology. Steve Jobs and Bill Gates, who, respectively, founded Apple and Microsoft, are entrepreneurs.

Professional psychology is at the low ebb, and because it continues to attract students, it was named in a recent poll as one of the nation's most overrated endeavors, with an average income at the bottom of all the doctoral professions in healthcare (Nemko, 2006). The next decade will decide whether professional psychology will survive, so innovation in defining itself to the public and in restructuring itself into a delivery system the public wants are crucial. In contrast to other healthcare organizations, our APA has failed to exercise leadership in training for and encouraging innovation in how we package and deliver our services. The long-outmoded 50-minute hour remains sacrosanct.

In order to fill this void, the Milton H. Erickson Foundation teamed with the Cummings Foundation for Behavioral Health and with considerable time and expense created a continuing education MBHA (master of behavioral health administration), all on video. The courses were all taught by renowned experts and were designed for practicing psychotherapists who could fulfill each course requirement one by one and do as many as they wished, all in their spare time. These courses all on disks were offered to licensed practitioners at a cost so minimal as to be unheard of in continuing education. To date only a relative hand-ful have taken advantage of the offer. This does not auger well for the future of psychotherapy, a profession desperately in need of innovation and creative change.

Entrepreneurship and Recognizing Business Opportunities in Psychology

One of the senior author's mentors, Henry J. Kaiser (who built the Los Angeles aqueduct from Hoover Dam, who was a major shipbuilder in World War II, and together with Sidney Garfield, built the Kaiser Permanente healthcare system), said that a first step in building a successful business was to "find a need and fill it." Obviously, psychologists need to find needs related to their expertise and interests—opportunities relating to mousetraps are of no interest. Fortunately, healthcare is currently about 15% of the GDP and increasing at a rate that is alarming (although behavioral health is only about 5% of the total healthcare dollar). Worries about these higher than the general rate of inflation increases, worries about demographic changes (the ever increasing proportion of the elderly who tend to be higher medical consumers), and worries about increases in lifestyle problems (e.g., obesity) form both important dimensions of the current healthcare crisis and the nexus of oppor-tunities for psychologists. We can see that these are central issues in every political campaign. In crises lie opportunities.

Psychologists missed both the first wave and the second wave defined by these crises. We have already discussed how psychologists missed the first wave—managed care. They also missed the second wave—disease management. Disease management arose when the healthcare industry examined how it was spending most of its money and found that approximately 40% of its funds were spent on chronic diseases such as diabetes, asthma, COPD, pain, and coronary problems (Cummings et al., 2005). In addition, it realized that the healthcare system was poorly organized to address these chronic conditions. The healthcare system was designed to take care of acute problems (broken bones, heart attacks), but not to address lifelong conditions that need a lot of self-management. Thus, individu-als with these chronic conditions were being poorly treated and not getting their healthcare needs met. This was a huge opportunity.

Unfortunately, beginning about 2 decades ago, physicians, MBAs, and nurses jumped in and now own the disease management industry, which is hundreds of millions of dollars. Dominant companies such as Healthways employ only a handful of psychologists even though disease management deals with problems such as self-control, social support, depression, treatment compliance, educa-tion, and lifestyle changes—i.e., problems that are in our expertise, not theirs. We missed this opportunity and we believe that psychologists and the patients of disease management both suffer because of this (Cummings et al., 2005).

What are the new wave opportunities? There are many but we want to mention two and discuss one a bit more. The two we see are gerontology and integrated care (and these intersect in interesting ways). What is clear is that due both to medical advances and better public health, individuals are living much longer. These elderly also require unique services (e.g., caregiver support related to Alzheimer's disease, bereavement counseling, behavioral health services in assisted living, and disease management tailored to their unique needs). However, psychologists are doing very little to address these. Only a very few programs offer any specialty in this, and only a few token gerontologists serve on the typical clinical faculty. Again, practically no psychologists lead businesses in addressing these opportunities (Hartmann-Stein, 1998). Entering students are interested in child psychology and only very rarely interested in the elderly. More education is needed to see the business opportunities related to providing high-quality services that meet the needs of this population.

Integrated care is needed in all primary care medical clinics. The business and ethical case for integrated care is this: integrated care can make patients healthier at lower costs. We believe for payers, patients, and providers it is a win-win-win situation. It does not attempt to artificially restrict the supply of medical services (as managed care attempted to do; but rather decreases the demand for integrated care services by making patients healthier). Payers are interested in economically efficient care (if they are not, again, proportionately more dollars go to healthcare and fewer are left over for education, food, etc.). Integrated care is efficient as it can give the patient care that they need (e.g., treatment for their panic disorder—instead of unnecessary coronary care) rather than treatment the medical system is designed to give them. For the patient, integrated care provides one-stop shopping and less stigma. And for the behavioral health provider, there is the provision of needed services in a high-volume setting, as well as the possibility of reaping financial rewards due to the value proposition that he or she is providing. Studies have shown that integrated care can produce decreases in medical costs in the range of 20–40% (Cummings et al., 2003). These savings can drive both contracts used to drive more dollars toward the profession of psychology and the creation of businesses owned and operated by psychology.

In addition, there are other business opportunities (the business that can provide high-quality and effective treatment of obesity will be worth billions of dollars; ehealth and telehealth also are the waves of the future). However, again, psychologists need to think like businessmen and not like economic victims to see and develop these. And the social welfare premise of our profession does not need to be lost—we should only develop businesses that provide high-quality services. Psychologists need to concentrate on maximizing benefits to the public when appraising businesses, rather than worrying if too much money is flowing into someone's pockets.

Summary and Conclusion

The senior author is often accused of having consistently predicted the future of healthcare, particularly behavioral healthcare, for the past 50 years. At this dire time, we would like to believe that somehow psychology will rally before it is too late, but we are far less sanguine. When psychology reaches the point of no return, two things will have happened: (1) the flow of practice referrals will slow to a trickle relative to the number of practitioners available, and (2) incoming students, whom the APA and academia to date have perhaps purposely shielded from the true decline in the profession, will awaken to the facts and cease to go into psychology. At that point the crisis will have hit academia, psychology departments will shrink, and finally those who have failed to train us for the future will feel the pinch.

Innovation is an adaptive process of evolution. When obsolescence sets in, the outmoded order is painfully replaced by the new and vigorous adaptation. Systems that fail to innovate die. But they are replaced by the adaptation. This always involves the interim loss of jobs, dislocation, resentment, and often panic. Such occurred when managed care replaced the healthcare provider as the determiner of practice, and most health professions have adapted and recovered. Psychology has not, and often such a failure is succeeded by gut-wrenching collapse out of which innovation will emerge. Yes, this sounds Darwinian, and psychologists as they continue to fight adaptation do not like the idea that, when all else fails, a new system can only rise from the ashes of a rigid system that refused to change or to die. We do not hesitate to point out to our patients the need for change. Psychologist, it is time to heal thyself.

References

Balint, M. (1957). *The doctor, his patient, and the illness.* New York: International Universities Press.

Barlow, D. H. (2004). Psychological treatments. *The American Psychologist, 59,* 869–878.

Cantor, D. (1993, August). *Will the solo independent practitioner be extinct by the year 2000?* Paper presented at APA Practice Directorate Mini-convention, American Psychological Association Annual Meetings, Toronto, Ontario.

Carnahan, I. (2002). Asylum for the insane. *Forbes, 169*(2), 33–34.

Cummings, N. A. (1985, August). *The new mental healthcare delivery system and psychology's new role.* Invited awards address to the American Psychological Association Annual Meetings, Los Angeles.

Cummings, N. A. (1986). The dismantling of our health system: Strategies for the survival of psychological practice. *The American Psychologist, 41,* 426–431.

Cummings, N. A. (2006). Psychology, the stalwart profession, faces new challenges and opportunities. *Professional Psychology, Research and Practice, 37*(6), 598–605.

Cummings, N. A. (2007). Treatment and assessment take place in an economic context always. In S. O. Lilienfeld & W. T. O'Donohue (Eds.), *17 great clinical ideas* (pp. 143–162). New York: Routledge (Taylor and Francis).

Cummings, N. A., & Cummings, J. L. (2000). *The essence of psychotherapy: Reinventing the art in the era of data.* San Diego, CA: Academic Press.

Cummings, N. A., Cummings, J. L., & Johnson, J. N. (Eds.). (1997). *Behavioral health in primary care: A guide for clinical integration.* Madison, CT: Psychosocial Press (International Universities Press).Cummings, N. A., & Fernandez, L. (1985). Exciting new opportunities for psychologists in the market place. *In Practice, 5,* 38–42.

Cummings, N. A., & Follette, W. T. (1968). Psychiatric services and medical utilization in a prepaid health plan setting. Part 2. *Medical Care, 6,* 31–41.

Cummings, N. A., & O'Donohue, W. T. (2008). *Eleven blunders that cripple psychotherapy in America: A remedial unblundering.* New York: Routledge (Taylor and Francis Group)

Cummings, N. A., O'Donohue, W. T., & Ferguson, K. E. (Eds.). (2003). *Behavioral health as primal care: Beyond efficacy to effectiveness. Cummings Foundation for Behavioral Health: Healthcare utilization and cost series* (Vol. 6). Reno, NV: Context Press.

Cummings, N. A., O'Donohue, W. T., Hayes, S. C., & Follette, V. (Eds.). (2001). *Integrated behavioral health: Positioning mental health practice with medical/surgical practice.* San Diego, CA: Academic Press.

Cummings, N. A., O'Donohue, W. T., & Naylor, E. V. (Eds.). (2005). *Psychological approaches to chronic disease management. Cummings Foundation for Behavioral Health: Healthcare utilization and cost series* (Vol. 8). Reno, NV: Context Press.

Dranove, D. (2000). *The economic evolution of American healthcare: From Marcus Welby to managed care.* Princeton, NJ: Princeton University Press.

Follette, W. T., & Cummings, N. A. (1967). Psychiatric services and medical utilization in a prepaid health plan setting. *Medical Care, 5,* 25–35.

Hartmann-Stein, P. E. (1998). *Innovative behavioral healthcare for older adults: A guidebook for changing times.* San Francisco, CA: Jossey-Bass.

Jones, K. R., & Vischi, T. R. (1979). The impact of alcohol, drug abuse, and mental health treatment on medical utilization: A review of the research literature. *Medical Care, 17*(suppl.), 43–131.

Nemko, M. (2006). Overrated career: Psychologist. *U.S. News & World Report,* pp. 51–52.

O'Donohue, W. T., Byrd, M. R., Cummings, N. A., & Henderson, D. A. (Eds.). (2005). *Behavioral integrative care: Treatments that work in the primary care setting.* New York: Brunner-Routledge (Taylor and Francis Group).

O'Donohue, W. T., Cummings, N. A., Cucciare, M. A., Runyan, C. N., & Cummings, J. L. (Eds.). (2006). *Integrated behavioral healthcare: A guide to effective intervention.* Amherst, NY: Humanity Books (Prometheus).

O'Donohue, W. T., Ferguson, K. E., & Cummings, N. A. (2002). Reflections on the medical cost offset effect. In N. A. Cummings, W. T. O'Donohue, & K. E. Ferguson (Eds.), *The impact of medical cost offset: Making it work you* (Vol. 5, pp. 11–28). Foundation for Behavioral Health: Healthcare Utilization and Cost Series. Reno, NV: Context Press.

Robinson, P. J., & Reiter, J. T. (2007). *Behavioral consultation and primary care: A guide to integrating services.* New York: Springer.

Saeman, H. (1996). Psychologists frustrated with managed care, economic issues, but plan to "hang tough." *National Psychologist, 5*(1), 1–2.

Sowell, T. (2003). *Applied economics.* New York: Basic Books.

Wright, R. H. (1992). Toward a political solution to psychology's dilemmas: Managing managed care. *In Practice, 12*(3), 111–113.

14 Getting Away from Professional Psychology's Sadomasochistic Marriage to Academia

Nicholas A. Cummings

Historians tell us that when Machiavelli was on his deathbed, a bishop went to see him, and immediately posed the question, "Machiavelli, are you ready to meet your maker?" There was silence. The bishop then asked, "Machiavelli, do you confess your sins?" The silence was deafening. Undaunted, the bishop continued, "Machiavelli, do you renounce Satan?" This time, Machiavelli responded in a loud, clear voice: "This is no time to make enemies."

In reflecting on my own almost 60 years of activism needed to create a profession where there was none, in which the APA openly spent 10 years demonizing me, when professors to their graduate students referred to me as psychology's Great Satan, it would seem a bit late for me to worry about whether I am making enemies. So please be forewarned that what you are about to hear is extreme. But extreme times require an extreme response. At an extreme moment in the history of America, Martin Luther King Jr. exclaimed, "The question is not whether we will be extremists, but what kind of extremists we will be. . . . The nation and the world are in dire need of creative extremists." On a more modest scale, and one close to home, psychological practice is languishing and is in danger of extinction, requiring creative extremism before it is too late.

I know who I am, a lifelong, dedicated practitioner who entered private practice in 1948 and was one of the World War II veterans who became interested in psychology from their war experiences, entered graduate school, and subsequently carved out a profession where there was none. Preceding us there were fewer than 200 psychologists in private practice, almost all women with master's degrees seeing only children. We entered doctoral programs created at the behest of the VA and NIMH, with the reluctant cooperation of psychology departments who hated the subject but welcomed the federal money and the bonanza of students on the G.I. Bill. They used most of this money to enlarge their experimental/research programs, and we found to our dismay that clinical programs had little or no clinical substance. We bootlegged our training by secretly paying friendly psychiatrists to teach us at night and on weekends. Soon we were paying them in kind by

Keynote Address, Annual Meeting of the National Alliance of Professional Psychology Providers (NAPPP), Las Vegas, Nevada, October 9, 2009.

providing psychological testing, something that was being taught in our clinical programs. Had our professors gotten wind of this arrangement, or even that we were contemplating independent practice upon graduation, we would have been dismissed from the program as this was happening to fellow students who complained of the lack of clinical training.

The success of psychological interventions on the front lines in World War II had aroused a sudden interest among the public in psychotherapy, creating a shortage of psychiatrists, and soon they were giving us their overflow patients. This is how, unbeknown to our professors, we surreptitiously slipped into private practice. Once we moved on from our secret psychiatrist mentors, things were tough, inasmuch as there was no societal recognition of psychologists, as well as an absence of licensure, third-party reimbursement, and malpractice insurance. Amazing, we succeeded by charging $10 an hour while psychiatrists charged $15. In my own case, a prospective patient would want reassurance I was a psychiatrist. When I responded that I was a psychologist, the caller would back away. I would invite them to come in for a visit, and if the caller concluded it was not worthwhile, there would be no charge and that would end the matter. But for only a few exceptions, the prospective patient found help in that first session and continued.

In the succeeding years, and against all odds, a handful of extremist known as the legendary Dirty Dozen forged a profession, having to fight all the way not only the American Psychiatric Association, but our own APA (Wright & Cummings, 2000). Our academically controlled profession opposed the very concept of independent practice, fighting in the state legislatures our attempts at licensure, while in health circles they spoke against third-party reimbursement for us. The same vehemence of this is now replicated as academia opposes prescription authority. In the mid-1960s, when one APA board member was asked why he was so opposed, he smugly replied, "I will not lift one finger to put another nickel in the pocket of a private practitioner." Colleagues, this attitude has not changed, but in most instances a "scholarly" veneer has been added in effective obfuscation of the underlying naked hostility. B. F. Skinner (1999) said it in his farewell address to the APA delivered weeks before he died. At one point, he interrupted his own speech and admonished professional psychologists, "they hate you, and there is nothing you can do to change that." I was in the auditorium and can still hear the gasp from the audience.

I believe I know who you are. You are dedicated practitioners who love your profession, but are dismayed by the APA's inability to restore professional practice to its rightful, integral place in the nation's health system. You saw your expensive dues being squandered in "hobby projects" without results, you resented the special assessment levied against members who are licensed, and you were outraged to learn that the ineffective head of the APA Practice Organization was being paid an annual salary of $640,000. You have quit the APA, you are thinking about quitting the APA, or you are maintaining your membership because you erroneously believe that leaving the APA would jeopardize your malpractice insurance. One must be a member to obtain APA insurance, but one does not have to be a member to continue it, a fact our national organization does not disclose unless asked directly.

I also know who our young colleagues are. They have a Disneyland view of practice imbued in them by their pseudo-clinician professors who tell them building a private practice is easy: just look at me. But anyone can obtain the one or two patients professors see, if they see any at all, whereas building a full-time practice takes work, dedication, and time. In many cases, we have recruited our own patients who followed in our footsteps as a substitute to resolving their transference toward their therapist. Too often they are the personality disordered and frequently intractable patients who seemingly so intrigue psychotherapists that they continue to see them interminably and eventually encourage them to join us as colleagues. Young practitioners take licensure, third-party payment, and societal recognition for granted, believing these were always there, knowing nothing of the 30 years of fighting it took to obtain these. Like their mentors, they are economic illiterates, and don't even realize that practice is a business rather than an eleemosynary endeavor. They are determined to do good deeds, but that is hard to do when you cannot even meet your overhead or your student loan payments. In short, professors admit students who are in their own image. Our graduates are not only economically illiterate, but they resemble nuns more than they resemble doctors. As one who has the highest regard for the dedication and self-sacrifice of nuns, I am, nonetheless grateful one is not flying the airliner I am on or surgically removing my tumor. When I ask professors why they don't tell prospective students the truth about declining practice, they respond, "Oh, no, that would scare students away." They fail to add, " . . . and that would cost me my job."

The Scientist/Professional Model: Our Sadomasochistic Marital Vow

Shortly after I entered private practice in 1948, I was called as an expert witness on behalf of a severely battered woman I was seeing. There was no psychology licensure then, and a sympathetic judge did his best to qualify me as an expert. I was unable to respond to his questions about a core curriculum for clinical psychology, to say nothing about the lack of competency standards. In the end, I was allowed only to testify that I had seen my patient's severe injuries, but not being an expert witness, I could not testify they were inflicted by her husband. Discouraged, I nonetheless brightened up when I learned the following year there would be a conference in Boulder, Colorado, to establish a core curriculum. Sadly, however, the Boulder Consensus Conference concluded that the science of psychology had not sufficiently progressed to allow a profession of psychology, and that psychologists must be trained primarily as scientists and only secondarily as professionals. Thus, a core curriculum was superfluous and the idea was rejected. Called the scientist/professional model, more than 80 similar conferences have taken place since Boulder, all of which except one have rejected a core curriculum as a threat to academic freedom. Thus the unconscionable stricture that the profession is not mature enough to exist independently of our academic guardians still prevails (Benjamin, 2001), and recently has been reiterated in belligerent form in the so-called Flexnor Report issued by the Association for Psychological Science. Interesting, this historian (Benjamin) who chronicled psychology's repeated rejection of a core curriculum failed to even mention the Vail Conference (early 1970s), which grew out of the professional school movement, and which outlined explicitly the Professional Model. The APA has not only failed to implement the recommendations of Vail, which did outline a practice core curriculum, but it seemingly buried all memory of it. No wonder: we stack our curriculum and competency conferences with the preponderance of scientists and academic pseudo-clinicians and then wonder why we get nowhere.

We as practitioners have for 6 decades passively allowed this Boulder Model in spite of its having been demonstrated that it produces mediocre scientists and less than skilled practitioners. It would be easy to call this our dodo-syndrome, but it is far more than that. Like a battered woman who clings to her brutal husband, we have a sadomasochistic marriage to the scientist/professional model, putting academic pseudo-clinicians in charge of not only training, but determining who gets trained, and ultimately determining how we should practice. Let us look at this egregious track record (Wright & Cummings, 2000):

- Academicians fiercely opposed psychology licensure, necessitating 25 years to go from the first state (Connecticut in 1952) to the last (Missouri in 1977). It could have been done in one third of the time if academic-scientific psychologists did not, state by state, oppose us in the legislatures, resulting in legislators time and time again denying licensure and telling us to go home to get our act together.
- APA President Jerome Bruner failed in 1965 to sign and transmit the letter as agreed upon by the APA, the Dirty Dozen, and Health Secretary Joseph Califano that would have made psychologists Medicare providers. Consequently, it was 25 years later (1990) before psychologists were granted that status, and then in a more limited capacity than that which was within our grasp in 1965 (Wright & Cummings, 2000).
- Our academic colleagues opposed our going into private practice, telling society we were not qualified to practice independently.
- They cautioned third-party payers that reimbursing psychologists would open a can of worms, leading to lawsuits and discredit.
- They consistently published questionable research that purported to demonstrate psychotherapy was no more efficacious than faith-healing or religious conversion. The popular press loved these and gave them broad coverage, much to the dismay of those of us trying to make a living as psychotherapists.
- They prevented practicing psychologists from holding faculty posts, and when the professional school movement knocked down that barrier, they "complied" by appointing academic pseudo-clinicians.
- They never raised a finger to help in our struggle for hospital privileges.
- Through their often irrelevant accreditation program they captured the professional schools and transformed them into their own image. This is another

instance of practitioners passively acquiescing to the scientist/professional model.

- At the present time they fiercely oppose prescription authority and write letters saying that as psychologists we unequivocally believe psychologists are not qualified for RxP. And much harm would befall the American people. The most recent was a signed petition by leading academic clinicians to the governor of Hawaii and the legislature of Missouri.

Yet in the face of all this, most practicing psychologists passively accept the Boulder Model as inevitable, while some even continue to believe in it. This is our sadomasochism.

We Are Not a Healthcare Profession

Taking advantage of the deep wounds inflicted on us by psychiatry when we were forging a profession, our academic/scientific colleagues have bamboozled us into thinking we are not, and should not be a healthcare profession. So pervasive has been this brainwashing that the fastest way to get a colleague to backtrack is to cry out, "Why, that's the medical model!" One automatically retreats, seemingly in shame. Our having let ourselves be so deceived has excluded us from our rightful place as an effective, integral part of our nation's health system. In the eyes of one historian, this abrogation, coupled with questionable and highly publicized debacles (e.g., multiple personalities, recovered memories of incest, rebirthing, victimology, reprogramming therapy, past lives therapy), has so lowered the respect of society that we are the only American occupation that has never had a commemorative postage stamp (Benjamin, 2001; Cummings & O'Donohue, 2008).

Nursing, once the lapdog of physicians, no longer sees itself as part of medicine, but as part of *healthcare.* Likewise, so does dentistry, podiatry, optometry, pharmacy, and every other doctoral-level healthcare profession, and all have prescription authority and an important role in the healthcare system except psychology and social work. This is now called the *health system,* not the medical system. By opting ourselves out of the health system it is no wonder that we are underfunded, underpaid, and underappreciated because the nation pays for healthcare, not mental healthcare. In contrast, look at nursing, which began as a para-profession to medicine, has now upgraded its nurse practitioners programs from the MA level to the doctorate, and is destined to become the de facto primary care profession by addressing the acute shortage of PCPs inasmuch as only 2% of medical school graduates are going into primary care. In the meantime, it matters not to our academia that the percentage of the national healthcare budget that goes to mental health dropped from more than 8% to 1.5% if one subtracts the portion that goes to psychotropic medication (Nemko, 2006).

Why has it behooved academic psychology to reject healthcare? In a number of ways, academia has profited off of professional psychology, all the while opposing its progress for reasons of its own, which can be summed up as disinterest and inability. Let us specifically address each.

- Academic psychologists are interested in their theories and their research and are disinterested in and unable to teach healthcare if called upon to do so. Especially this is true of psychopharmacology.
- The highly successful model of 1969–1976 at the California School of Professional Psychology in which all instruction was part time was scrapped at the behest of APA accreditation, which requires full-time faculty. The original design enabled CSPP to so flourish economically that it plowed back 20% of its income into scholarships. Each class was taught by someone who made his/her living doing what was being taught, thus not only providing the epitome of practical knowledge, but saving CSPP from unnecessarily expensive full-time tenured professors. The professional schools have abandoned their promise and have become "me-too" APA-approved traditional programs, churning out thousands of master's degrees to stay economically viable.
- As presently constituted, the majority of psychology doctoral students are in clinical psychology, and their numbers support the other doctorates (e.g., behavioral analysis, social and experimental psychology, I/O psychology).
- Terminal master's programs are cash cows for psychology departments, so as early as the 1970s they successfully opposed any efforts to adopt the California licensing model in which MA-level practitioners would practice as psychological assistants under the direction of licensed psychologists. This would have been similar to how physician assistants work in medicine. However, this would have drastically reduced the number of students seeking such a career, curtailing academia's cash cow.
- It matters not to academia that there is now a glut of more than 750,000 MA-level psychotherapists, most of whom trained in psychology departments and professional schools. Managed care panels are composed largely of such master's-level psychotherapists, and because the APA has failed to demonstrate the value-added of the PhD, the pay scale for psychotherapy is a sub-doctoral one for psychotherapy.
- Since professional psychologists comprise the majority of the APA membership, we are paying a disproportionate amount of the money through our dues to support the vast number of esoteric psychology journals with little readership so that academics can publish, thus assuring tenure and eventual promotion to the rank of full professor. By the way, the term "full-time professor" is not only a misnomer, but a costly one as well.

A Proposal: A Redefined Profession

The paradigm shift about to be proposed may at first be seen as extreme, until one realizes it is the simple and logical structure found in all healthcare professions except our own.

Each healthcare profession determines its own direction, but derives knowledge from science and applies it as it pertains appropriately to practice. Biology and its many scientific derivatives (physiology, chemistry, embryology, genetics, etc.) are the scientific basis for practice in all healthcare, providing knowledge but not dictating practice. In healthcare, each profession determines its own practice procedures, deriving knowledge from science, and supplementing it with the practical (practice) research that is necessary and that scientists are incapable of or disinterested in doing. Thus the biological sciences supply the physiological and anatomical basis, but they do not dictate, for example, how a surgeon removes a patient's appendix or transplants a heart. Medicine, nursing, dentistry, podiatry, and optometry are dependent on the biological sciences, but it is each profession's responsibility to determine how knowledge is translated into practice. Not so in psychology, where for 6 decades academic psychologists have dominated our accreditation, training, certification, licensure, and all too many other aspects of what should be determined by practitioners, all the while denying us the core curriculum that would advance practice and increase societal respect and appreciation.

Additionally, all healthcare uses different names for the science than for the practice. Biologists contribute to medicine, but they do not call themselves physicians, and conversely physicians do not call themselves biologists. It is time to break the stranglehold this overlapping has placed on our practice. Psychology should continue to be the science for the psychological professions, but the practice itself should be called *behavioral health*. A new degree is called for, *doctor of behavioral health* (DBH), freeing it from the plethora of irrelevant requirements the APA imposes on the PhD and even the PsyD. The mission is to train behavioral care providers who are skilled practitioners as well as intelligent consumers of science, something all other healthcare professions have been doing all along. The DBH would be an integral part of the health system, serving in all healthcare settings, and serving as primary behavioral care providers (BCPs) right in the primary care setting with PCPs with equal importance. It is time also to end the internecine warfare among several so-called psychological professions, all of which purport to do psychotherapy and are independently licensed: clinical psychology, counselors, social workers, marriage and family therapists. These should be given the opportunity to upgrade to the DBH, placing all behavioral healthcare practitioners on the doctoral level, and in keeping with the intent we are to serve as *primary* behavioral care practitioners (BCPs) side by side with *primary* care physicians (PCPs).

The good news is that such a program exists (Cummings, 2008). It was launched in the 2009–2010 academic year by the forward-looking, innovative Arizona State University with 57 practicing MA-level psychotherapists with an average of 7.4 years of experience (O'Donnell, 2009). Ronald O'Donnell, PhD, serves as director, and Janet Cummings, PsyD, as his co-director. And there is continued good news, as the NAPPP has established accreditation and certification boards to usher in the new era (Caccavale, 2009a, 2009b). After years of inertia, practitioners are beginning to take rightful possession of their profession. Let us not allow this momentum to be derailed as was the case in the professional schools.

The Science of Psychology: An Addendum

It may startle many to hear this author state that scientific/academic psychologists have a right to be doing what they have been doing. It is we practitioners who have been derelict in not taking charge of our profession, while allowing the scientist/professional model through academia to take charge of our destiny and run it into near extinction. After doing so, they now complain we are inadequately trained, but who trained us? The dictum "let a thousand flowers bloom" (Benjamin, 2001) is appropriate for science. This is how science progresses, with competing theories often in contentious disagreement. On the other hand, practice requires standards and procedures that meet the needs of practice and the patients it serves. But a realistic assessment of how little useful knowledge scientific/academic psychology has really contributed to practice needs to be stated.

None other than past APA president Ronald Fox (2003), in bemoaning the paltry contributions of psychology to the understanding of such imperatives as poverty, violence, why our children do not learn, and societal disorganization in general, laments that our research has been obsessed with "picking lint out of our navels." This scathing assessment is not alone, as the list of similar observations compiled by Cummings and O'Donohue (2008) discloses.

In a publication soon to appear, none other staunch academician Larry Beutler (2009) concludes the following:

I became convinced that scientists were intentionally obscuring many important results because of an unwarranted devotion to a limited number of scientific methods. In fact, I came to believe that they may be using methods and defining psychotherapy and research informed practice in ways that hindered clinicians from being optimally effective. (p. 301)

And:

The degree that the effort to identify EST or research-informed psychotherapies is viewing evidence through a single or preferred research methodology, when there are several competent methods available, is the degree to which the scientist has fallen prey to worshipping the method rather than the "truth." (p. 302)

No small wonder that practice has been declining both economically and in the eyes of the general public. It is time we shake off the shackles!

References

Benjamin, L. (2001). Psychology's struggles with its curriculum: Let a thousand flowers bloom. *American Psychologist, 56*(9), 715–742.
Beutler, L. E. (2009). Making science matter in clinical practice: Redefining psychotherapy. *Clinical Psychology: Science and Practice, 16*(3), 301–317.

Caccavale, J. L. (2009a, April). Why clinical psychology needs to be reframed, renewed and restored. *The Clinical Practitioner, 4*(4), 1–4.

Caccavale. J. L. (2009b, May). Why specialty certification is a must for clinical psychologists. *The Clinical Practitioner, 4*(5), 1–3.

Cummings, N. A. (2008, September). A new model for training BCPs: A paradigm shift. *The Clinical Practitioner, 3*, 8–9.

Cummings, N. A., & O'Donohue, W. T. (2008). *Eleven blunders that cripple psychotherapy in America: A remedial unblundering.* New York: Routledge (Taylor and Francis Group).

Fox, R. (2003, September/October). Psychology's failures a tragedy. *The National Psychologist, 12*(5), 1, 3.

Nemko, M. (2006). Overrated career: Psychologist. *U.S. News and World Report,* pp. 51–52.

O'Donnell, R. (2009). The Doctor of Behavioral Health program at Arizona State University. Personal Communication, September 11, 2009.

Skinner, B. F. (1999). Farewell address to the APA. As audiotaped by this author.

Wright, R. H., & Cummings, N. A. (2000). *The practice of psychology: The battle for Professionalism.* Phoenix, AZ: Zeig, Tucker and Theisen.

Index

acceptance-commitment therapy (ACT) xv, 145
Ackerman Institute 148
adaptation 93
addiction: alcoholism 43, 44, 45–6; drug addiction 43–4; genetic predisposition 45; intervention phase 1: withdrawal 48–52; intervention phase 2: the games 52–4; intervention phase 3: the working through 54–5; intervention phase 4: self-responsibility 54–5; medical model 44, 56; mental health clinics 56–7; morphine addiction 44; psychological model of 44–8; special cases 55–6; substitute addiction 44; tobacco addiction 55
addiction treatment programs 46
Adler, Alfred 144
Aetna, Inc. 37
Affordable Care Act (Obamacare) xxi, xxv
Albee, G.W. 35
Alcohol, Drug Abuse and Mental Health Administration (ADAMHA) 114–15
alcoholic clinics 28
alcoholics 28
Alcoholics Anonymous 28
alcoholism 43, 44, 45–6
American Academy of Pediatrics (AAP) 82
American Biodyne xxii, xxiv, 68, 69, 70, 71, 78, 84, 104–5, 156–7, 167, 175
American Dental Association (ADA) 169
American Medical Association 96
American Psychiatric Association 144, 152, 181
American Psychiatric Association Guidelines 76
American PsychManagement 68
American Psychological Association (APA): Boulder Model 182–4;

convention xvi; Council of Representatives xxiii; espousal of integrated care by xxv; formation of 144; against inclusion of psychotherapy in national health insurance 32, 181–2; integration of psychology in primary care 143; managed care organizations and 89, 167; medical cost offset effect research xvii; presidential address xix; program accreditation 185; recognition of professional psychologists 58; requirements for approval of professional psychology programs xv, 1, 4
"anniversary reactions" 15
antidepressant medication 76
anxiety 69
arbitrary session limits xvii
Arizona State University (ASU) xxvi, 186
artificial demand 155
Asian Americans clients 34
Association for Psychological Science 183
attention deficit/hyperactivity disorder (ADD/ADHD) 79, 80–2, 84, 152
Automated Multiphasic Screening Examination 25, 30, 72

behavioral care providers (BCPs) 110–11, 141, 171, 186
behavioral healthcare: behavioral care practitioner of the future 110–11; discovery of somatization 113–14; downsizing 92; evidence-based 96; growth of 88; human services model 92–3; impact of information age 91–2; integration in Medicare 104–7; integration with primary care xxi–xxii, 90–1, 108–9, 113–25, 171; medical cost offset 114–22; new psychologists 91; new vision of 95–6; reason for